D1379732

Electoral Incentives in Congress

David Mayhew's (1974) thesis regarding the "electoral connection" and
its impact on legislative behavior has become the theoretical foundation for much of the existing research on the modern US Congress.
Recently, a number of scholars have begun to independently suggest
that the electoral incentive may apply to politics in earlier congressional eras as well. To assess these disparate claims more systematically,
Carson and Sievert investigate whether legislators in earlier historical
eras were motivated by many of the same factors that influence their
behavior today, especially with regard to the pursuit of reelection. In
this respect, they examine the role of electoral incentives in shaping
legislative behavior across a wide swath of the nineteenth century. This
entails looking at patterns of turnover in Congress across this period,
the politics underlying renomination of candidates, the changing role
of parties in recruiting candidates to run and its broader effect on candidate competition, as well as electoral accountability across a variety of
dimensions. The results have wide-ranging implications for the evolution of Congress and the development of various legislative institutions
over time.

Jamie L. Carson is Professor of Political Science at the University of
Georgia.

Joel Sievert is Assistant Professor of Political Science at Texas Tech
University.

LEGISLATIVE POLITICS & POLICY MAKING

Series Editors

Janet M. Box-Steffensmeier, Vernal Riffe Professor of Political Science, The Ohio State University

David Canon, Professor of Political Science, University of Wisconsin, Madison

For a complete list of titles in this series, please see www.press.umich.edu.

ELECTORAL INCENTIVES
IN CONGRESS

Jamie L. Carson and Joel Sievert

University of Michigan Press
Ann Arbor

First paperback edition 2019

Published in the United States of America by the
University of Michigan Press
Manufactured in the United States of America
♾ Printed on acid-free paper

First published in paperback July 2019

A CIP catalog record for this book is available from the British Library.

Library of Congress Cataloging-in-Publication Data

Names: Carson, Jamie L., author. | Sievert, Joel, author.
Title: Electoral incentives in Congress / Jamie L. Carson and Joel Sievert.
Description: Ann Arbor : University of Michigan Press, 2018. | Series: Legislative politics and policy making | Includes bibliographical references and index. | Identifiers: LCCN 2017057640 (print) | LCCN 2018002009 (ebook) | ISBN 9780472130795 (hardback : alk. paper) | ISBN 9780472123759 (ebook)
Subjects: LCSH: United States. Congress—History—19th century. | United States. Congress—Elections. | Legislators—United States—History—19th century. | BISAC: POLITICAL SCIENCE / History & Theory. | POLITICAL SCIENCE / Government / General.
Classification: LCC JK1021 (ebook) | LCC JK1021 .C368 2018 (print) | DDC 324.973/05—dc23
LC record available at https://lccn.loc.gov/2017057640

ISBN: 978-0-472-03750-6 (pbk. : alk. paper)

To Jamie Carson's friends Tom and Mary Jane Clark
To Joel Sievert's parents, Craig and Janet

Contents

Illustrations

TABLES

FIGURES

Acknowledgments

Writing a book is often a labor of love, and the writing of this book was no exception. Several years ago, during weekly lunch meetings, the two of us started discussing ideas that would eventually culminate in this project. We were both familiar with Mayhew's classic argument about the electoral connection and with a variety of attempts to try to test his argument in an earlier historical context. One potential limitation of such previous research was that the scholars engaged in this enterprise seemed to be looking for evidence more typical of the modern era (i.e., advertising, credit claiming, and position taking) but probably less common in the past. As a result, we decided to try to "unpack" the main factors associated with an electoral connection, to try to better understand whether it could be applicable in earlier political eras. The end result is this book, including a series of tests of the electoral connection that leverages some of the rather unique aspects of the electoral system throughout the nineteenth century.

We incurred a number of debts while working on this book project and owe thanks to a variety of individuals who offered us valuable comments and feedback on various chapters. The broader project was presented to the American Politics Working Group at the University of North Carolina, and we are especially thankful to John Aldrich, Frank Baumgartner, Tom Carsey, Michael McKuen, Jason Roberts, Sarah Treul, and Stuart McDonald for their extremely helpful remarks. Chapter 4 was originally presented at the 2016 Midwest Political Science Association Conference in Chicago, and we thank James Gimpel for helpful comments on the early draft. We presented an early version of chapter 5 at the 2016 Southern Political Science Association Conference in Puerto Rico and thank Anthony Fowler for pushing us to refine our argument about legislative turnover. Chapter 6 was originally presented as a paper at the 2014 Congress and History Conference at the University of Maryland and the 2014 American Political Science Association Conference in Washington, DC. We thank David Brady, Gerald Gamm, Greg Koger, Daniel Schlozman, Wendy Schiller, Charles Stewart, and Ryan Williamson for their helpful comments on that paper. Finally, chapter 7 was presented at the 2016 American Political Science Association Conference in Philadelphia, and we wish to thank Linda Powell for her insights on enhancing our argument on electoral accountability. We are particularly thankful to Bryan Black and Jana Kelnhofer for their assistance with data collection.

We especially thank Chuck Finocchiaro, who assigned reading a draft of our manuscript to his Congress class for graduate students at the University of South Carolina during the 2017 spring semester. Chuck and his students carefully read over our manuscript and offered us both substantive and stylistic suggestions for making the argument even better. We are grateful to Chuck and his students for their incredibly thoughtful remarks, and the manuscript is significantly more polished as a result of their suggestions.

Joel thanks John Aldrich and Dave Rohde, who offered him a postdoctoral position in the Political Institutions and Public Choice Program at Duke University during the 2015–16 academic year. Much of this book was written while Joel was serving as a postdoctoral student at Duke, and he is grateful for the many conversations and favorable work environment he had in the Old Chemistry Building.

We are extremely grateful to Melody Herr, who took interest in our original idea and convinced us to seek out an advance contract from the University of Michigan Press to publish this book. Although Melody left the press before the book's completion, we appreciate her inspiration early in the process. We also thank Meredith Norwich, Scott Ham, Danielle Coty, Mary Hashman, and the anonymous reviewers at the University of Michigan Press, for their excellent comments and suggestions. Scott, Danielle, and Mary worked with us during the final stages of the manuscript preparation process, and each of them played an important role in bringing this book to completion. We are particularly indebted to series editors Jan Box-Steffensmeier and David Canon, who were incredibly supportive of our efforts to produce this book. We also appreciate the careful copyediting done by Jill Butler Wilson and wish to thank Tammy Carson for compiling the index for the book.

Chapter 3 builds on and extends prior work by Jamie Carson and Jeffery Jenkins on the theoretical components of the electoral connection, published in 2011 in "Examining the Electoral Connection across Time," *Annual Review of Political Science* 14: 25–46. Parts of chapter 6 extend earlier research by Jamie Carson and Joel Sievert, published in 2017 in "Congressional Candidates in the Era of Party Ballots," *Journal of Politics* 79 (2): 534–45. We gratefully acknowledge permission from the journals to reuse portions of those earlier works here.

ONE

Introduction

American politics has been characterized by heightened electoral competition and volatility over the last several decades (Lee 2016). In 1994, the Republicans captured control of both the US House and Senate for the first time in 40 years. A mere six years later, Republicans won control of the White House, which produced their party's first extended period of unified government since the 1920s. After 12 years out of power, the Democrats, leveraging the national tide created by the declining popularity of the Bush administration and the increasing number of casualties from the Iraq War, regained control of both chambers of Congress in the 2006 midterm elections. Four years later, during the 2010 midterms, the Democrats once again lost control of the House, in what President Obama ultimately described as a "shellacking." By 2014, the Democrats also lost control of the Senate, as a result of economic uncertainty and midterm voters' increasing frustration with the Obama presidency. Although the Democrats had an opportunity to win back control of Congress in 2016, they made only minor inroads in both chambers and lost the presidency to political neophyte Donald Trump, resulting in a unified Republican government for the first time in 10 years.

Despite these rather dramatic upheavals in American electoral politics, one thing has remained constant during this period—the ability of self-interested legislators to get reelected. Since 1994, nearly 95 percent of House incumbents who sought reelection have managed to win another term in Congress. Given the smaller number of senators running in an election year, the percentage of senators winning reelection during this

same period has been lower (87 percent), but it still suggests that legislators have fine-tuned the strategic aspects of determining when to run
for reelection and when to retire. This raises a provocative question: how
do we reconcile the rather high degree of electoral instability in American politics with individual legislators' relative success in getting reelected
from one election cycle to the next?

In many respects, the relatively high reelection rate among legislators
is consistent with what David Mayhew (1974) originally described as the
"electoral connection." In its most basic form, Mayhew's theory contends
that once in office, legislators want to continue to get reelected and will
pursue whatever actions put them in the best possible position to achieve
this important, overriding goal. Since Mayhew's seminal book was first
published, his argument has gained a lot of traction among scholars seeking to understand legislative behavior and how Congress is organized.
While not everyone agrees with this simplistic view of member behavior
(see, e.g., Fenno 1973), it is difficult to argue that Mayhew's argument has
not had an enormous influence on those who study Congress and individual member behavior.[1]

Notwithstanding its prominence in the study of Congress, the electoral
connection was, until fairly recently, primarily thought to be largely a modern phenomenon. Mayhew's account of Congress is based on his personal
observations from the late 1960s and early 1970s, when both chambers
were beginning to undergo remarkable transformations (Rohde 1991).
Many scholars believe that the politics of earlier eras were far too different
to support the type of electoral connection Mayhew describes, especially
given the greater electoral and political upheaval during these eras in history. From 1840 to 1888, for instance, partisan control of the US House
switched a total of 10 times, suggesting considerable electoral instability
during this political era. At first glance, this widespread turnover in Congress might lead one to conclude that an electoral connection would be
difficult to envision throughout the nineteenth century.

Our earlier discussion about electoral volatility during the past few
decades leads us to reevaluate this conventional wisdom. Few would question the applicability of Mayhew's argument about the electoral connection in the context of the contemporary era, yet the electoral instability
we have observed during the past few decades is surprisingly similar to
what was regularly seen throughout the nineteenth century. In fact, this
similarity raises a very important consideration that previous scholars have
overlooked. If an electoral connection in Congress has been present across
time, this has important implications for our understanding of both con-

gressional and American electoral development. A more systematic understanding of the electoral connection and its effects on member behavior is thus worth additional scholarly attention and serves as the central focus of this book.

The Electoral Connection

In his influential book on Congress, Mayhew (1974) views members of Congress as "single-minded seekers of reelection." While he acknowledges that this strict assumption represents an abstraction from reality, he contends that it provides a useful mechanism for evaluating the behavior of elected representatives. As formulated by Mayhew, the link between legislators and constituents is electoral in nature; representatives are selected by constituents and can be voted out of office, in frequently occurring elections. If legislators value their political positions and seek to remain in office (as all indications suggest), they must seek and win reelection. This requires legislators to make efforts to address and meet the needs of their constituents. When an election occurs, voters are given the chance to reward or punish their elected representatives, by using votes as blunt instruments of accountability. This process repeats itself every two years, and members who remain responsive to their constituents are typically rewarded with another term in office.

Mayhew's conception of the electoral connection is contemporary in nature and has come to be viewed largely as a post–World War II phenomenon. Though Mayhew does not address the question of whether an electoral connection might operate outside of the contemporary era,[2] the conventional wisdom among legislative scholars is that earlier eras were far too different to accommodate a strong electoral linkage between individual representatives and their constituents (Polsby 1968; Formisano 1974; Price 1975; Skeen 1986; Swift 1987; Huckabee 1989). Scholars argue, for example, that most nineteenth-century legislators were not interested in pursuing a career in Congress (Polsby 1968; Price 1975) and that they therefore lacked strong incentives to heed the wishes of their constituency. Other scholars maintain that nineteenth-century voters evaluated candidates based on party affiliation rather than legislative actions (Skeen 1986) and did not generally hold public officials accountable for their individual behavior in office (Formisano 1974).

The preceding arguments about Congress and legislative behavior have been refined by research suggesting that individual accountability dramatically increased following the adoption of various antiparty reforms between 1890 and 1920, such as the Australian (secret) ballot and the direct primary (Rusk 1970; Kernell 1977; Katz and Sala 1996). The secret ballot had a profound effect on the electoral environment, providing voters with a greater opportunity to punish or reward candidates individually, while also giving incumbents the institutional means to develop a personal vote (Cain, Ferejohn, and Fiorina 1987; Ansolabehere, Snyder, and Stewart 2000). With the "party ballot" in place prior to these reforms, voters were selecting less between different candidates than between different parties (Engstrom and Kernell 2005). Moreover, the direct primary provided voters with the ability to choose party nominees directly, rather than allowing party elites to dictate the choices, as had been the case during the convention era (Ware 2002; Reynolds 2006). Although not stated explicitly, a direct implication of much of this research is that an individual electoral connection emerged at some point during the twentieth century but was tenuous, at best, prior to the reforms of the Progressive Era.[3]

Since the first edition of Mayhew's book was published in 1974, a number of scholars have found, despite the aforementioned arguments, that some variant of the electoral connection was present *throughout* the nineteenth century and potentially even earlier. For instance, while members of Congress may not have always been the "single-minded reelection seekers" that Mayhew describes in the contemporary age, there is evidence that they have *always* been ambitious (Stewart 1989).[4] Moreover, multiple studies have suggested that nineteenth-century members of Congress pursued behavioral strategies similar to those of the contemporary period (advertising, position taking, and credit claiming), striving to be responsive to constituents' demands, even though nineteenth-century electoral dynamics were somewhat different (see, e.g., Finocchiaro and MacKenzie, 2018; Finocchiaro and Jenkins 2016; Reynolds 2006; Wilson 1986a, 1986b). Finally, there is evidence that voters in the nineteenth century rewarded and punished incumbents based on their performance in office (Bianco, Spence, and Wilkerson 1996; Carson and Engstrom 2005). As a result, scholars in this revisionist tradition point to the similarities between nineteenth-century and contemporary politics and contend that some version of an electoral connection may have been present across much of US congressional history.

Unfortunately, studies investigating the electoral connection outside of the modern era have been largely individualistic in nature, as a more theoretically oriented perspective of how the electoral connection might have operated prior to World War II has not emerged. This uneven development may be partly attributable to fundamental ambiguities: specifically, a precise elaboration of the necessary components that underlie the modern electoral connection, along with corresponding evidence, does not appear in the literature. An accurate assessment of the breadth and scope of the electoral incentive requires us to unpack the individual components of the concept. Only by clearly identifying the critical domains of the contemporary electoral connection can we begin to trace out the historical progression and pinpoint changes that were significant to its development. We can then begin to examine the relative importance of specific institutions or legislative behaviors, as they relate to the electoral connection. In doing so, we can assess and perhaps challenge the "traditional" accounts of when specific components of the contemporary electoral connection were actually fulfilled.

In seeking to unpack the electoral connection, we identified four theoretical components that we believe are essential to understanding its potential applicability across time. First, we believe that members of Congress must be *ambitious*; they should desire a career in Congress or, at the very least, in public service. Second, we believe that representatives must possess some degree of *autonomy*, defined simply as the ability to shape their own political futures in the absence of broader political constraints. Third, we believe that members must be *responsive* to their constituents, in that they desire to assist them when interacting with the federal government. Finally, we believe that legislators must be in a position to be held *accountable*; that is, they can be rewarded or punished for their performance in office, based on the individual preferences of their constituents.

We discuss each of these four conditions in greater detail in chapter 3, where we evaluate the types of evidence needed to support each one. Later in the book, we assess these components more systematically by investigating whether legislators during the nineteenth century were motivated by many of the same factors that influence their behavior today (especially with regard to the pursuit of reelection). In this respect, we agree with the following claim made by Bianco, Spence, and Wilkerson (1996: 147) in their research on the electoral connection and the Compensation Act of 1816:

> Our premise is simple. It is one thing to argue that a congressional career was less attractive or less feasible in an earlier time than it is today, but another to conclude that members of the early Congress were unconcerned about the electoral consequences of their behavior. We do not believe that the politics of the modern and early Congresses are as different as the conventional wisdom suggests.

The present study's focus on electoral politics throughout much of the nineteenth century gives us an opportunity to examine the role of electoral incentives in shaping legislative behavior across a much broader time frame than has previously been explored. By investigating the four theoretical conditions previously outlined, we are able to systematically evaluate whether the preconditions for an electoral connection were indeed present in earlier eras. This entails examining patterns of candidate entry and turnover in Congress in the nineteenth century as well as exploring the politics underlying renomination of candidates during this same period. This investigation also gives us a chance both to better understand the changing role of parties in recruiting candidates to run for elective office and to evaluate the broader effects of party influence on candidate competition. Finally, we can look for evidence of electoral accountability during that era before the adoption of a number of progressive reforms.

Why Study the Electoral Connection in the Nineteenth Century?

To be clear from the outset, the purpose of this book is more than simply confirming the existence of an electoral connection in earlier eras. By analyzing congressional politics and elections in the context of the four theoretical conditions we discuss in chapter 3, we hope to better understand how electoral incentives may have shaped important developments in Congress throughout much of the nineteenth century. Most accounts of institutional development in Congress explain development by focusing on policy preferences of members, relations between the major political parties, and fluctuations in workload and the policy environment. Although we do not discount the importance of these explanations, we believe that an electoral connection is also an important piece of the puzzle for fully understanding institutional development in Congress. Indeed, we are not alone in believing that an electoral story underlies the origins of various institutions, such as committees and property rights (Jenkins 1998), or procedural developments (Meinke 2007). It may well be that viewing developments through the lens of the electoral connection can help explain these changes in the nineteenth century, just as it often does for the twentieth century and beyond.

We believe that the series of empirical analyses we employ across our various chapters can provide insights about institutional development, by demonstrating how electoral factors served to motivate legislative behavior on a variety of key dimensions. This book is ultimately a story about how institutions serve to both influence and constrain political behavior as well as affect political outcomes when those institutions are reformed. Nineteenth-century elections were markedly different affairs than what we are accustomed to today. Throughout much of that era, presidential elections were not always held on the same day as congressional elections (and were often scheduled months apart). Voting did not become a private act until late in the nineteenth century, and registration was not required to vote until approximately the same time. Until the 1890s, voters in much of the country selected candidates at the polls by way of party ballots that were supplied by the respective party organizations, rather than created by individual states.

Perhaps the biggest difference in elections from the nineteenth century to the modern era is political parties' substantial role in influencing elections. Prior research largely focuses on the role played by parties in nineteenth-century elections (see, e.g., Bensel 2004; Carson and Roberts 2013; Silbey 1991; Ware 2002), which is not surprising given the various electoral norms and rules in place at the time (i.e., the use of nominating conventions, the party ballot, machine politics). Until numerous progressive reforms were enacted during the late nineteenth century, party organizations maintained a tremendous degree of control over both candidates and voters in US elections. Unlike parties in the modern era, which may be better understood as being in service to candidates (Aldrich 2011), parties during the nineteenth century often dictated who was allowed to run for office, who could participate in elections, and when elections would be scheduled. One potential implication of such an arrangement is that there seems to be little room for individual politicians to matter without thinking of them in purely partisan terms.

The preceding discussion about the role of parties during the nineteenth century raises a number of important questions. What exactly would an electoral connection look like in an era of strong party organizations? Is there room for individual politicians to matter in the way that Mayhew (1974) originally described? We firmly believe that the answer to the second question is yes. By focusing on the fact that parties were incredibly influential in the nineteenth century, especially with respect to slating candidates, prior scholarship has focused disproportionately on the role of party as *gatekeeper*. Although parties did exercise a considerable amount of control over both the ballot and individual candidates in that era, scholars have sometimes overlooked the fact that parties still needed (or at least wanted) strong candidates who would consent to appear on the ticket for a specific office. The disproportionate focus on the *demand side* of the equation is unfortunate, because candidates were selected not on an ad hoc basis but on the basis of their prior qualifications and desire to serve in elective office (Carson and Roberts 2013). Our objective here, then, is to focus on the career decisions of individuals, whether they were incumbent legislators or potential challengers, as a means of better understanding the *supply side* of the equation. By focusing on the electoral connection and its underlying components, we hope to better understand how the behavior and actions of individual legislators and candidates might have also influenced elections in the nineteenth century.

A Brief Word about the Senate

Given the absence of direct election in the Senate during the nineteenth century, the main tenants of our argument are primarily about the House. Nevertheless, some of our theoretical claims could gain traction in the Senate during that era. Although selection by state legislatures meant that nineteenth-century senators lacked a direct connection to the statewide electorate, it did not mean they were unresponsive to this constituency. Indeed, there is growing evidence that nineteenth-century senators engaged in many of the same electorally motivated behaviors as contemporary senators (Schiller 2006; Schiller and Stewart 2014). Indirectly elected senators introduced constituency-oriented legislation (Meinke 2008; Schiller 2006) and worked diligently to secure patronage and appropriations dollars for their state (Rogowski 2016; Schiller and Stewart 2014).

Schiller (2006) contends that these activities were important for senators who wished to solidify support among party officials and the statewide constituencies. In light of the high rates of turnover in state legislatures during the nineteenth century (Schiller, Stewart, and Xiong 2013), this base of support could be crucial for senators who wished to serve another term in the Senate. Schiller elucidates the logic behind building a base of support among the mass electorate.

> The key to winning a Senate seat was forming a solid coalition inside the legislature that was reinforced by personal popularity among constituents and party officials in legislators' home districts. These external bases of support were particularly crucial to secure reelection because senators would frequently outlast most of the members of the state legislature who initially voted for them. . . . Then, as now, senators used their legislative tools, including com-

mittee assignments and bill introduction, to craft legislative agendas that would increase their popularity among potential voters. These legislative efforts constituted a significant portion of their public reputation, and they used their record of responsiveness to continuously cultivate support to bolster their reelection chances. (Schiller 2006: 197)

These activities helped senators build a base of support among party officials and the statewide constituencies that could reinforce their support in the state legislature. Even if direct elections increased senators' interest in building a reputation with their statewide constituency, it does not mean that they ignored these voters prior to the adoption of the Seventeenth Amendment.

In addition to responding to constituent interests, nineteenth-century senators were also ambitious politicians. While the move to direct elections may have increased the electoral value of prior governmental experience for senators (Crook and Hibbing 1997; MacKenzie 2014), nineteenth-century senators were hardly political neophytes. Like their counterparts in the House, most senators came to Washington, DC, with at least some previous service in elected office. According to MacKenzie's (2014) calculations, around 90 percent of senators who served between 1868 and 1895 held public office before being elected to the Senate. The primary distinction between nineteenth-century senators and those of the early twentieth century appears to be the length of their pre-Senate political career, with the latter having served for longer before the start of their time in the Senate. For our purposes here, the important point is simply that senators who were indirectly elected fit the broader career path of a progressively ambitious politician (Schlesinger 1966).

The Organization of This Book

Chapter 2 of this book surveys the growing literature on the electoral connection outside of the modern era, in an effort to put our broader theoretical argument into the appropriate historical context. It begins with a brief summary of Mayhew's tenants about the electoral connection in Congress and its applications during the past 40 years. From there, we discuss research that has begun to examine the electoral connection from a historical perspective, as well as the specific challenges associated with such research. In short, most of the prior research on this subject focuses exclusively on a subset of narrow or salient cases that may not be truly generalizable. Alternatively, a subset of existing research makes broad claims about the electoral connection in the past that are not empirically tested. We use chapter 2 to define what is meant by the electoral connection (in terms of both the underlying incentives legislators respond to and the associated electoral consequences) and to discuss why additional empirical research is necessary to examine behavior in the nineteenth century more systematically.

In chapter 3, we present the theoretical framework for our broader argument about examining the electoral connection across a much longer period of history. In that chapter, we draw on research by Carson and Jenkins (2011), who have outlined four critical conditions that they believe are necessary for establishing an electoral connection outside of the modern era: *ambition*, *autonomy*, *responsiveness*, and *accountability*. Given the difficulty associated with testing the electoral connection in any historical context (let alone in the nineteenth century), we argue that these four established criteria are useful for evaluating both the causes and the effects of legislative behavior. Additionally, we seek to leverage a variety of electoral and institutional changes throughout the nineteenth century, in an effort to examine our underlying hypotheses more systematically. We do not just make assumptions about how an electoral connection might have operated in the nineteenth century. Rather, the subsequent chapters in the book set out to directly test each of these four criteria as systematically as possible.

Chapter 4 offers us the chance to illustrate that individual candidates were ambitious throughout much of the nineteenth century. That chapter builds on previous work by Carson and Roberts (2013), by extending the argument much further back into the nineteenth century. Showing that candidate experience or quality mattered in that era and that party organizations actively recruited more experienced candidates to run for elective office demonstrates that ambition is not tempered by historical eras and that strong challengers can enhance competition in congressional elections. We believe that this argument is especially important, as it calls much of the past historical discussion about elections from that era into question. We also show in chapter 4 that elections were more competitive throughout most of the nineteenth century than in much of the modern era, given the significant influence that the party organizations had in recruiting the strongest possible candidates to run in individual House races.

Chapter 5 provides an opportunity to speak to the issues of both ambition and autonomy in the context of nineteenth-century elections. Specifically, most congressional scholars argue that nineteenth-century legislators were not interested in careers within Congress (i.e., they either lacked political ambition or were not autonomous in their decisions to seek reelection). To support this claim, previous research points to greater turnover among legislators during the nineteenth century in contrast to the modern Congress. As we discuss in more detail in chapter 5, we think it is both important and necessary to differentiate between careerism in Congress and careers in the parties. Many legislators were unable to pursue careers in Congress like we regularly observe today, but that does not mean that they were less interested in pursuing careers at other levels within the party organizations. We document these trends in chapter 5 and suggest that such pursuit was a viable alternative for many ambitious politicians during that period in history.

Additionally, much of the prior work on nineteenth-century careers does not account for the different sources of turnover in Congress. In chapter 5, we define turnover as consisting of two unique components: involuntary and voluntary departure. Most prior studies treat turnover and voluntary departure (an incumbent declining to seek another term in office) as roughly analogous quantities. We argue that a complete understanding of both turnover and legislators' incentive structure during the nineteenth century requires an examination of involuntary departure—that is, whether an incumbent unsuccessfully sought another term in office. Our analysis reveals two important and related findings. First, an incumbent was one of the candidates in a majority of the elections held during the period we analyze, which suggests that many incumbents valued continued service in Congress as far back as the nineteenth century. Second, a sizable portion of legislative turnover during that period was due to greater electoral competition, which means that involuntary departure was an important driving force behind high turnover rates during that era.

In chapter 6, we investigate the preconditions for a personal vote in nineteenth-century elections. In particular, we focus on two factors that should influence the personal vote for representatives serving in the US House. First, election timing was quite variable before 1872, as many House races were not held concurrently with presidential elections, which raises broad implications for understanding congressional elections during that era. Second, House candidates' position on the ballot varied depending on whether a presidential or gubernatorial race was being contested at the same time. To investigate the effects of these factors, we examine House elections prior to the adoption of the Australian ballot and find strong evidence of a personal vote for incumbents during that period. Our findings raise important implications about electoral accountability and legislators' ability to cultivate a personal vote in a more party-centered era. The results in chapter 6 also speak to the possibility of reverse coat-tail effects throughout much of the nineteenth century, since the quality of House candidates could have benefited presidential candidates as well.

Chapter 7 focuses on one of the most important aspects of the electoral connection, legislative accountability. Much of the existing research on the electoral connection in different eras makes rather strong assumptions or tests Mayhew's argument in a limited historical context. We here seek to examine electoral accountability across a much longer period of time, using historical elections data we have been collecting for the past few years. This gives us the opportunity to evaluate the effect of a variety of institutional changes—such as changing congressional norms regarding property rights, shifts toward single-member districts, variability in election timing, and ballot reforms—on incumbent electoral performance. We also have the chance to examine more specific questions, such as legislators' propensity to seek and win reelection, support the party on important legislative issues, and engage in participatory shirking.

The final chapter of this book briefly reviews the preceding discussion and focuses on the broader lessons for American institutional and political development. Among the potential implications of our analysis, one particularly stands out. The uncovering of more systematic evidence that an electoral connection has been present across congressional history may lead legislative scholars to revisit our understanding of the institutional development of Congress. Indeed, this evidence could help explain why specific congressional institutions were adopted at certain points in time: they may have been created with the express purpose of enhancing or "firming up" the existing constituency-representative linkage in Congress. An electoral incentive in Congress may have always existed in some form, but the adoption of institutions or reforms such as standing committees, the secret ballot, and the direct primary served to augment the linkages already in place.

TWO

Contemporary and Historical Evidence for an Electoral Connection

> Specifically, I shall conjure up a vision of United States congress-
> men as single-minded seekers of reelection, see what kinds of activi-
> ties that goal implies, and then speculate about how congressmen so
> motivated are likely to go about building and sustaining legislative
> institutions and making policy. (Mayhew 1974: 5)

In 1974, David Mayhew published these famous words that would go on
to revolutionize the way students of congressional politics analyze legislative behavior and institutional change. For years, legislative scholars
had searched for a simplifying assumption to understand how members
of Congress behaved once they were in office. The quest for reelection
discussed by Mayhew offered a powerful starting point for evaluating legislative behavior and the types of policies representatives would ultimately
pursue once elected. While he acknowledges that this strict assumption
represents an abstraction from reality, Mayhew contends that it provides
a useful mechanism for evaluating the behavior of elected representatives.
After all, reelection is simply a "proximate" goal that legislators pursue.
They clearly may also seek influence within the chamber or specific public
policies, but they cannot achieve those goals until they can secure their
own reelection.

The tenets of what is typically considered the "electoral connection"
rest on the candidate-centered politics of the contemporary era, in which

members of Congress can establish their own campaigns independent of the party, raise their own money, and appeal directly to voters in their reelection campaigns. Voters, in turn, can punish or reward incumbents directly, by splitting their tickets and voting for candidates of different parties when necessary. These dynamics lead members of Congress to pursue various "electorally useful" strategies, such as advertising, credit claiming, and position taking. Throughout his book, Mayhew demonstrates that the electoral connection explains a considerable amount of variation in member behavior and goes a long way in helping us understand the development of the modern Congress.

During the past few decades, students of legislative politics have marshaled a considerable amount of evidence in an attempt to broadly test Mayhew's assertion regarding legislators acting as "single-minded seekers of reelection." In this vein, much of the initial interest focused on the modern, post–World War II era of politics, and the bulk of the literature examined the three major activities that Mayhew discussed in the first part of his book. Here, we briefly review Mayhew's characterization of each of these activities, given their relevance to existing empirical tests in the literature.

Mayhew begins his discussion with advertising.

> One activity is *advertising*, defined here as any effort to disseminate one's name among constituents in such a fashion as to create a favorable image but in messages having little or no issue content. A successful congressman builds what amounts to a brand name, which may have a generalized electoral value for other politicians in the same family. The personal qualities to emphasize are experience, knowledge, responsiveness, concern, sincerity, independence, and the like. (Mayhew 1974: 49)

Much of the early work on the electoral effects of advertising sought to link the emphasis more directly to potential explanations for the incumbency advantage, especially as it related to increased name recognition for incumbents over challengers (see, e.g., Abramowitz 1975; Alford and Hibbing 1981; Cover and Brumberg 1982). Eventually, the debate evolved into increased attention to the "personal vote," the portion of a candidate's vote share that was unique to the specific candidate rather than to a political party (Cain, Ferejohn, and Fiorina 1987; Ansolabehere, Snyder, and Stewart 2000; Desposato and Petrocik 2003). Candidates more familiar to the voters as a result of successfully building a favorable "brand name" were viewed as more successful in cultivating a stronger personal vote with their constituents. More recent research (see, e.g., Prior 2006; Schaffner 2006) illustrates the nature of this advantage accruing to incumbents as a result of their use of media, such as television and newspapers, to better inform voters about themselves, thus raising their level of constituents' awareness of and familiarity with them.[1]

Getting one's name out to constituents is only part of the equation, according to Mayhew. Legislators must also find ways to remind voters that they are the ones personally responsible for positive actions that have occurred and that there is no guarantee that the same things would occur if someone else were to replace them in Congress. This leads us to the next electorally useful activity, credit claiming.

> A second activity may be called *credit claiming*, defined here as act-
> ing so as to generate a belief in a relevant political actor (or actors)
> that one is personally responsible for causing the government, or
> some unit thereof, to do something that the actor (or actors) con-
> siders desirable. The political logic of this, from the congressman's
> point of view, is that an actor who believes that a member can make
> pleasing things happen will no doubt wish to keep him in office so
> that he can make pleasing things happen in the future. The empha-
> sis here is on individual accomplishment (rather than, say, party or
> governmental accomplishment) and on the congressman as doer
> (rather than as, say, expounder of constituency views). Credit claim-
> ing is highly important to congressmen, with the consequence that
> much of congressional life is a relentless search for opportunities to
> engage in it. (Mayhew 1974: 52–53)

Although the electoral effects of advertising have received their fair share of attention in the literature, the bulk of research testing the electoral connection has focused specifically on the concept of credit claiming. Interestingly enough, however, the record in this regard is somewhat mixed. The number of studies that purport to find evidence of credit claiming paying off at the polls (see, e.g., Alvarez and Saving 1997; Bickers and Stein 1996; Fiorina 1989; King 1991) is roughly the same as the number suggesting that it does not (see, e.g., Feddman and Jondrow 1984; Johannes and McAdams 1981; Serra and Moon 1994). This is especially revealing since most members of Congress strongly believe that forms of credit claiming, such as casework on behalf of individual constituents, yield tangible electoral rewards.

In an effort to clarify these seemingly inconsistent results, recent research examining the electoral effects of credit claiming have offered several potential explanations. Bickers and Stein (1994), for instance, argue that not all representatives are equally motivated to allocate pork back to their districts. In fact, they find that marginal legislators are the most likely to engage in credit claiming, since "safe" legislators do not receive the same electoral benefits from such activities. In a similar fashion, Sellers (1997) argues that certain representatives (typically Republicans) tend to abstain from credit-claiming activities, since they are more likely to reap electoral benefits from being fiscally consistent as opposed to distributing pork-barrel projects to their district. Grimmer, Messing, and Westwood (2012) contend that a complete understanding of credit claiming requires looking not just at the allocation of benefits but also at how members take credit for their actions. According to those scholars, "[F]requently claiming credit for small amounts of money is a much more efficient way to cultivate support among constituents than increasing the total amount claimed" (715). More recently, Clemens, Crespin, and Finocchiaro (2015: 111) argue that there is a geographic component to distributive politics, such that there is "substantial spatial heterogeneity in traditional models of pork-barreling."

Besides advertising and credit claiming, Mayhew argues that members of Congress also find it electorally useful to make frequent public pronouncements in their capacity as legislators.

> The third activity congressmen engage in may be called *position taking*, defined here as the public enunciation of a judgmental statement on anything likely to be of interest to political actors. The statement may take the form of a roll call vote. . . . The congressman as position taker is a speaker rather than a doer. The electoral requirement is not that he make pleasing things happen but that he make pleasing judgmental statements. The position itself is the political commodity. (Mayhew 1974: 61–62)

While the electoral effects of advertising and credit claiming have been widely explored in the literature, substantially less attention has been given to the electoral consequences of position-taking behavior in Congress.[2] Since the early 1970s, the effects of legislative position taking have generally been analyzed in terms of roll-call voting and almost exclusively with respect to the House (see, e.g., Erikson 1971; Jacobson 1993a; Pritchard

1986; Wright 1978).[3] Moreover, as Mayhew (1974: 69–70) and others have noted, it is difficult to find systematic evidence of legislators' position-taking behavior affecting election results.

The preceding discussion about position taking offers an interesting puzzle to students of congressional elections. Surveys of individual members consistently show that legislators believe that the positions they take on roll-call votes impact their electoral fortunes (see, e.g., Froman 1963; Clausen 1973; Matthews and Stimson 1975; Kingdon 1989; Sullivan, Shaw, McAvoy, and Barnum 1993). Other studies find little or no evidence of legislative behavior affecting elections, suggesting that legislators may not need to be very concerned about the potential electoral implications of position taking (see, e.g., Ansolabehere, Snyder, and Stewart 2001; Gaines and Nokken 2001; Kuklinski 1977). If the latter situation is indeed the case, why might members of Congress worry about the potential electoral effects of position taking? Mayhew (1974), Fiorina (1974), Kingdon (1989), and Arnold (1990) all emphasize that incumbents are extremely sensitive to the potential electoral implications of their votes and that they behave strategically when announcing a position on a roll-call vote. Even after a vote has been cast, legislators will be attentive to the electoral consequences of particular positions and, bearing these potential considerations in mind, will craft an explanation of their legislative behavior (Grose, Malhotra, and Van Houweling 2015).

More recently, legislative scholars have uncovered evidence of position-taking behavior affecting representatives' electoral fortunes. Bovitz and Carson (2006), for instance, show that a wide range of roll-call decisions have significant effects on incumbents' electoral margins. In fact, their results suggest that the extent to which a particular roll call is controversial, salient, and a catalyst for intraparty disagreement affects whether it has electoral implications. Another study concludes that electoral sanctions only result when legislators' positions on salient roll calls lead constituents to believe that the incumbent is more ideologically distant from themselves (Nyhan et al. 2012). The basic mechanism outlined in this study is also consistent with analyses focusing on legislators' aggregate roll-call behavior. Canes-Wrone, Brady, and Cogan (2002) investigate the relationship between members' electoral margins and their revealed ideological position, to ascertain whether legislators are punished for being "out of step" with their constituents. Their findings suggest that legislators are indeed held accountable for roll-call voting behavior that does not align with constituent preferences.[4] Building on these findings, Carson, Koger, Lebo, and

Young (2010) argue that, all else being equal, voting with one's party is often more detrimental to a member's electoral fortunes than is ideology.

Historical Evidence for the Electoral Connection

Mayhew's (1974) concept of the electoral connection, with its underlying potential for retrospective punishment by voters, has shaped much of the contemporary research on the US Congress. There is very little scholarly consensus, however, about whether his argument accurately portrays politics outside of the post–World War II era. Though Mayhew does not address this question in his classic work, the conventional wisdom suggests that the politics of the nineteenth century was far too different from that of the modern era to accommodate a strong electoral linkage between individual representatives and their constituents (Formisano 1974; Huckabee 1989; Polsby 1968; Skeen 1986; Swift 1987). Most legislators did not appear interested in pursuing a career in Congress (Polsby 1968; Price 1975), which leads some scholars to conclude that nineteenth-century members of Congress lacked the incentives to heed the wishes of their constituency. Some believe that voters during that era would be disinclined to hold electorally disinterested officials accountable, which would further complicate the linkage between representatives and constituents (Formisano 1974). Instead of retrospective evaluations of legislators' actions, voters' evaluations of candidates are thought to have been based solely on party affiliation (Skeen 1986).

The arguments discussed above comport with evidence suggesting that individual accountability increased following the adoption of antiparty and progressive reforms, such as the Australian ballot and the direct primary, between 1890 and the early part of the twentieth century (Kernell 1977; Rusk 1970). The secret ballot had a profound effect on the electoral environment, not only giving voters a greater opportunity to punish or reward candidates individually, but also affording incumbents the institutional means to develop a personal vote with one's constituents (Ansolabehere, Snyder, and Stewart 2000; Cain, Ferejohn, and Fiorina 1987). Although not usually stated explicitly, a direct implication of these findings is that before the transformation of the American elections from a party-dominated process to a more candidate-centered system, the electoral connection was tenuous at best.

A few legislative scholars have nevertheless suggested that Mayhew's notion of an electoral connection might still be valid in earlier eras. Katz and Sala were among the first to investigate whether an electoral connection might have existed during the nineteenth century, as well as how it might have influenced the institutional structure of Congress. In their 1996 study, they develop and test their hypothesis based on an electoral rationale for the emergence of property rights among congressional committees. More specifically, they examine tenure patterns on committees before and after the adoption of the Australian ballot in the early 1890s. According to Katz and Sala, legislators may have had greater incentive to engage in personal vote seeking following adoption of the secret ballot, since its passage created new incentives to reward or punish individual members selectively. Based on their analysis, Katz and Sala find an increase in committee assignment stability after 1892, when a majority of the states had adopted a version of the secret ballot that was in use in national elections. They also reject two competing explanations—the institutionalization and realignment hypotheses—that received some attention in previous literature with respect to the organizational structure of Congress.

Katz and Sala offer an interesting perspective on the existence of an electoral connection during the nineteenth century, but it is not without potential limitations. First, they assume that members of Congress were motivated by reelection as far back as the late nineteenth century, with little or no evidence in support of such a contention. Although it is never stated directly, Katz and Sala's theoretical argument suggests that an electoral connection did *not* exist prior to this time. They then show how the adoption of the secret ballot and the corresponding establishment of property rights in the process of committee assignments would support their argument, without explicitly demonstrating that legislators used their committees to engage in more credit claiming or position taking, consistent with Mayhew's (1974) original argument. Katz and Sala also assume that property rights did not exist prior to the ballot reforms, which is somewhat surprising since other studies find that committee property rights were securely in place decades before the ballot reforms were adopted (Gamm and Shepsle 1989; Jenkins 1998). That this assumption may not be true should call into question some of the other arguments made by Katz and Sala.[5]

Bianco, Spence, and Wilkerson (1996) provide one of the first empirical tests of an electoral connection during the early nineteenth century. In particular, they examine whether legislators who supported the controversial Compensation Act of 1816—which would have raised legislators' salaries from $6 per day to an annual salary of $1,500 per year—resulted in a greater number of defeats and retirements. Based on a careful analysis of the votes on this highly salient piece of legislation, they found that, all else being equal, the most electorally vulnerable legislators were much less likely to support this legislation. Their examination also revealed that representatives who voted in support of the bill were less likely to seek reelection compared with legislators who voted nay, which suggests a greater degree of electoral accountability than expected during that era. As a result, Bianco, Spence, and Wilkerson (1996: 147) conclude,

> The conventional wisdom has it that contemporary notions of the electoral connection cannot be applied to the early Congress. Our analysis, admittedly of only one case, suggests that an electoral connection may have operated in the early Congress as well. That the Compensation Act was unusually controversial and clearly an exception to the normal politics of the period is not in question. The point is that the conventional wisdom sees no role for the electoral connection in any analysis of the early Congress. Did an electoral connection operate in the early Congress? The contribution of this paper is to move the conventional wisdom from answering "no, never" to saying "perhaps on occasion." Additional work will be needed to say more. Judging from our results, however, we feel that there is considerable value to pursuing this line of research.

Building on the evidence from the Compensation Act, Carson and Engstrom (2005) offer a test of the electoral connection in early American politics by examining the electoral aftershocks of the disputed presidential election of 1824. Using county-level presidential voting data, along with the unique circumstances associated with the presidential contest, Carson and Engstrom investigate the connection between representative behavior, district public opinion, and electoral outcomes. Based on their analysis, they find that representatives who voted for John Quincy Adams yet represented congressional districts supporting Andrew Jackson were targeted for ouster and suffered a substantial vote loss in the subsequent midterm elections. They also find that the entry of an experienced challenger in the 1826–27 elections had a sizable impact on the fortunes of incumbent legislators. From this finding, Carson and Engstrom conclude that some form of an electoral connection did exist in the early nineteenth century, although they caution that the effect could be limited to hypersalient votes in Congress.

Congressional scholars have also examined the passage of the Pendleton Act of 1883, another piece of major legislation, for evidence of an electoral connection in the nineteenth century. Johnson and Libecap (1994) argue that legislators enacted this bill in an effort to more efficiently secure their own reelection. More specifically, they argue that the dramatic growth in the patronage system during the post–Civil War era rapidly began to outstrip the ability of individual representatives to dole out federal appointments. In response, representatives opted to create a new civil service system that would more efficiently serve their reelection interests. Although some historians argue that the elimination of the patronage system undermined legislators' ability to get reelected, Johnson and Libecap disagree with this characterization. They maintain that with skilled politicians now employed by the new civil service, legislators could actually get more out of political appointees who remained in the existing patronage positions.[6]

In their attempt to explain the postal reforms in the late nineteenth century, Kernell and McDonald (1999) investigate why members of Congress would shift from the use of fourth-class postmasters to greater reliance on rural free delivery (RFD). The change is especially puzzling since legislators chose to abandon an entrenched patronage system that had served them well for decades and replaced it with one largely insulated from political control. Kernell and McDonald contend that electoral motivations provide the best account for this rather dramatic turn of events. Specifically, they argue that the simultaneous electoral changes, especially the recent adoption of the secret ballot, led career-minded legislators to search for a better method of serving their constituents. RFD provided such a means, since it gave constituents something they had desired for a number of years. Additionally, Kernell and McDonald find that vulnerable Republicans were much more likely than other legislators—especially Democrats in the South—to receive an increased number of RFD routes in their districts. Kernell and McDonald (1999: 809) conclude,

> In a political system run by self-reliant officeholders, the urge for reelection is assumed to influence every aspect of a politician's life (Mayhew 1974). By the close of the nineteenth century, members of the House appear to have been following this urge no less than do today's representatives.

Rogowski and Gibson (2015) also examine federal post offices during the late nineteenth century, but they do so under the guise of examining whether legislators were rewarded or punished for their behavior. In seeking to better understand electoral accountability during the Gilded Age, they examine the relationship between distributive politics and electoral outcomes, using new data on locations of federal post offices. Based on their analysis of the allocations for post offices between 1876 and 1896, Rogowski and Gibson find that electoral competition and institutions directly influenced the relationship between legislative behavior and accountability. Like Carson and Engstrom (2005), they find evidence of an electoral connection prior to the adoption of the Australian ballot. Rogowski and Gibson maintain that the effects are limited to counties with more marginal members and to legislators in the majority parties. After passage of the secret ballot, however, the relationship between behavior and electoral outcomes with respect to the distribution of post offices becomes much more pronounced. As such, they conclude that the electoral connection was clearly enhanced by the adoption of the Australian ballot late in the nineteenth century.

In her examination of electoral politics during the nineteenth century, Anzia (2012) focuses specifically on the role of machine politics and election timing in local elections. Based on her analysis of politics in the 1800s in three major US cities—New York, Philadelphia, and San Francisco—she illustrates that political parties frequently manipulated the timing of city elections in an effort to secure an electoral advantage over their opponents. She found that whereas party machines occasionally preferred simultaneous or on-cycle elections when their candidates were popular in state and national politics, they more often favored off-cycle elections, since the lower levels of voter turnout in those elections gave parties a significant advantage in mobilizing voters. Based on this important consideration, Anzia (2012: 25–26) argues,

> By changing the time at which city elections were held, party elites could increase or decrease the number of voters who participated in city elections, potentially tipping the balance of party vote share in their favor. This finding lends support to the claim that even in the early nineteenth century, political parties were organized to win elections, and they actively worked to create electoral rules that helped them do so. Not only did election timing have a role in shaping the American party system, but the parties, in turn, had a role in shaping electoral institutions.

In seeking to evaluate specific tenants of the electoral connection across time, Baughman and Nokken (2011) analyze rates of roll-call abstention, from the antebellum era through the early part of the twentieth century, to better understand whether marginal members were more likely to miss the occasional roll call to focus more directly on their constituency. Baughman and Nokken ultimately find that legislators who pursued reelection during the era studied were much more likely to participate on roll calls than those members who decided not to seek reelection. They also note that abstention rates differed by party, with members of the majority much more likely to show up for important roll-call votes. As such, they provide evidence that electoral considerations helped to explain legislative behavior as far back as the early days of the Republic and during a period of important electoral and institutional reforms. Baughman and Nokken also consider how varying election timing and lame-duck sessions impacted legislative voting behavior. They find that abstention dropped in the post-election period in around two-thirds of the Congresses between the 33rd and 61st Congresses.

Finocchiaro and Jenkins (2016) examine the electoral connection during the early antebellum era, by focusing specifically on legislators' increased use of federal military pensions. Based on an analysis of distributive legislation during this period, they find that representatives were responsive to requests for military pensions following the Revolutionary War, as members' electoral interests resulted in increased particularistic activities in the period from 1818 to 1832. What originally started as a simple program for disabled Revolutionary War veterans grew, over time, into a much larger program that provided benefits for anyone with prior military service. Finocchiaro and Jenkins find that the key particularistic elements of veterans' pensions originated here, as members of Congress who represented geographic units with a higher concentration of pension-eligible adults actively sought a greater distribution of benefits.

Limitations of Existing Research on the Electoral Connection

The discussion in the preceding section is not meant to review all of the existing research exploring the electoral connection in earlier political eras. Rather, it serves to illustrate that a growing number of scholars have begun to investigate the possibility that an electoral connection might actually exist outside of the modern era. One limitation of such work, however, is that most of the studies conducted to date have been either individualistic in nature or have only examined a very specific aspect of the electoral connection. Indeed, some of the research simply assumes that an electoral connection existed during the nineteenth century, without explicitly testing for it (e.g., Katz and Sala 1996). When the electoral connection is subject to greater empirical scrutiny, the resulting evidence is very limited in nature.

As a result, we do not have systematic evidence of a broader electoral connection during this specific period in history.

As noted in chapter 1, we believe that the uneven development in our understanding of how an electoral connection might operate in earlier political eras is a function of fundamental ambiguities in the existing literature. Most research to date has focused on the three components that Mayhew discusses in his 1974 book—advertising, credit claiming, and position taking. Although this is a useful starting point for evaluating Mayhew's argument, a more complete understanding of how the electoral connection operates involves unpacking the theory's various individual and theoretical components. Our argument is that we must explicitly identify the "critical" elements of the Mayhewian electoral connection before we can begin to more fully understand how such incentives might have motivated legislative behavior throughout the nineteenth century. An additional benefit of refocusing the discussion on these key theoretical building blocks is that we can more clearly assess how specific political institutions have been created and adapted to further legislators' electoral interests. In doing so, our ultimate objective is to systematically assess and perhaps even challenge the conventional wisdom about the electoral connection and how it came to shape representative behavior in Congress.

In sum, we believe that legislative scholars either have been looking in the wrong place or have focused on the wrong attributes of the electoral connection when trying to understand its applicability to legislative behavior in earlier political eras. In the next chapter, we unpack what we believe to be the four main components of the electoral connection. We define what is meant by the electoral connection (in terms of both the underlying incentives legislators respond to and the associated electoral consequences) and discuss why additional empirical research is needed to examine legislative behavior in the nineteenth century more systematically. These four theoretical concepts then serve, individually or in combination, as the central theoretical motivations for the series of empirical tests throughout the remainder of this book.

THREE

Unpacking the Electoral Connection

with Jeffery A. Jenkins

Mayhew's (1974) argument concerning the electoral connection and the legislative behavior associated with it has become the theoretical basis for much of the existing work on the US Congress. In its simplest version, reelection serves as the "proximate" goal for members of Congress, since it must be achieved before they can pursue other important goals such as good public policy or influence within the chamber (Fenno 1973). In their attempt to get reelected, legislators rely on certain familiar behaviors—advertising, credit claiming, and position taking—that create favorable and potentially durable impressions with their constituents. All of this is familiar ground for anyone who has closely read Mayhew's classic work. In this chapter, we investigate Mayhew's thesis more thoroughly in an attempt to answer even more fundamental questions about this dynamic. For instance, what actually constitutes an "electoral connection"? More specifically, what are some of the underlying assumptions that drive Mayhew's thesis?

Assumptions Underlying the Electoral Connection

At its heart, Mayhew's notion of an electoral connection is derived from the linkage between representatives and their constituents. In a typical representative democracy, policy agents serve the citizens; in the case of the

US Congress, legislators (US representatives or senators) serve geographic constituencies (districts or states). The linkage between constituents and their representatives is electoral in nature; representatives serve at the behest of constituents and, theoretically, can be voted out of office in frequently occurring elections. If legislators value their political positions and seek to remain in office—which most accounts of the contemporary electoral connection assume—they must win elections; this requires a regular attempt to meet the needs of their constituents. When an election occurs, constituents evaluate the performance of their representatives, assess whether their specific interests and needs have been adequately fulfilled, and use their votes as blunt instruments of accountability—rewarding or punishing their representatives accordingly.

With the representative-constituency linkage forming the basic template for an electoral connection, specific conditions must be met to fulfill Mayhew's original formulation. We argue that four such conditions exist. First, an electoral connection is premised on the notion that legislators are politically ambitious (e.g., that they desire reelection). Indeed, this ambition principle is the central assumption in Mayhew's theoretical framework. From legislators' aspiration to be reelected, we can presume that they desire a career in Congress—at least for some extended period of time; otherwise, they would not endure the rigors of the political campaign every two or six years. Multiple reelection victories provide additional opportunities for power (and further stoke ambition): the longer a member serves in the House or Senate, the more likely he or she is to gain influence within the chamber, as a function of existing seniority norms. This gain, in turn, makes it far easier for legislators to influence policy outcomes, especially if they serve as key members of the party leadership or the committee structure.

A second condition to fulfill Mayhew's formulation is that members of Congress must possess autonomy; that is, they must be in a position to control their own destiny. Legislators can be said to possess autonomy when two conditions are met. First, access to the electoral process must be open and exercised at the member's discretion, which means a legislator cannot be prevented from seeking reelection. Stated differently, no specific barriers (institutional or otherwise) should stand in the way of a member's ambition. Second, a member must maintain a large degree of independence in his or her pursuit of reelection. As Mayhew asserts, legislators in the modern era can build and sustain their own electoral coalitions largely independent of the party organization. More specifically, members of Congress can establish their own campaign themes, based on their own record of accomplishments, as well as raise their own money and appeal directly to their constituents. Although party affiliation provides legislators with an important "brand" name, along with a variety of services (see Aldrich 2011), it is not meant to restrict the appeal of the representative or senator to their constituents.[1] After all, legislators may be forced to appeal to more diverse constituencies (i.e., senators), and they do not want to be labeled too extreme relative to the voters that they represent.

A third condition of the electoral connection is that legislators must possess the ability to be responsive; that is, they must be able to meet the needs of their constituents. More simply, legislators must be able to provide their constituents with a variety of "benefits" that enhance the legislators' chances of reelection. In Mayhew's world, responsiveness is conceptualized in terms of three electorally useful activities that legislators frequently engage in: advertising, credit claiming, and position taking. For instance, to curry favor with their constituents, members of Congress can utilize casework, express favorable positions on symbolic votes, or funnel pork-barrel projects to their home districts. A legislator's position in Congress— whether as a party leader or a key member of a relevant committee—offers him or her the opportunity to engage in these types of activities. Moreover, legislative actions must be salient or visible, so that constituents fully recognize the important role that the legislator played in securing these particularized benefits for them (Arnold 1990; Fiorina 1974; Kingdon 1989). In the end, the primary goal for legislators with respect to responsiveness is to represent constituents' interests so that the citizens are more likely to vote for their representative in the next election.

A fourth condition, which focuses more directly on the constituency side of the electoral connection, is that voters must possess the ability to keep legislators accountable; that is, they must be able to evaluate legislators and punish or reward them appropriately. Additionally, Mayhew (1974: 28–38) suggests that a representative's particular electoral circumstances should influence his or her legislative behavior. Electorally vulnerable or marginal legislators, for example, should be less likely to support legislation that is politically unpopular. At the same time, we should observe higher rates of retirement among those legislators voting for unpopular legislative initiatives, and we should find lower rates of reelection among those who support such policies. Indeed, these expectations are borne out in studies examining the electoral consequences of position taking and roll-call voting during the contemporary era, when legislators are penalized for extreme behavior relative to the constituency they represent (Bovitz and Carson 2006; Canes-Wrone, Brady, and Cogan 2002; Carson, Koger, Lebo, and Young 2010; Jacobson 1993a).

In sum, we contend that four specific conditions must be fulfilled in order for an electoral connection, along the lines that Mayhew (1974) first elaborated, to operate. In the rest of this chapter, we examine the four theoretical conditions in detail, identifying when each was satisfied in a strict sense. We also allow for flexibility in our assessment of each condition, to determine if it operated differently than what we have become accustomed to in the contemporary context. In doing so, we discuss the specific conditions under which an electoral connection that was weaker or less formalized may have existed even further back in time.[2]

Ambition

Political ambition is the first and probably most fundamental component of the electoral connection. The claim that ambition is central to the electoral connection may, at first, appear to be counterintuitive, given that it is sometimes portrayed in an unfavorable light. For instance, candidates for public office sometimes cite their opponent's perceived political ambition as evidence that the opponent is unfit for office. In his foundational work on ambition theory, Schlesinger (1966) contends that this view of ambition overlooks the important role that ambition plays in compelling elected officials to be attentive to their constituents: "Representative government, above all, depends on a supply of men so driven; the desire for election and, more important, for reelection becomes the electorate's restraint upon its public officials" (2).[3] Schlesinger goes on to observe that the absence of political ambition can ultimately result in an inattentive government, composed of individuals who take whatever actions they desire because they are not restrained by considerations about their political futures.

When ambition is viewed as a desire for and interest in a future political career, it is easier to discern how the desire to achieve reelection and maintain a career in Congress, which is the basic building block of Mayhew's thesis, follows directly from an assumption about members' political ambition. Indeed, Schlesinger's (1966: 10) definition of static ambition, a politician who seeks to secure a long career within a specific office, is consistent with Mayhew's argument that legislators desire a career within Congress. How long have members of Congress been politically ambitious? Or (a question perhaps more in keeping with Mayhew's thesis) how long have members valued a career in Congress and thus actively sought reelection?

Although some might equate these two questions, a review of the congressional literature reveals that they are, in fact, two distinct ones, with two distinct answers.

There is general agreement among legislative scholars—using different measures such as the average number of terms served (Polsby 1968), the percentage of more senior members (Price 1971), the percentage of incumbents replaced by new members (Fiorina, Rohde, and Wissel 1975), and the percentage of incumbents running in the general election (Brady, Buckley, and Rivers 1999)—as to when members sought to establish roots in Congress and make it the basis of their careers. Brady, Buckley, and Rivers (1999: 490) succinctly summarize the findings as follows:

> The literature generally dates the rise in careerism as beginning in the 1890–1910 period. . . . After 1900, the number of freshman House members sharply declined and the average years of incumbent service grew dramatically. . . . [B]y 1920 the House had been transformed from a body of amateur members to a modern legislature of professional politicians with established careers in Washington.

While the 1890–1910 era seems to have been a significant moment in the rise of congressional careerism—thanks partly to a variety of changes, both endogenous to Congress (the growing importance of seniority) and exogenous (declining party competition, tied directly to various electoral reforms)—there is also evidence that a careerist trend had begun before then. Kernell (1977: 671), for example, contends that House membership began stabilizing as early as 1860 and that there was a "near linear growth of congressional careerism" from the Civil War through the 1920s.[4] Elsewhere, Kernell (2003) notes that the proportion of newly elected legislators in the House dropped from 60 percent to 24 percent between the 1850s and the turn of the twentieth century.

There are difficulties, however, in ascribing "desire for a congressional career" with each of these presumptive measures of careerism. In particular, these measures conflate nomination and election—which effectively means that members counted as careerists or career-seeking were those who sought reelection *and previously won renomination*. There is strong reason to believe that incumbents likely sought reelection—and desired a career in Congress—but were denied renomination by their respective parties; we explore this phenomenon more directly in chapter 5. Moreover, incumbents could not seek nominations directly during the nineteenth century; rather, nominations were determined by party conventions and were sometimes subject to informal term limits (i.e., rotation). These encumbrances on the discretion of incumbents are discussed in the next part of this chapter. The larger point here is simply that measures of congressional careerism in the literature are limited in what they can tell us about the rates at which incumbents in either the House or Senate desired reelection and a career in Congress more generally.

A broader question is, were nineteenth-century representatives ambitious? If ambition is given a broader definition than "desiring a career in Congress" or "single-minded reelection seeking," Mayhew's formulation is potentially applicable during an era of high turnover in Congress. For instance, Stewart (1989: 9–10) argues,

> [T]he extent of the nineteenth-century congressional revolving door has frequently been over-interpreted. The high turnover rates mask the extent to which late-nineteenth and early-twentieth century MCs were professional politicians, but politicians with a higher priority on local careers than on national ones. Thus, the "election pursuit" hypothesis that drives current congressional research in this tradition can be applied to past congressional behavior if the conceptualization of election pursuit is made more general, allowing for a broader notion of what MCs wanted to do with their future careers.

Based on Stewart's argument, careerism in the nineteenth century might be conceived better as "political careerism" than as "congressional careerism." Ambitious office seekers in the nineteenth century typically pursued a leapfrog strategy in building their political careers, with a seat in Congress constituting just one stop along the way. Members often moved from a local (state) position to Congress and then back again. A nonlinear career path might be considered unusual in the modern era—when progressive ambition, the desire to obtain high office, has become the norm (Schlesinger 1966; Rohde 1979)—but during the nineteenth-century political era, governorships, mayoralties, and judgeships were common employment destinations after serving in Congress.[5] Moreover, access to these positions often hinged on members' congressional performance, as party leaders back home kept a close eye on Washington politics (Stewart 1989: 57–58).[6]

Stewart (2001: 138–39) explores the ambition and back-and-forth structure of nineteenth-century politicians. Looking at a sample of two nineteenth-century Congresses, the 1st (1789–91) and the 47th (1881–83), he finds that 95.4 and 80.7 percent of freshman representatives, respec-

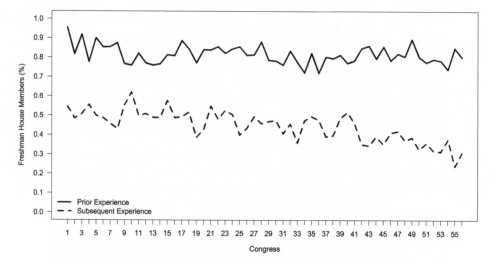

Figure 3.1. Percent of freshman House members with prior/subsequent political experience, 1st through 56th Congresses. (Data from Inter-University Consortium for Political and Social Research and McKibbin 1997.)

tively, had previous (local) political experience. Moreover, for many of those freshmen, their political careers did not end in Congress, as 53.8 and 44.3 percent, respectively, held another political position after serving in the House. In figure 3.1, we examine Stewart's argument across all Congresses through the turn of the twentieth century—the 1st through 56th Congresses (1789–1901). Consistent with Stewart's argument, freshman House members throughout the period possessed prior political experience, with a per-Congress average of 81.6 percent previously holding a political position. The findings on subsequent political experience are also interesting and hint at the rise of congressional careerism. Between the 1st and 24th Congresses (1789–1837), 50.3 percent of House freshmen went on to hold another political position; the number drops to 45.1 percent between the 25th and 41st Congresses (1837–71) and to 35.2 percent between the 42nd and 56th Congresses (1871–1901).[7] These data suggest that a small move toward House careerism occurred during the early part of the Second Party System and that a considerably larger move began during Reconstruction.[8]

Even if nineteenth-century members of Congress were not careerists in the same way as their modern counterparts, the patterns evident in figure 3.1 are still consistent with an important component of ambition theory. Indeed, Schlesinger (1966) contends that the "central assumption of ambition theory is that a politician's behavior is a response to his office goals," which lead the ambitious elected official to engage in "political acts and make decisions appropriate for gaining office" (6). The evidence that most members of Congress valued a career in politics suggests that they should still be responsive to local and state interests, since they would need to appeal to these voters in order to win a future office. In this way, political ambition, broadly defined, has the potential to induce similar behavior as that observed by modern legislators who exhibit static or progressive ambition.

Before moving on, we want to briefly entertain a related question: why was careerism more political than congressional during much of the nineteenth century? Although this question has not yet received significant attention in the literature, there are two potential answers. First, much of the political-economic development prior to the Civil War occurred at the state and local levels—this is where the bulk of the money resided and where political decision making had the greatest effect on public policy (Wallis 2004; Wallis and Weingast 2005). It was only after the Civil War that the federal government expanded appreciably and that large revenue surpluses (brought on by protective tariffs) provided members of Congress with substantial distributive policy-making authority (Kernell 1977). Second, congressional salaries were low throughout the nineteenth century, and several attempts to raise them significantly were quickly rescinded (Bianco, Spence, and Wilkerson 1996; Alston, Jenkins, and Nonnenmacher 2006). Thus, serving in Congress was not a lucrative venture in the nineteenth century, and other political offices, even many at the state level, often paid considerably more.

Autonomy

While ambition may be the most fundamental component of the electoral connection, it must be combined with autonomy to reach the conception that Mayhew describes. It is not enough that members want to achieve reelection (and to maintain a career in Congress), they must also be in a position to make it happen. They must possess discretion to pursue reelection, should that be their choice, and to do it largely on their own terms. Additionally, they must be able to craft their own reelection campaigns, based on their knowledge of their geographic units and the political dynamics therein, largely unhindered by external (partisan) requirements.

Stated simply, Mayhew's thesis requires that members of Congress must be able to control their own electoral destinies.

Discretion is the first element of the autonomy component. Members must be able to pursue reelection on their own accord; the option must be available for them to exercise. Given the considerable influence that parties exercised over elections throughout much of the nineteenth century (Carson and Roberts 2013), this type of discretion is a fairly modern development. Regardless of the electoral institutions in place, however, an incumbent's choice to run for reelection has long necessitated seeking a party's nomination. Since election viability is often based on running under the banner of one of the two major parties, renomination is a crucial step in the larger quest for reelection. In a strict sense, an incumbent's ability to directly seek renomination originated with the direct primary movement of the early twentieth century. Primary elections allow candidates to compete actively for a party's nomination by appealing directly to party-identifying citizens of the underlying geographic constituencies, who are in the position of making selection decisions.[9] During the first two decades of the twentieth century, the vast majority of states adopted direct primary laws, which covered congressional party nominations as well as party nominations for most other state offices (see Ware 2002: 123). Thus, for much of the last century, a legislator's ability to seek reelection has been a two-stage process, with renomination (the initial stage) essentially required for reelection.[10]

Prior to the rise of direct primaries, state party conventions—which first emerged in the 1830s—selected a party's slate of candidates. Party nominees for House seats were chosen in district conventions, with delegates selected from the district's various counties (Reynolds 2006). The convention system was an indirect nomination process, as candidates for office (including incumbents) were left to the mercy of the convention delegates that determined party slates. There was little room for the average voter in such a system; voters may have had a say over initial delegate selection (although the openness of this process varied by county), but they had no direct say over the choice of congressional nominees.

In addition to the indirect nominating system in use during the convention era, some nineteenth-century congressional incumbents also had to deal with state-level norms that served as de facto term limits. The practice of "rotation" allowed party leaders to distribute offices among the many party faithful (Kernell 1977) and generally meant that members of Congress were restricted to a finite period of service—often two terms. Because rotation was an informal party rule, data on which states regularly employed rotation and over what period of time this practice was utilized by state party organizations is sketchy at best. Despite the well-known case of Abraham Lincoln being restricted to one House term in Illinois (per the Whig Party rule in place at the time), Kernell (1977) argues that rotation was a relatively minor problem, in that it was not employed widely and thus affected relatively few incumbents.[11]

While party conventions served as a potential barrier to ambitious politicians, reelection-minded incumbents and other potential candidates did not behave passively during the convention era.[12] Rather, they acted rationally and adjusted to the institutional environment. During much of the convention era, active politicking and campaigning by candidates was frowned upon, as a culture of reticence and decorum was perpetuated. Still, as Reynolds (2006: 9) notes, "Prospective nominees and their friends worked quietly behind the scenes." By the end of the nineteenth century, however, the culture had changed, and candidates for nomination behaved much more aggressively, courting convention delegates openly and actively. By 1900, Reynolds (2006: 10, 72–73) contends, candidates for congressional seats "had learned that it paid to be assertive in promoting one's availability for party honors," and "it was expected that persons desirous of a nomination had to spend extra time, money, and energy to win it." Thus, the emergence of the "hustling candidate" occurred well in advance of the direct primary era.

One additional facet of discretion deserves mention. While the indirect nature of the nomination process could hamper incumbents' ability to seek reelection, incumbents could circumvent their party if they failed to gain renomination. During much of the nineteenth century, the balloting process was informal, which meant that parties were largely responsible for printing and distributing ballots. If an incumbent failed to receive the party's nomination, it was possible to "bolt" the party (and the convention's decision) and run a splinter campaign in the general election. All that was required was for the incumbent to print and distribute ballots of his own. As Bensel (2003: 8) argues,

> Unlike contemporary politics where a new party would have to circulate petitions, pay filing fees, and meet deadlines months before an election takes place, a party faction could become an effective contender at the polls even if it bolted only hours before the voting started.

Moreover, the lack of ballot rules allowed a splinter candidate to reconfigure the regular party slate of nominees and insert his own name in place of the party's chosen congressional nominee (Ware 2002). Doing so required no special skills or talents. As Reynolds (2006: 127) explains, "[A]nyone could prepare and distribute 'mixed' or 'irregular' tickets." Thus, if an incumbent member of Congress was popular enough with voters and controlled enough resources to print ballots and hire workers to distribute them, he could still credibly vie for reelection without the party's official nomination.

Independence is the second element of the autonomy component. Congressional scholars typically view candidates or campaigns as independent when they are at least somewhat outside the control of the party organization. Although it is often held, per Mayhew's thesis, that candidate-centered campaigns did not emerge until after World War II, other evidence suggests that the process began much earlier, with the adoption of the direct primary. The creation of an open nomination process led to a Darwinian struggle among potential party candidates. According to most accounts of congressional politics, this heightened competition gave way to an increased importance for the attributes of individual candidates. In particular, a candidate's ability to raise sizable sums of money is thought to have become more valuable over time. As election costs rose prodigiously during the era of the direct primary, candidates needed pay for campaign managers, agents in the field, local workers, and political advertising, in order to remain electorally competitive (Reynolds 2006: 190–92). Under this new system, candidates with strong financial backing—and who could raise money consistently—were considerably advantaged.[13]

It would be incorrect to conclude that money was unimportant to the nomination process before the spread of the direct primary, however.[14] The rise of hustling candidates increased the flow of money into the nominations process, as this new type of candidate, eager for nomination, distributed funds to lobby and sway convention delegates. As Summers (2004: 8) states about the late nineteenth century, "Money was everywhere. A campaign could not get along without it." Potential candidates' financial independence was an important consideration even during the height of the convention era. While party leaders had a strong hand in selecting candidates, the process could still be quite candidate-centered, since potential candidates made themselves viable based on the degree to which they could independently finance their pursuit of office. According to Reynolds (2006: 189), "Politicians salivated at the prospect of nominating a rich man for office who could liberally fund the fall campaign." With financial independence came general campaign independence, as candidates were typically given a wide berth to establish their own campaign messages (within the very general auspices of the party platform).

Aside from financial independence, congressional candidates during the nineteenth century were, at times, afforded greater discretion with regard to the campaign itself. Prior to 1872, election timing was quite variable, as many House elections were held months before (or even months after) November (Engstrom 2012). In some off-November elections, the House candidates were at the top of the party ballot (Engstrom and Kernell 2014), which meant that the choice of ballots in the congressional race did not require the voter to first choose among the presidential candidates. The substantive consequences of holding separate presidential and congressional elections were, at times, considerable. In 1844, North Carolina held its congressional elections in August, and Democrats won 6 of the state's 9 seats. In November of that year, Henry Clay, the Whig presidential candidate, carried North Carolina with a little over 52 percent of the vote. Similarly, Lewis Cass, the 1848 Democratic presidential candidate, won Virginia with 50.8 percent of the vote, but Democrats won 14 out of the state's 15 seats in the congressional elections held five months later, in April 1849. These races clearly demonstrate the potential advantages and consequences of holding off-cycle elections (Anzia 2012). We have examined the importance of variable election timing in previous research (Carson and Sievert 2017), and we return to this important subject in chapter 6 of the present study.

Responsiveness

In addition to being both ambitious and autonomous, members of Congress must also be responsive. The third assumption underlying Mayhew's conception of the electoral incentive, responsiveness means that incumbents must be able to fulfill the needs and requests of their constituents. As reelection requires constituent ratification, members have to be in a position to provide the types of benefits of concern to constituents. Mayhew contends that legislators in the contemporary Congress frequently engage in three types of behaviors in their pursuit of constituent support: advertising, credit claiming, and position taking. A mixture of these three fundamental activities, Mayhew suggests, helps to ensure that members of Congress continue to get reelected.

To what extent are these types of reelection-oriented activities actively facilitated by the institutional structure within Congress? At the beginning of the second half of his text, Mayhew offers an important insight about the institutional design of the legislature in conjunction with the electoral connection and addresses this question in particular.

[T]he organization of Congress meets remarkably well the electoral needs of its members. To put it another way, if a group of planners sat down and tried to design a pair of American national assemblies with the goal of serving members' electoral needs year in and year out, they would be hard pressed to improve on what exists. (Mayhew 1974: 81–82)

What makes this statement of particular interest in this context is that many of the recognizable congressional institutions—the standing committee system, the property rights norm, and the seniority system—have been in place as far back as the early nineteenth century (Gamm and Shepsle 1989; Jenkins 1998; Polsby 1968; Stewart and Canon 2001). Even so, when we discuss the electoral connection in conjunction with these legislative institutions, we often do so in terms of the contemporary Congress. For instance, when focusing on legislators engaging in credit-claiming activities, we often think about how effective they are in terms of funneling pork-barrel projects back to their home state or district. We often also emphasize how members of Congress take advantage of the media to advertise themselves or their accomplishments to their constituents.

Were legislators in a position to utilize these types of activities to provide "benefits" to their constituents outside of the contemporary era, albeit to a somewhat more limited extent than we regularly observe today? As noted earlier, Reynolds (2006) describes how candidates during much of the nineteenth century were expected to rise above the political fray—as raw political ambition was considered a "vice" during that era—by not actively soliciting public support for their campaigns. By the latter part of the nineteenth century, this cultural (and behavioral) norm was no more, as candidates actively adjusted their behavior in an attempt to earn and retain the nomination for office (Reynolds 2006: 62–67). In much the same way that Mayhew claims for congressional incumbents today, these "hustling candidates" valued the importance of getting their name out to delegates. Once they secured a seat in Congress, they could then utilize their legislative accomplishments to justify why they should be reelected.

Evidence for member advertising also exists in the antebellum era. Cooper and Young (1989) argue that changes to the rules of bill introduction in the House, going back to the late 1830s, were made at least partly to generate additional opportunities for members to promote their legislative efforts. Committees had always been privileged in their ability to introduce bills, and members' opportunities to gain the floor for advertising purposes had always been limited. This created pent-up member demand, and the rule changes in 1837–38 only whetted members' appetites. Alexander (1916: 217) states,

> [By the 1840s] members clamored for more time for the introduction of bills. At first bills were not numerous. The modern habit of using them to advertise a member's activities did not then obsess the legislative mind. . . . But when the fact developed that a bill introduced, though not passed, benefited the member, since it evidenced a disposition to serve his constituents, the House (1860) set apart each alternate Monday for their introduction and ordered them referred without debate. This radical change, encouraging members to present bills on all possible subjects, created such a Monday rush that it increased their number nearly twenty-fold in twenty years.

Institutional development in the House thus followed directly from members' self-interest. Beginning in the 1830s and continuing over the next few decades, the procedures of bill introduction in the House changed to make it easier for members "to introduce business of interest to their states and localities" (Cooper and Young 1989: 98). Regarding constituency-induced member self-interest as the driving force for institutional development in the House is quite consistent with Mayhew's (1974) elaboration of the electoral connection.

In addition to advertising, members of Congress also find it advantageous to engage in various forms of position taking. As Mayhew (1974: 62) reminds us, the "congressman as a position taker is a speaker rather than a doer," since "the position itself is the political commodity." In the age of 24-hour cable news stations and the Internet, incumbents have a far easier time getting their message out today than they did in the past. Nevertheless, the reach of the party press was extensive in the nineteenth century (Smith 1977), and events in Congress were covered in great detail (Kernell 1986; Kernell and Jacobson 1987). Well before the era of mass technological communications, these party newspapers provided incumbents with an outlet to take positions on issues of concern to the public.

An interesting case of antebellum position taking that has been explored extensively in the literature is the petition movement against slavery in the 1830s (see Carpenter and Moore 2014; Carpenter and Schneer 2015; Miller 1995; Jenkins and Stewart 2003; Meinke 2007). From the federal government's founding, petitions, or memorials, sent from citizens to their members of Congress had been a regular part of the representative-constituency linkage. In the mid-1830s, the petition movement escalated considerably, as antislavery constituents in the North flooded their members of Congress with requests that the South's "peculiar institution" be eliminated and that slaves be freed (Carpenter and Moore 2014). These efforts eventually led to a series of "gag rules" in Congress, wherein petitions regarding slavery would not be publicly read. After years of argument and mounting pressure in the North, the continuing petition drive led to the repudiation of the congressional gags; many Northern politicians who had previously supported the gag rules switched their positions, fearing constituent retribution (Meinke 2007). In the 1840s and 1850s, fear of taking the wrong position on slavery issues affected speakership elections and candidate choice (Jenkins and Stewart 2001, 2012). Position taking on "racial issues" more generally cropped up again in the 1870s and has been the basis for a number of recorded cases of "killer amendments" across American history (Jenkins and Munger 2003).

The final activity that incumbents regularly employ in an attempt to get reelected is credit claiming. Here the goal is simple: the member needs to accomplish certain objectives on behalf of his or her constituents that will make them want to continue to support the representative in upcoming elections. In the contemporary era, there are plenty of opportunities for credit claiming—such as funneling pork-barrel projects to constituents, preventing a military base from being closed, and performing casework for voters—many of which stem directly from a committee on which a representative sits. Ultimately, the representative needs to convince his or her constituents (1) that the representative is personally responsible for making something desirable happen and (2) that the outcome would be significantly less likely to occur if the representative were not currently serving in Congress.

As noted above, much of the recognized institutional structure in Congress that facilitates credit claiming was in place long before the modern (post–World War II) era. This suggests that incumbents may have found it advantageous to utilize their positions on legislative committees far earlier than is generally accepted, to try to achieve "benefits" for their constituents. Indeed, committee assignments and committee chairs were hotly contested during the antebellum period—probably, at least in part, for credit-claiming purposes (Jenkins and Stewart 2003). In the postbellum years, committee assignments and committee chairs formed the glue that held party organizations together; assignments and chairs were doled out to different factions in the party, based on members' particular district (constituent) needs, and thereby cemented organizational decisions made in caucus (Jenkins and Stewart 2003).

The late nineteenth-century congressional agenda created the basis for many credit-claiming opportunities, as particularistic issues gained in importance.[15] For example, legislation on rivers and harbors emerged in force in the early 1880s and typically "contained significant appropriations for improvements designed to benefit only particular localities" (Stathis 2002: 122). Indeed, members of Congress in the late nineteenth and early twentieth centuries frequently claimed credit for their district's respective piece of the rivers-and-harbors pie (Wilson 1986).[16] Protective tariffs were perhaps the major political-economic issue in the postbellum Congress, as a variety of producers and manufacturers of raw materials forcefully lobbied their particular members of Congress for favorable trade terms. Members were cognizant of such lobbying efforts and actively sought to signal that they were being responsive (often with speeches on the floor of Congress and with their roll-call votes) and to claim credit for specific elements in the tariff schedules (Brady 1973; Conybeare 1991; Brady, Goldstein, and Kessler 2002; Schiller 2006). Civil War pensions were also a major element of congressional policymaking in the postbellum years.[17] Civil War veterans were a large client group, and members of Congress (mostly Republicans, but also Northern Democrats) worked very hard to pass general pension bills and to meet the individual needs of pensioners (and potential pensioners) in their districts (Finocchiaro 2005, 2006).

Interestingly, the antecedents for the particularistic congressional programs in the post–Civil War era were rooted in the pre–Civil War era; that is, constituent demand, congressional policymaking, and member credit claiming were active components of political life in antebellum America. For example, protective tariffs were as hotly contested prior to the Civil War as they were after, and geographically centered constituent pressure and congressional responsiveness were very much in operation (Pincus 1975, 1977; Irwin 2006). In addition, the template for Civil War pension legislation could be found in the Revolutionary War pensions of the 1810s and 1830s. The particularistic elements of veterans' pensions originated here, as members of Congress who represented geographic units with a higher concentration of pension-eligible adults actively sought a greater distribution of benefits (Finocchiaro and Jenkins 2016).

Additional evidence of credit claiming in the antebellum era can be illustrated by examining the number of public and private laws produced. These data are presented in figure 3.2. As the series suggest, the number of private laws trailed the number of public laws until the 1830s, when members of Congress clearly viewed opportunities for credit claiming by providing Revolutionary War pensions to particular constituents (and their

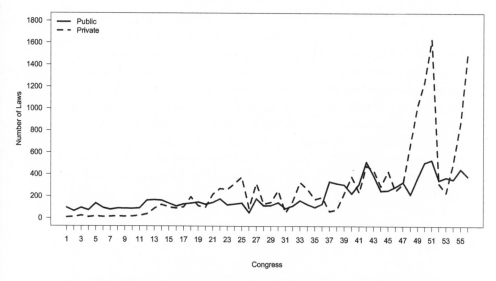

Figure 3.2. Public and private laws, 1st through 56th Congresses. (McIver 2006. © Cambridge University Press.)

families) via private bills. This private pension strategy continued through the late 1850s (as veterans of the Mexican-American War were also targeted). After the Civil War, the number of potential pensioners was enormous, and Congress generally worked to provide for their needs through public acts. But by the 1880s, members of Congress once again turned to private bills to provide individual pensioners (and their families) with relief, and they did so with gusto and fervor, as the number of private bills (and laws) skyrocketed. This massive increase coincided with the trend toward congressional careerism that began in the late nineteenth century. By the 1880s, as Cooper and Young (1989: 99) state, "the Civil War made private business in the form of pensions and relief from political disabilities more relevant to [members' immediate] career interests."

In looking back through time for evidence of member responsiveness, one need not stop with the early nineteenth century. Indeed, one can find evidence of constituency-based decision making in Congress going back to the late *eighteenth century*. For example, the apportionment of congressional seats after the decennial census, which precipitated battles in Congress through the 1940s, first emerged as an issue in 1791, as members debated a new House size and ratio of representation (Balinski and Young 2001; Schmeckebier 1941; Zagarri 1987). Inevitably, different bills were presented, stipulating different House sizes (105 and 112) that appeared to favor different regions and economic constituencies. As Balinski and Young (2001: 13) note, "The contest over division of seats arose from deep political divisions: the emerging conflict between North and South, between Republican and Federalist, between agricultural and industrial interests." The stakes were high, and while the bill establishing a House of 120 seats passed both chambers, it led to the first presidential veto in US history, as President George Washington preferred the 105-seat measure. In addition, bankruptcy policy, which was a major issue in Congress throughout the nineteenth century (as well as the twentieth), had its roots in the eighteenth century, with the first major bankruptcy law in the United States passed in 1800. Roll-call votes on bankruptcy issues had a distinct constituency basis, the nature of which was both regional (North vs. South) and economic, as it was supported by banking and trading interests (Berglöf and Rosenthal 2005, 2007; Poole and Rosenthal 2007).

These various findings raise an important question: why would legislators endeavor to be responsive to constituents in the premodern era if they were not interested in pursuing a career in Congress? The answer may be relatively simple: perhaps incumbents were not focused on a career in Congress per se but, rather, were politically ambitious and interested in a *political career*. Since nineteenth-century careers were largely viewed as residing within the party organization (Aldrich 2011), it would make sense that legislators would want to do things to keep their constituents happy, like taking favorable public positions on roll-call votes and routinely engaging in credit claiming. Indeed, Bianco, Spence, and Wilkerson (1996: 147) note,

> We do not believe that the politics of the modern and early Congresses are as different as the conventional wisdom suggests. Studies of the modern Congress emphasize the fact that legislators are held accountable for their individual behavior. In this paper, we show that the same sort of accountability arose in at least one instance in the 19th century Congress.

The same voters that incumbents represented in the House might very well be their constituents at some future date, when they ran under the banner of the party organization for a state-level position.[18]

The preceding argument is crucial in explaining why incumbents were responsive in the nineteenth century, even though they were not congressional careerists in the modern sense. As political careerists, they had to please their constituents, and a representative could serve the same constituents when a member of Congress and when a member of the state house or senate. Also, party organizations cared about making sure that constituents were happy; they wanted to keep congressional districts within their party column, regardless of whether that district was represented by the same person. Ultimately, incumbent members of Congress cared if party leaders were satisfied during much of the nineteenth century (and earlier), since those leaders could affect their chances of maintaining a successful political career, whether inside or outside of Congress.

Accountability

The final component of Mayhew's conception of the electoral incentive is accountability; members of Congress must be accountable to voters, who evaluate their performance in office and punish or reward them accordingly, by voting to remove or reelect them. Accountability thus requires that voters have the means to evaluate individual incumbents, as well as the general aptitude or capacity to make a choice, within a competitive electoral environment. Thus, unlike the three components previously discussed, which focus on the member of Congress specifically, this final component focuses on the voters in the member's geographic constituency. Voters possess the ultimate say in whether members will achieve their proximate goal of reelection.

Voters were first provided with the means to evaluate *individual* members of Congress directly in the late nineteenth century, with the advent of the Australian ballot. As noted above, an official balloting system did not exist in the United States throughout most of the nineteenth century; instead, ballots were printed and distributed largely by the parties themselves and provided a list of only the party's candidates for all available offices.[19] Starting in the late 1880s and stretching into the 1910s, the balloting process was taken over by the states themselves, and the unofficial party ballot was replaced by an official government ballot.[20] The new, state-generated ballot—known as the Australian ballot, as it was first instituted in Australia, earlier in the nineteenth century—listed *all* candidates for *all* offices, from which the voters could pick and choose by both candidate and office. The Australian ballot made ticket splitting more straightforward and thus made it much easier for voters to punish or reward candidates individually (Rusk 1970; Katz and Sala 1996). The Australian ballot thus firmed up the agency relationship by increasing accountability; members of Congress now had a greater incentive to be responsive to the needs of their geographic constituencies.[21]

During the pre-Australian ballot days, the agency relationship was considerably softer, as the structure of the party ballot often constrained voters' ability to hold individual incumbents accountable. The parties constructed their ballots to promote straight-ticket voting; thus, if a voter wanted to punish a particular party candidate, the ballot structure made it somewhat difficult to do so without punishing the entire party slate. We say "somewhat" because voters still had the ability to split their tickets and punish or reward candidates: it simply required a more manual effort. For example, voters could scratch out a candidate's name and write in another name; they could cover candidates' names on the ballot with small strips of paper bearing unofficial candidates' names, called "pasters" and often hawked at voting places; or they could create their own ballot at home and simply bring it to the polling place (Bensel 2004; Reynolds and McCormick 1986; Reynolds 2006; Summers 2004; Ware 2002).

There were dangers associated with *not* voting a straight party ticket in the era of party ballots, however. Voting was not secret, and party workers (i.e., henchmen) were positioned at the polling places, ever watchful of how voters behaved. In addition, party ballots were often color coded, giving the party henchman a clear cue of voters' intentions. Pressure or outright violence could be directed toward those who bucked the system of straight party voting.[22] Nevertheless, as Reynolds (2006: 128) notes concerning that era, "Anecdotal evidence of rampant ticket splitting is abundant. It also finds ample support in the election data." He surveys two Colorado precincts in 1888 and 1904 and finds that, respectively, 29.6 and 37.4 percent of ballots were of the split-ticket variety (130–31). Bensel (2004: 32) looks at an Ohio county in 1868 and uncovers more moderate results: 17 percent of ballots cast were split tickets.[23] Thus, while ticket splitting was clearly easier during the Australian ballot era (when the ballot was designed for such and when voting was secret), voters could still reward or punish candidates during the era of party ballots, should they so choose.

Did voters possess the *capacity* to punish or reward individual incumbents during the nineteenth century? Many studies hold that this period well before the era of mass communications—radio and television were many decades away—was characterized by very strong citizen attachments to party (see, e.g., Silbey 1985, 1991), with any significant election-to-election deviations (when they occurred) resulting from voters punishing the majority party *generally* for negative economic conditions (Holt 1992). Still, the availability of political news was substantial; as noted previously, newspapers were plentiful throughout the country, and national events (principally actions taken by the president and Congress) made up the lion's share of newspapers' political coverage (see Kernell 1986; Kernell and Jacobson 1987). News—especially news that involved a district or state's members of Congress—was a hot commodity. Thus, information about political affairs in Washington and particularly in Congress was plentiful in nineteenth-century America, and available evidence suggests that citizens were sufficiently engaged politically to keep track of their elected members of Congress.[24]

One might be tempted to read the literature on congressional elections as concluding that electoral accountability is rare, even in the modern era. Because legislators cast hundreds of votes in a congressional session, one should not expect the vast majority of roll calls to have significant electoral effects, for instance. As Carson, Finocchiaro, and Rohde (2010) show, as much as two-thirds of legislation considered in the House is highly consensual. It is rare for behavior on these low-variance roll calls to have any noticeable electoral effects, since they do little to help voters or special interest groups distinguish legislators from one another. Moreover, only a fraction of roll calls with variance in legislative behavior may become important enough to play a significant role in an election, since voters generally tend to be largely unaware of how their representatives vote on much of the legislation considered in Congress (Kingdon 1989). While voters may recognize the significance of a few important roll calls in Congress each year, they are less likely to learn or recall exactly how their member voted with respect to those bills. In nearly all cases, the public's information about positions taken by legislators is often limited to a few extremely salient issues (Arnold 1990).

Given the relative obscurity of most House roll calls and the fact that voters are generally unaware of legislators' voting behavior, why, then, might legislators worry about which positions they take on the House floor? Chances are that any single roll call will remain outside of the electoral arena. However, studies of legislative behavior suggest that members of Congress are risk averse and worry about the positions they take because they suspect some roll calls *may* become electorally salient (see, e.g., Mayhew 1974; Jacobson 1987; Arnold 1990), and they can never be absolutely sure about which ones will emerge. Therefore, legislators have significant incentive to make choices as if every roll call could become a factor in their reelection bid, and over forty years of Congress scholarship, since Mayhew (1974), contends emphatically that they generally act accordingly.[25]

To date, various explanations have been offered to address the hypothesized link between House floor roll-call voting and citizens' voting behavior at the polls. In some instances, voter awareness implies a thorough and sophisticated understanding of an incumbent's specific roll-call choice; however, a second level of awareness is sufficient to link legislative behavior to electoral outcomes. Some voters gain a more general sense of awareness of a specific roll-call decision. For example, in some cases, proposed legislation garners significant attention inside the beltway, stimulating elite action, which, in turn, provides voters with some (relatively generic) understanding of their legislators' decisions on hot-button issues. These voters may not necessarily be cognizant of all the details of the vote, but they are at least somewhat familiar with the nature of a *specific* position their legislator has taken on an issue that is salient to them. This awareness can be sufficient for the roll call—the official articulation of the position taken—to have an impact on election day.

Arnold (1990: 46) argues that legislators must be careful when casting roll calls, because citizens may use any number of the incumbents' actions when engaging in retrospective voting. Additionally, Wright (1978: 446) claims, "Issues do not need to explain most of the variance in election outcomes; they just need to have enough of an impact to give congressmen— who are surprisingly insecure about their own re-elections . . .—an incentive to heed the general policy wishes of their constituents." Moreover, incumbent legislators must develop voting records that prevent challengers from being able to expose inconsistencies in their position taking. As Jacobson (1987: 139) argues, taking "a prominent position on the wrong side of a major issue" can "galvanize potential opponents."

In sum, positions on roll calls can have significant electoral consequences, not because voters are necessarily aware of legislators' specific roll-call choices, but because legislators' roll-call behavior affects the actions of political elites (e.g., the media, special interest groups, and experienced challengers), which, in turn, affects voters' choices. This conceptualization of the accountability process, involving various potential links between roll-call decisions and voters as well as different levels of voter awareness, leads to the prediction that a significant proportion of *key* votes on the House floor should have observable effects on electoral margins. Although much of the preceding discussion is related to electoral accountability in the modern era, it has analogs to accountability in earlier political eras as well. Indeed, existing research on the nineteenth-century Congress supports the accountability component of the electoral connection. Three examples stand out.

Bianco, Spence, and Wilkerson (1996) examine the Compensation Act of 1816—which retroactively increased congressional pay by as much as 100 percent—and find (a) that members who were more electorally vulnerable were less likely to support the legislative compensation plan and (b) that members who chose to support the plan were less likely to seek reelection, due to the apparent electoral risks of such action. Moreover, those scholars note that the congressional pay raise was sufficiently salient for voters to become informed about it, even during that era of limited news outlets, and thus made it easier to hold representatives accountable for their support of the controversial legislation. In general, based on their findings, Bianco, Spence, and Wilkerson argue,

> [V]oters in the 1816 elections did not indiscriminately punish incumbents . . . nor did voters focus their anger on the party in power. Rather it appears that as far as the Compensation Act is concerned, incumbents were held accountable for their individual behavior, much as in the modern era. (147)

As a result, Bianco, Spence, and Wilkerson conclude that "the politics of the modern and early Congresses are [not] as different as the conventional wisdom suggests" (147).

In a similar vein, Carson, Jenkins, Rohde, and Souva (2001) examine the congressional elections of 1862–63—which took place during the American Civil War—to determine the extent to which the electorate's dissatisfaction with the Republican-organized war effort led to a systematic backlash against the Republican House candidates. They find that, much like in modern elections, both national forces (i.e., the course of the war) and district-specific conditions (i.e., entry of quality challengers against marginal incumbents, district-level war casualties, and the timing of races) affected incumbents' electoral fortunes in predictable ways. More generally, their findings "confirm the importance of district-specific effects on electoral outcomes in the nineteenth century" (894).

Finally, Carson and Engstrom (2005) examined the electoral aftershocks of the disputed presidential election of 1824. The election was controversial, as no candidate received a majority of the popular vote, and the winner had to be decided in the House of Representatives. As a result, the House contest was an extremely high-profile race, and citizens throughout the country awaited the outcome. Carson and Engstrom find that legislators who (a) voted for John Quincy Adams (the eventual winner) in the

House contest and (b) represented districts that supported Andrew Jackson in the popular election were targeted for ouster and suffered a substantial vote loss in the subsequent midterm election. They also find that the entry of a quality challenger had a sizable impact on the fortunes of incumbent legislators. These results, they contend, "serve to confirm that representatives could be held accountable for their behavior in office during the antebellum era" (746).

Overall, then, there is evidence suggesting that incumbents could be held accountable for their behavior in earlier eras, much as we have found evidence supporting this contention in the contemporary era (see, e.g., Bovitz and Carson 2006; Canes-Wrone, Brady, and Cogan 2002; Jacobson 1993a). Lacking, however, is more systematic evidence from the premodern era that directly compares legislative accountability to the modern era. Most of the accounts described above deal with isolated events of an exceptional nature that were especially salient to voters from that era. Without a more systematic analysis to determine whether accountability was present on other, less atypical votes in Congress, it is difficult to fully assess the extent to which this component of the electoral connection was present generally across time.

Discussion

So far in this study, we have sought to better understand how an electoral incentive might have manifested itself in Congress well before the mid-twentieth century. While our discussion in this chapter lays out the theoretical components of an electoral connection in Congress and how it might have operated in earlier political eras, it is entirely suggestive at this point. As such, there is still much work to be done to evaluate what an electoral connection might have looked like during the nineteenth century and how it may have changed over time. In the next four chapters, we conduct a series of empirical analyses and case studies to examine each of these four components of our broader argument about the electoral connection. By examining each facet of the electoral connection during the period from the 1820s to the 1880s, we hope to provide a more comprehensive account of how electoral incentives informed and motivated legislative politics during the first century of American political development.

There are two reasons why these seven decades are particularly well suited for our present endeavor. First, previous studies suggest that the strength of nineteenth-century political parties undermined the existence of key components of the electoral connection (see, e.g., Polsby 1968; Swift 1987). However, political parties were not uniformly empowered as engines for mass electoral politics throughout the nineteenth century. "Proto-electoral" parties began to organize in the wake of the 1824 election, and truly nationwide mass electoral parties did not form until the 1840s (Aldrich 2011; Formisano 1974). As a result, we are able to examine congressional politics in the period before mass electoral parties, during the era of strong parties, and in the early stages of the breakdown in party strength that began in the late nineteenth century.

While some scholars point to the late nineteenth century as the starting point for the rise of candidate-centered politics (Reynolds 2006; Ware 2002), our examination of a significantly longer time period can shed light on whether it was truly a new development or a return to the dynamics of an earlier era. We expect that the latter account has greater explanatory power than previous explanations would suggest. Indeed, our argument has parallels to studies on the role of political parties *within* Congress where congressional scholars talk about the relative balance of power between committees and parties. While there can certainly be differences between committee and party government, both institutions provide structure to what could otherwise be an unstable process. Similarly, the continuum between candidate and party-centered elections can be understood in terms of a shift between which factor helps to structure outcomes. In much the same way that different institutional developments shift the balance of power between committees and legislative parties, we would expect to find a similar pattern in electoral politics. Of course, the elections of earlier eras are not perfectly comparable to modern ones, but differences are more likely to be in magnitude than in form.

The second factor making the 1820s to the 1880s a suitable period for the present study is that institutions make an important contribution toward satisfying some of the components of the electoral connection. Indeed, both the Australian ballot and the direct primary were important reforms that helped to put in place some of the conditions needed for the modern, Mayhewian electoral connection (Carson and Roberts 2013; Carson and Sievert 2015). As we have discussed in this chapter, these institutional reforms may not have been necessary for the existence of some form of electoral connection. During the decades we examine, however, there was variation in other types of institutional arrangements. Perhaps the most intriguing for our current study is the fact that congressional elections were not held on a uniform date throughout large swaths of the nineteenth century. In earlier work, we examined how variable election timing conditioned the party-centered nature of nineteenth-century congressional elections (Carson and Sievert 2017). In the chapters that follow, we build on this foundation to more fully document the impact of nonuniform election timing on both intralegislative and electoral politics. Similarly, the timing of congressional sessions was far different during the nineteenth century, which has important implications when viewed in conjunction with the variability in the timing of elections.

FOUR

Candidates and Competition in US House Races, 1820–88

In the summer and fall of 1854, the nation once again found itself fiercely divided over the question of slavery. The passage of the Nebraska-Kansas Act, which allowed the newly organized territories to vote on the question of whether to allow slavery, had the practical (though informal) effect of repealing the Missouri Compromise. Although both Democratic and Whig legislators voted for passage of the bill, the vote divided the Whig coalition more clearly along regional lines. Northern Whigs unanimously opposed the bill, while the party's Southern faction largely lined up in support of the legislation. Despite the clear intraparty division on the Nebraska bill, some Northern Whig politicians hoped the legislation would revitalize the party and lead them to victory in upcoming congressional and statewide elections (Holt 1978). Unfortunately for these optimistic Whig politicians, they were not responsible for the Democrats' major electoral defeat in the ensuing congressional elections. Instead, a coalition of anti-Nebraska forces dominated both state and congressional elections throughout the year (Gienapp 1986; Holt 1978).[1] The Democrats' seat share was slashed from 157 seats in the 33rd Congress (1853–55) to 83 seats in the 34th Congress (1855–57).[2]

Unlike some members of the opposition coalition that took control of the House, the Republican Party had not been active in any previous election.[3] A lack of prior electoral organization did not keep the Republicans from riding the anti-Nebraska tide to considerable success, however. In Michigan and Wisconsin, the two states where the party first organized, the

Republicans won five of the seven available seats. Of the five newly acquired Republican seats, four were won by defeating a Democratic incumbent, and only one Democratic incumbent, Daniel Wells of Wisconsin, managed to survive the anti-Nebraska tide. Although the success of these and other Republican candidates has been well documented (Aldrich 2011; Gienapp 1986; Holt 1978), prior accounts often focus on the broader historical significance of these victories, rather than considering how they fit into broader theories about electoral competition in congressional elections. Aldrich (2011: 150), who describes these candidates and their contemporaries in the anti-Nebraska coalitions as "midlevel ambitious politicians," comes the closest but limits his focus to state-level electoral outcomes. What remains unclear is whether these "ambitious politicians" were strategic actors who sought to capitalize on favorable electoral circumstances or amateurs who were merely swept into office by national tides.[4]

If the first Republican congressional candidates were primarily experienced politicians and not amateurs, strategic politicians theory (Jacobson and Kernell 1983; Jacobson 1989) could provide a useful framework for understanding key elements of this historic election. While the theory was originally developed to describe post–World War II elections, a growing body of research suggests that it is applicable across a larger swath of history (Carson, Engstrom, and Roberts 2007; Carson and Roberts 2013; Carson and Sievert 2015). An examination of the prior electoral backgrounds of Republican candidates in four states—Illinois, Maine, Michigan, and Wisconsin—largely comports with the expectations of strategic politicians theory.[5] Republican candidates were on the ballot in 20 of the 22 congressional districts across these four states. Illinois was the only state in which the Republican Party did not field a candidate in every congressional race. In total, 14 of these 20 Republican candidates had previously been elected to public office.[6] The Republicans won four of the five districts in which an incumbent legislator switched parties to join the Republicans, and they won six of the nine races where they nominated a nonincumbent candidate with elective experience. In contrast, the Republicans won only three of the six races in which they fielded a candidate with no previous electoral experience. Overall, these cases suggest that several members of the first wave of Republican candidates were strategic politicians in precisely the manner posited by strategic politicians theory.

As the above story suggests, having a large pool of "quality" challengers is a necessary condition for competitive congressional races. During the modern era, a relatively large number of incumbents face either a weak, inexperienced challenger or no opponent at all. Yet this has not always been the case across the history of this nation. Throughout much of the nineteenth century, as many as 40 or 50 percent of incumbents ran against strong or experienced challengers in the general election. Why were congressional elections so much more competitive in the past than they are today? If this competition was indeed manufactured, as some scholars have suggested (Carson and Roberts 2013; Engstrom and Kernell 2014), what factors contributed to its decline over time? Additionally, what implications does the decline in competition in House races have for our broader understanding of representation and electoral accountability in the legislative process?

This chapter builds on the theoretical discussion in the preceding chapter with respect to the existence of an electoral connection in the nineteenth century, by focusing specifically on the issues of ambition and responsiveness. In particular, we here seek to better understand whether the preconditions for greater competitiveness in House elections in the nineteenth century can offer us leverage in our efforts to uncover the potential electoral motivations for recruiting experienced or higher-quality candidates to run for elective office. In addition to issues of candidate emergence, we focus on electoral responsiveness among the voters of the day. In particular, we evaluate whether voters are more likely to support candidates with prior elective experience and if voter turnout is higher in elections where at least one highly qualified candidate is running for office. Uncovering systematic evidence of these phenomena will offer us leverage in our effort to demonstrate the presence of an electoral connection throughout the nineteenth century.

We begin this chapter by briefly reviewing prior work on changing patterns of candidate competition in House races over time. From there, we discuss the theoretical factors that have played a role in shaping the competitiveness of elections across different political eras. We then turn to a discussion of the empirical data used in our analysis, before presenting our more systematic analyses on candidate emergence, electoral competition, and factors related to voter turnout in the nineteenth century. After summarizing our central findings, we discuss the broader implications of our results with respect to how an electoral connection might have operated during that political era.

Strategic Candidates

Much of the early literature on candidate emergence focused principally on the question of ambition and who decides to run for office (see, e.g.,

Schlesinger 1966; Rohde 1979). In building on this rich literature, Jacobson and Kernell (1983) were among the first to examine whether political candidates exhibit strategic behavior in deciding whether to seek office. Through an examination of aggregate patterns of candidates' career decisions, they speculate about the underlying motivations for politicians' behavior. As their theory is premised on rational calculations, they argue that experienced candidates are more likely to run for the House when national and partisan conditions are more favorable in terms of their likelihood of success. Jacobson and Kernell test their theory of strategic behavior on data from the 1974, 1980, and 1982 congressional elections and find convincing evidence in support of their hypotheses concerning strategic politicians. Not only do they conclude that experienced challengers wait until circumstances are optimal before they decide to run, but these scholars also find that strategic politicians play a pivotal role in determining the results of both district-level elections and the overall partisan composition of Congress.

Jacobson (1989) offers additional support for the strategic politicians theory by testing it against congressional elections data from 1946 to 1986. Through his examination of elections data during that 40-year period, Jacobson finds that experienced challengers do not emerge arbitrarily; rather, their likelihood of running varies with their perceived chance of winning (775). Jacobson concludes that a greater proportion of experienced candidates emerge when their party's prospects appear favorable. As a result, he argues that strategic decisions by congressional candidates—based on factors such as likelihood of victory, value of the seat, and opportunity costs—both reflect and enhance national partisan tides. In support of his contention that experienced politicians act strategically, Jacobson recognizes that quality candidates are more likely to run in an open-seat race and that they rely increasingly on an incumbent's prior margin of victory as an important cue in deciding whether to run (778).[7]

Jacobson and Kernell provide invaluable insights about strategic candidate behavior in the post–World War II era. Surprisingly little attention, however, has been given to House or Senate elections outside of the modern era. On one level, this should not come as a great surprise. Collecting data on candidate quality back to 1946 was labor intensive, and extending Jacobson's work requires a considerable investment of time and energy. Indeed, historical elections data, such as party affiliation and vote shares, were not readily available for systematic analysis by students of congressional elections until the publication of invaluable resources like Dubin's *Official Results* (1998) and Martis's *Historical Atlas* (1989). Even with these data, there was no guarantee that a similar analysis would yield insights into historical elections, given how fundamentally different those elections are supposed to be from elections in the post–World War II era. As such, scholars' lack of attention to earlier elections was largely pragmatic.

Despite these practical considerations as well as potential data limitations, Carson and Roberts (2005) were among the first to systematically analyze a subset of House elections during the late nineteenth and early twentieth century. They find that much like candidates in the modern era, candidates with previous electoral experience were more successful at securing votes and were more likely to seek office when national and/or local conditions favored their candidacy. Factors such as national economic conditions, an incumbent with a small prior electoral margin, and the presence of an open seat were all related to experienced candidates' entry decisions. Carson and Roberts argue that these effects are consistent with what we would expect to observe in the contemporary era (which is characterized by candidate-centered elections) but that they do not necessarily correspond to the conventional perception of elections from earlier eras.

More recently, Carson and Roberts (2013) extended their previous analysis of strategic candidate behavior, to include all congressional elections from 1872 to 1944. They find that candidates exhibited strategic behavior across this broader range of elections and were responsive to many of the same considerations as candidates in the modern era. Carson and Roberts also demonstrate that the adoption of the Australian ballot had observable effects on candidate and voter behavior. At the same time, the proportion of quality challengers declined precipitously after states began utilizing the direct primary. Once parties ceded control over the nomination process to voters, experienced candidates became far more risk averse about seeking higher office, since running and losing could put an end to an otherwise promising electoral career. When coupled with the gradual elimination of patronage positions the party machines had used to entice reluctant candidates to run for office, the proportion of strategic candidates running for office continued to decline throughout the early twentieth century.

In light of the valuable insights about historical elections offered by Carson and Roberts, we here extend their analysis even further back in time in an attempt to answer a number of important questions. For instance, was increased competition largely a function of increased party strength during the machine era, or should we expect to find similar patterns in previous decades as well? Did the parties value the recruitment of experienced candidates during the antebellum period as much as they did during the Gilded Age? Did the emergence of quality challengers affect candidate competition during earlier eras as it regularly does today? Was turn-out higher in those races where strong candidates ran for elective office? Finally, does the pattern of candidate emergence and party recruitment of challengers help us understand whether an electoral connection may have indeed been present in earlier eras? In the remainder of this chapter, we turn to these important questions.

Emergence of Experienced Candidates

What factors do potential candidates consider when evaluating their chances of running a successful campaign for the House? Jacobson and Kernell (Jacobson and Kernell 1983; Jacobson 1989) find that an incumbent's margin of victory in the last election and the underlying partisan preferences of the district are important in influencing a potential challenger's decision calculus. The decision by an incumbent to forgo another term in office is another issue of consequence for potential candidates, since the presence of a well-entrenched incumbent is often a deterrent to candidate emergence. Several studies find that experienced candidates are more likely to emerge in open-seat contests, thus increasing the overall level of competitiveness of these races (Banks and Kiewiet 1989; Carson and Roberts 2005, 2013; Gaddie and Bullock 2000; Jacobson 1989).

It is prudent to describe the relationship between these factors and candidate emergence before we discuss our more systematic analysis. We begin by examining the relationship between incumbency and candidate emergence. There are several advantages to starting our analysis by comparing candidate emergence in incumbent-contested and open-seat races. First, it is largely accepted that strategic candidates of today would prefer to run for an open seat rather than challenge an incumbent (Cox and Katz 1996). If we observe a similar pattern in earlier historical periods, it can be seen as suggestive evidence that the influence of ambition on legislative and candidate behavior is arguably a general phenomenon rather than a modern development. Second, the dichotomy of open seat versus incumbent is relatively straightforward and does not require making assumptions about the continuity of partisan alignments. As such, we can easily examine patterns of candidate emergence back to 1820.

In figure 4.1, we plot the proportion of experienced candidates in both incumbent-contested races (black dots) and open-seat races (open dots). As in modern elections, candidates with previous electoral experience were considerably more likely to wait for an open seat before running for Con-

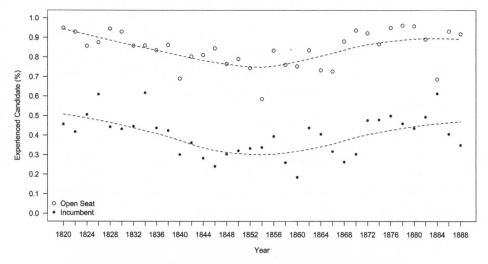

Figure 4.1. Experienced candidate by race type, 1820–88. Black dots and open dots denote the proportion of experienced candidates in incumbent-contested and open-seat races respectively. The dotted lines represent the trend as estimated by a lowess regression.

gress. Approximately 40 percent of incumbent-contested races featured a challenger with prior electoral experience. In contrast, just over 84 percent of open-seat races included at least one candidate who previously served in an elected position. Furthermore, across the seven decades examined here, there is not a single election year where the proportion of experienced challengers who ran in incumbent-contested seats was higher than the proportion of experienced challengers running in open-seat races. On average, the difference was almost 45 percentage points. The 1884 election was the only year where the difference between open-seat and incumbent-contested races was under 10 percentage points, and there were only three other elections—in 1826, 1834, and 1854—where the difference is less than 30 percentage points.

Another notable pattern in figure 4.1 is the decreasing supply of experienced candidates in the late 1830s and 1840s that is followed by a resurgence starting in the 1860s. These trends are notable partly because mass political parties, which first began to take form during the election of 1828 (Aldrich 2011), did not fully form until sometime around the late 1830s or early 1840s (Formisano 1974; McCormick 1966). One interpretation of figure 4.1 is that the creation of mass political parties led to a momentary suppression in the entry of ambitious politicians to congressional elections. Indeed, such an interpretation would be consistent with the adoption of rotation and with greater elite control of electoral politics, both of which came with the establishment of mass political parties (Kernell 1977). However, it is especially interesting to note that the proportion of quality candidates was relatively high during the early decades, well before the emergence of strong party organizations. This suggests that strong parties may be sufficient but are not necessary to recruit more high-quality challengers. Similarly, the subsequent increase in the entry of experienced candidates in later decades fits with the observation that increased ambition in the late nineteenth century had the potential to undermine or at least challenge partisan control (Kernell 1977; Reynolds 2006).

Although the differences between open-seat and incumbent races is informative, the behavior of strategic politicians should also be informed by the district-level electoral context. In particular, higher-quality candidates should be most likely to run in districts where the underlying electoral circumstances are most favorable. Both lagged congressional vote and the district-level presidential vote are commonly used to capture any district-specific electoral conditions. Prior to 1840, however, the national party organizations were not established in all states (McCormick 1966), which poses issues for calculating either measure of district-level electoral competition across the entire population of congressional races.[8] As a result, we limit much of the analysis that follows to elections between 1840 and 1888. We can, however, examine two states—Ohio and Pennsylvania—where party competition can broadly be defined in terms of Jacksonians versus anti-Jacksonians throughout the 1830s. In doing so, we are able to control for multiple factors that might influence candidates' decision making.

Political parties in Ohio organized around national party labels in 1828, and competition was limited to these two factions from that point onward (McCormick 1966: 258–79). Pennsylvania was slower to adopt national party labels, and the anti-Jacksonians were split between the Adams/Whigs coalition and the Anti-Masonic Party (McCormick 1966: 134–47). Despite these differences between the states, electoral competition can still generally be defined in terms of the basic partisan divisions erected by Jackson and his opponents. Furthermore, the observed differences in the level of party organization provide a unique opportunity to examine how the creation of mass parties influenced candidate decisions. One additional advantage to focusing on these two states is that their elections were always held on the same day, which is notable given the greater variability in election timing prior to the 1870s (Carson and Sievert 2017; Engstrom and Kernell

2005, 2014). As such, we can be more confident that we have adequately controlled for other factors, such as national tides, that might influence candidate decision making.

Our outcome variable for the analysis of elections in Ohio and Pennsylvania and the full set of elections between 1840 and 1888 is Cox and Katz's (1996) Democratic quality advantage (DQA). The measure is coded 1 when the only candidate with prior electoral experience is the Jacksonian/Democratic candidate, –1 when only the non-Democratic candidate is experienced, and 0 when both or neither candidates have prior electoral experience.[9] There are advantages to using DQA to measure candidates' experience and entry decisions. First, as we discussed in an earlier study (Carson and Sievert 2015), candidates' entry decisions in the nineteenth century can be thought of, at least partly, as capturing partisan recruitment efforts. Since the parties were responsible for slating candidates, it is reasonable to think about candidates' experience and entry decisions in terms of whether one party was advantaged over another or if the parties were evenly matched. Second, DQA makes it easier to examine both incumbent and open-seat races in the same analysis. A number of studies rely on a dichotomy of experienced versus nonexperienced candidates, but this dichotomy was primarily developed to examine incumbent-contested races. If we think about candidacy in terms of partisan advantages, however, it is easier to construct an outcome variable that will be the same for both incumbent and open-seat races.

To account for differences between open-seat and incumbent-contested races, we include two binary variables to account for whether a race featured a Democratic or a non-Democratic incumbent, with open-seat races treated as the reference category. These incumbent-specific variables allow us to gauge whether potential challengers were strategic and waited for an open-seat race to emerge before deciding to run for Congress. A positive coefficient estimate for the Democratic incumbents or a negative one for the non-Democratic incumbents would be evidence that experienced candidates were less likely to challenge an incumbent. We also control for the lagged Democratic congressional vote. A positive coefficient estimate for this variable would be consistent with the expectation that electoral context, particularly expected competitiveness, should influence candidates' entry decisions. For now, we do not include district-level presidential vote as a predictor, because the same two candidates were not always on the ballot in the presidential election in both states.[10] We also include year-fixed effects, to account for any temporal differences in candidates' entry decisions.

In table 4.1, we report the results of a series of regression models that predict the emergence of quality challengers in elections in Ohio and Pennsylvania.[11] The first and third columns report the coefficient estimates for regression models that examine elections in each state between 1830 and 1838. During that period, both national political parties were formally organized in Ohio, but the Whigs had yet to firmly establish themselves in Pennsylvania. The second and fourth columns report estimates for models that examine elections from 1840 to 1852. Both national parties were formally organized in Ohio and Pennsylvania by 1840, and the Democrat-Whig division lasted through the 1852 election.

The results for Ohio are fairly consistent across the time periods. Experienced candidates were less likely to challenge an incumbent, which indicates that a party was more likely to have a quality advantage when an incumbent sought another term in office. It also appears that the parties were fairly evenly matched in Ohio with respect to candidate entry. The coefficient estimates for incumbency are of comparable magnitude across both time periods, which suggests that any potential deterrent effect of incumbency was symmetric. Electoral context, as captured by the previous Democratic vote share in a district, also has a comparable effect across the time periods.

Our analysis of Pennsylvania, however, suggests that there were interesting differences in candidates' entry decisions before and after the establishment of formal party organizations. Although incumbency did appear to deter experienced candidates from entering a race, the effect is almost

TABLE 4.1. Candidate emergence in Ohio and Pennsylvania, 1830–52

	Ohio		Pennsylvania	
	Est. (*SE*)	Est. (*SE*)	Est. (*SE*)	Est. (*SE*)
Dem. inc.	0.41*	0.56*	0.30*	0.72*
	(0.19)	(0.18)	(0.16)	(0.12)
Non-Dem. inc.	−0.47*	−0.56*	−0.56*	−0.60*
	(0.19)	(0.17)	(0.17)	(0.12)
Dem. vote$_{t-1}$	0.02*	0.02*	0.03*	0.02*
	(0.01)	(0.01)	(0.01)	(0.01)
Constant	−1.07*	−1.12*	−1.64*	−0.92*
	(0.53)	(0.77)	(0.43)	(0.35)
N	77	113	123	141
R^2	0.58	0.41	0.47	0.61
Time period	1830–38	1840–52	1830–38	1840–52

Note: Cell entries are regression coefficients from an OLS regression model, with robust standard errors in parentheses. Year-specific fixed effects were estimated but are not reported here.

*$p < .05$

two times larger for non-Democratic incumbents than for Democratic incumbents. In contrast, the estimates for incumbent-contested races are quite similar once both major parties were formally organized in Pennsylvania. Furthermore, the magnitude of the estimate for Democratic incumbents more than doubles once the national Whig party establishes a foothold in the state. These findings fit with patterns observed in figure 4.1, which suggests that the creation of mass political parties may have led to a decrease in the supply of experienced candidates.

While the findings in table 4.1 provide insights about the consequences that formal party organizations had on ambition, we wish to understand ambition more broadly. For the analysis that follows, we focus on elections held between 1840 and 1888. We begin in 1840 (rather than the 1820s) because national party organizations were firmly established by that date, which makes it easier to pool observations from all states. Although party identification was more fluid during that time period, the Democrats were a constant throughout that era. We therefore code the two-party vote with reference to the top Democratic finisher and the top finisher from an opposition party.[12] In the 1840s and 1850s, the opposition candidate is typically a Whig; from the 1860s onward, Democrats typically faced a Republican.[13] Our measure of district-level presidential vote is constructed in the same manner. Unlike in recent elections, however, presidential vote returns are only available at the county level during that period. We therefore aggregate the votes across counties within a district to obtain the total vote for each presidential candidate, then calculate the two-party vote with these vote totals.[14]

In table 4.2, we report the results of a series of regression models for elections in all states between 1840 and 1888, where DQA is once again the outcome variable. The first column reports the coefficient estimates for a model that pools open-seat and incumbent-contested races. We still find evidence of a deterrent effect in incumbent-contested races, and the effect for incumbency appears to be symmetric across parties. We also find evidence that electoral context influenced candidate emergence, as both the lagged congressional vote and the district-level presidential vote are positive and statistically significant. When we pool all elections together, presidential vote does have a notably larger impact on candidate emergence than does lagged congressional vote.

Given the clear differences between incumbent and open-seat contests, we also examined the effect of electoral context in each type of election. The results for the regression model including only incumbent-contested races are in the second column of table 4.2. For these cases, the estimates for both electoral context variables are essentially identical. In contrast, the effect for presidential vote is considerably larger in open-seat races. One plausible interpretation of these findings is that when an incumbent ran for reelection, the opposition party and potential candidates considered both the electoral security of the incumbent and the district's partisan undercurrents. By contrast, district partisanship mattered considerably more than past congressional results in open-seat races.

In sum, decisions regarding candidate emergence during the middle and later nineteenth century look surprisingly similar to the behavior observed in today's more candidate-centered elections. Indeed, higher-quality candidates and the parties who selected them to run during that era were sensitive to some of the same electoral factors as their modern counterparts. While we are not suggesting that candidates in that era were exhibiting strategic behavior in the exact same manner as those envisioned by Jacobson and Kernell (Jacobson and Kernell 1983; Jacobson 1989), our findings suggest that they were more similar than many previous accounts would suggest. This also indicates that an electoral connection may have been present, especially with respect to candidate ambition.

Electoral Competition and Experienced Candidates

As noted earlier, prior work on the electoral impact of congressional candidates primarily examines the post–World War II era. Although scholars

TABLE 4.2. Emergence of experienced candidates, 1840–88

	All (SE)	Inc. (SE)	Open (SE)
Dem. inc.	0.448*		
	(0.022)		
Non-Dem. inc.	−0.417*		
	(0.022)		
Dem. vote$_{t-1}$	0.005*	0.022*	0.004*
	(0.001)	(0.001)	(0.002)
Dem. pres.	0.018*	0.023*	0.028*
	(0.001)	(0.001)	(0.002)
Constant	−1.130*	−2.248*	−1.367*
	(0.062)	(0.08)	(0.10)
N	4591	2902	1689
R^2	0.47	0.43	0.18

Note: Cell entries are regression coefficients from an OLS regression model, with robust standard errors in parentheses. Year-specific fixed effects were estimated but are not reported here.
*$p < .05$

have begun to document the relevance of these factors in historical eras (Carson and Roberts 2013; Carson, Engstrom, and Roberts 2007), the conventional wisdom suggests that individual candidates should matter little in earlier historical eras. Scholars have argued that voters during that period evaluated candidates almost entirely on the basis of party affiliation rather than experience (Skeen 1986) and generally did not hold public officials accountable for their behavior in office (Formisano 1974; Swift 1987).

The arguments for a more limited role for individual congressional candidates during that period is buttressed by research suggesting that the party ballot manufactured greater levels of voter responsiveness to the parties (Engstrom and Kernell 2005, 2014). Since the party ballot made split-ticket voting difficult, if not impossible, voters were selecting not between different candidates as much as between different political parties (Rusk 1970). In discussing the importance of this institutional arrangement, Engstrom and Kernell (2005: 535) conclude that "coattail voting occurred by default" under the party ballot unless voters went to extraordinary lengths to split their vote.

While nineteenth-century electoral institutions likely led to voting that was more partisan and nonpersonal than in contemporary elections, a growing body of research highlights the important role of candidates in nineteenth-century congressional elections. Carson, Jenkins, Rohde, and Souva (2001) show that voters in the 1862 congressional election held legislators accountable for both national conditions and district-specific factors, such as battle casualties during the course of the Civil War. There is even evidence, as far back as the early nineteenth century, of voters rewarding or punishing incumbents based on legislative performance (Bianco, Spence, and Wilkerson 1996; Carson and Engstrom 2005). Furthermore, a number of recent studies demonstrate that the attributes of the candidate who was chosen to be a party's nominee for Congress could be quite consequential in nineteenth-century elections (see, e.g., Carson and Hood 2014; Carson and Roberts 2013; Carson and Sievert 2017).

We begin our analysis of electoral competition by exploring descriptive evidence of the electoral effects of candidate-specific attributes. As with candidate emergence, we want to examine the lengthiest time series we can. One limitation to looking at elections from the 1820s and the 1830s, of course, is that it can be difficult to systematically code our measure of candidate experience, DQA, in elections where the major parties have not yet organized. We therefore start by looking at how incumbents performed when they did and did not enjoy a recruitment advantage. In this case, an incumbent has a recruitment advantage when he is the only candidate

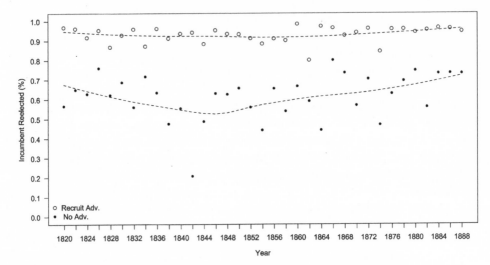

Figure 4.2. Proportion of incumbents reelected, 1820–88, by challenger type. Open dots and black dots denote the proportion of incumbents who won reelection when they did and did not have a recruitment advantage respectively. The dotted lines represent the trend as estimated by a lowess regression.

with prior service in an elected office. Conversely, an incumbent does not have a recruitment advantage when he runs against a challenger who has previously won an elected position. We measure electoral competition by calculating the proportion of races in which an incumbent was reelected, by the type of challenger faced. Our findings are reported by election in figure 4.2, where the open dots denote the calculations for incumbents with a recruitment advantage, while the black dots represent incumbents without a recruitment advantage.

The first notable pattern evident in figure 4.2 is that incumbents nearly always won when they ran against a candidate without prior experience. In 29 of the 35 elections considered, at least 90 percent of incumbents who had a recruitment advantage were reelected, and in 15 of these elections, over 95 percent won. The low point for these incumbents was the 1862 election, when only 80 percent were victorious, but even then, these legislators still outperformed their counterparts who faced a quality challenger, by almost 15 percentage points. There is very little change over time in the electoral fortunes of these incumbents, which is evident from the estimated fit from a loess regression, denoted by the dashed line in figure 4.2.

The second notable finding in figure 4.2 is that although incumbents still often won when they faced an experienced challenger, they never out-performed incumbents who did not. Indeed, there were six elections in which over half of the incumbents who faced a quality challenger were defeated. The low point was the 1842 election, when only 20.6 percent of these incumbents were reelected. However, there is considerable variability over time in the electoral success of these incumbents. By the 1870s and 1880s, it was not uncommon for over 70 percent of incumbents who faced an opponent with prior electoral experience to win. There were years during these decades, such as 1874 and 1882, when that number dipped to around 50 percent, but these outcomes were outliers. In contrast, electoral competition in these races was much higher in the 1840s and 1850s. During these decades, it was common for a third or more of incumbents who ran against a quality challenger to lose. In short, incumbents did not lose to just any party candidate but were more likely to be replaced by a challenger with prior elective experience. This evidence suggests that, contrary to some previous accounts of nineteenth-century electoral politics, parties valued prior political experience when recruiting candidates to run for office, since experienced candidates regularly outperformed their inexperienced counterparts.

An important implication of figure 4.2 is that incumbents and their parties would appear to have a strong interest in dissuading an experienced candidate from challenging an incumbent. While most incumbents in most years could survive a challenge from a higher-quality opponent, their likelihood of victory went up considerably if they could scare off these experienced candidates. One way to discourage these types of challengers would almost certainly be for incumbents to engage in behavior or develop a reputation that would signal that they would be difficult to beat. In this sense, nineteenth-century legislators who wanted to continue to serve in office faced an electoral landscape that was similar to their counterparts in the twenty-first century.

Although figure 4.2 is highly suggestive, our earlier analysis indicates that experienced challengers were more likely to target vulnerable incumbents, which could lead our descriptive analysis to overstate the effect of candidate experience. It is therefore important to ascertain whether the effect of candidate quality remains once we control for other factors that might influence electoral competition. Additionally, we want to compare incumbent-contested and open-seat races in order to develop a more complete understanding of how candidates influenced electoral competition. We therefore once again limit our analysis to elections held between 1840 and 1888. The outcome variable for our analysis is the Democratic share of the two-party vote. If candidates' entry decisions impacted electoral margins, we would expect DQA to be positive and statistically significant. To account for electoral context, we control for the lagged congressional vote and the district-level presidential vote.

In table 4.3, we report coefficient estimates for a series of ordinary least squares (OLS) regression models. The first two columns of the table contain the estimates from a model that pools all observations, while the third and fourth columns report estimates for incumbent-contested and open-seat races respectively. For all four models, there is a sizable and statistically significant effect for candidate quality. In the first two models, a candidate recruitment advantage is expected to provide a boost of approximately three percentage points to the advantaged party's vote share. The estimated effect of candidate quality is slightly higher in incumbent-contested races, nearly half of a percentage point. In sum, candidates' entry decisions had a consistent impact on electoral competition even after we control for other key factors.

The results reported in table 4.3 reveal that candidate experience was not the only way in which attributes of individual candidates could impact election outcomes. First, incumbency appears to have a small but independent effect, at least for Democratic incumbents, separate from electoral context and candidate quality. One potential explanation for this apparent advantage of Democratic incumbency is differential election timing, which we discuss in greater detail in chapter 6. Second, although the magnitude

TABLE 4.3. Democratic vote share, 1840–88

	All (SE)	All (SE)	Inc. (SE)	Open (SE)
DQA	2.96*	3.34*	3.48*	2.83*
	(0.21)	(0.20)	(0.28)	(0.29)
Dem. vote$_{t-1}$	0.15*	0.17*	0.22*	0.06*
	(0.02)	(0.02)	(0.03)	(0.03)
Dem. pres.	0.57*	0.58*	0.54*	0.64*
	(0.03)	(0.03)	(0.04)	(0.04)
Dem. inc.	1.21*			
	(0.34)			
Non-Dem. inc.	−0.43			
	(0.28)			
Constant	13.95*	13.31*	12.35*	15.42*
	(1.13)	(1.09)	(1.51)	(1.51)
N	4409	4409	2770	1639
R^2	0.60	0.60	0.63	0.55

Note: Cell entries are regression coefficients from an OLS regression model, with robust standard errors in parentheses. Year-specific fixed effects were estimated but are not reported here.

*$p < .05$

of the coefficient estimate for DQA is comparable in incumbent-contested and open-seat races, there are notable differences in the estimated effect for electoral context. While the coefficient for presidential vote in incumbent-contested races is still larger than the one for lagged congressional vote, the magnitude of the estimate for presidential vote in open-seat races is over ten times greater than the one for lagged congressional vote. When an incumbent was one of the candidates for Congress, his previous electoral performance was a better predictor of current levels of electoral competition than when it was an open-seat race. While we may not be able to definitively conclude that nineteenth-century incumbents enjoyed a personal vote in the same manner that they did in the modern era, these two findings are at least suggestive evidence that incumbents were able to marshal some base of support that was not strictly tied to their party.

In sum, we find clear and robust evidence that candidate-specific attributes played an important role in congressional elections throughout the middle and late nineteenth century. Previous studies argued that the party ballot made individual candidates less relevant during that era, because voters were forced to choose between parties rather than between individual candidates. While we do not dispute these previous claims about the nature of the party ballot, our evidence demonstrates that individual candidates were hardly irrelevant during that era. Furthermore, the structure of the party ballot itself should make it difficult to find *any* evidence of candidate-specific effects, which implies that the period of the middle and late nineteenth century represents a particularly difficult test case for uncovering evidence of an electoral connection. Given the robustness and substantive significance of our results, it is reasonable to conclude that candidate experience was an important factor in shaping electoral competition throughout that period.

Candidates and Turnout in Congressional Elections

Although voter turnout in modern elections has received considerable attention (see McDonald and Popkin 2001), we know surprisingly little about voter turnout in earlier eras. Engstrom (2012) helped to fill this gap by analyzing turnout patterns in congressional races from 1840 to 1940. The puzzle he sets out to explain is why voter turnout in congressional elections during that era is so much higher and variable when compared with elections in the post–World War II period. To gain leverage on this important issue, Engstrom takes advantage of variation in electoral rules and political competition throughout much of the period he considers. In particular, he examines variation in ballot format, electoral calendars, district size, electoral competition, and districting arrangements, to better understand why voter turnout was significantly higher then than it is today.

Based on his careful analysis of congressional elections during the 100-year period considered, Engstrom identifies a number of important trends with regard to electoral turnout. First, he finds that the adoption of the Australian ballot had a detrimental effect on voter turnout but that the extent of the effect varied depending on the type of ballot adopted by individual states (i.e., the office-bloc ballot reduced turnout by nearly 9 percent, while the party-column ballot reduced turnout by much less, 3.7 percent). Engstrom also finds that turnout in congressional elections held at the same time as presidential elections was much higher than in states with elections occurring before or after November. Additionally, his results suggested that larger district populations reduced turnout, as did less competitive statewide presidential contests. Finally, Engstrom finds that the costs of voting had a negative relationship with voter turnout—once states adopted registration requirements, the likelihood of voting in congressional elections declined by nearly 2 percent.

Engstrom's results are especially instructive for understanding how candidates influenced electoral competition in nineteenth-century elections. Specifically, we build on Engstrom's findings by adding an additional variable to the analysis, candidate recruitment advantage. Our argument may seem surprising given the conventional views about the primacy of the party organization for mobilizing nineteenth-century voters. We see our theoretical contention more as an extension of the conventional view than as a competition claim. Specifically, we posit that experienced candidates facilitated the parties' mobilization efforts. As with much historical analyses, we face considerable limitations in causally identifying the exact mechanism at work. We suspect, however, that two factors, separately or together, help to produce the hypothesized effect. First, candidates with prior electoral experience could leverage their own personal political networks to benefit the party. As with modern congressional candidates, these connections were likely the product of having already won an election to obtain political office. Second, candidates with prior electoral experience increased the overall appeal of a given party's ballot (Carson and Roberts 2013; Carson and Sievert 2017). In doing so, these candidates could help to reduce uncertainty among voters about the party's position.

We expect voter turnout will be higher in races where no party has a recruitment advantage, all else being equal. For incumbent-contested races, this means that the emergence of an experienced challenger will increase turnout. In these cases, we expect that increased voter turnout may work against the incumbent. The dynamic may be more complicated in open-seat races, for which turnout will already be higher. Indeed, during the period we examine, turnout was around 68.5 percent in open-seat races and approximately 63.7 percent in incumbent-contested races. It is therefore possible that the impact of candidate quality on turnout will be limited to races where an incumbent is seeking another term in office.

To test for the effect of candidate emergence on turnout, we utilize Engstrom's (2012) measure of district-level turnout in congressional elections as our outcome variable. As noted before, our main covariate of interest is candidate recruitment advantage, which we code by collapsing DQA into a binary measure. In addition to candidate quality, we include a number of other relevant predictors and controls so that our regression models are consistent with Engstrom's empirical analysis. First, we include the lagged margin of victory and the presidential margin of victory, to account for expected electoral competition. Second, we include a control for the number of eligible voters, to account for both differences in district size and the fact that cost of voter mobilization increases with the number of potential voters. Lastly, we include a number of covariates to account for the larger electoral context in which an election was contested. These include variables that capture whether it was a presidential election year and whether a gubernatorial election was occurring at the same time, since we expect higher turnout during these elections. We also include controls for election timing, as well as state-fixed effects to account for differences in turnout between states.

In table 4.4, we only report the estimates for candidate recruitment advantage, since that is our main variable of interest. For the interested reader, the full model results are available in the appendix to this chapter (table 4.A1). Since we expect to find differential effects for candidate experience in incumbent and open-seat races, we examine these elections separately. For incumbent-contested races, turnout was nearly three percentage points lower in races where a quality challenger did not emerge. When we focus the analysis on presidential election years, the effect drops by around one percentage point. The weaker effect in presidential election years is arguably not surprising, since turnout is markedly higher, on average, in these contests (see appendix). In contrast, the impact of candidates' entry decisions increases to almost four percentage points in years with midterm elections. As expected, we find no substantive effect for candidate recruitment in open-seat races.

To demonstrate the substantive significance of these results, we examined the electoral consequences that an increase in turnout had for incumbents. We estimated both a pooled model and separate models for midterm and presidential election years. The specification for these regression models is the same as the models reported in table 4.3, but we use incumbent vote share, rather than Democratic vote share, and recode the presidential vote share to denote how the incumbent's party performed in the most recent presidential election. We also control for whether the incumbent faced a quality challenger. In the interest of space, we report only the coefficient estimates for turnout in table 4.5. The full model results are reported in the appendix at the end of this chapter (table 4.A2).

The estimated effect of an increase in voter turnout on an incum-

TABLE 4.4. Candidate recruitment advantage and voter turnout, 1840–88

	All (SE)	Pres. (SE)	Midterm (SE)
Incumbents			
Recruitment adv.	−2.84*	−1.63*	−3.87*
	(0.49)	(0.62)	(0.78)
N	4558	2214	2384
R²	0.36	0.31	0.36
Open seat			
Recruitment adv.	−1.03	−0.98	−0.57
	(0.61)	(0.87)	(0.85)
N	4558	2214	2384
R²	0.36	0.31	0.36

Note: Cell entries are regression coefficients from an OLS regression model, with robust standard errors in parentheses. Year-specific fixed effects were estimated but are not reported here.
*$p < .05$

TABLE 4.5. Effect of turnout on incumbent margin of victory

	Est. (SE)	N	Δ predicted vote share
All	−0.15*	2518	−3.45
	(0.02)		
Presidential	−0.13*	1384	−2.77
	(0.02)		
Midterm	−0.16*	1134	−3.57
	(0.02)		

Note: Cell entries are regression coefficients from an OLS regression model, with robust standard errors in parentheses. Year-specific fixed effects were estimated but are not reported here.
*$p < .05$

bent's vote share is nearly identical across all three models. For a one-point increase in voter turnout, an incumbent's share of the two-party vote decreases by around 0.15 points. While the effect size is comparatively small, the fact that we find an independent effect for turnout after controlling for other key factors, such as challenger quality and electoral context, is notable.[15] The range of the turnout variable is considerable, which means that differences in turnout could add up to have a sizable impact on election outcomes. In the final column of table 4.5, we report the estimated change in the incumbent's vote share over the interquartile range of turnout when we hold all other variables constant. For example, in the pooled model, this means calculating the difference in the expected incumbent vote share when turnout was 55.74 percent and when it was 78.50 percent. Across all three models, the predicted decrease in the incumbent's vote share is around three percentage points.

While there is a growing body of evidence concerning the importance of congressional candidates throughout the nineteenth century (Carson and Hood 2014; Carson and Roberts 2013; Carson and Sievert 2017), our analysis provides an important step forward in understanding the mechanism that produced candidate-specific effects during that era. Previous scholars noted the importance of the party organization for mobilizing voters. Our results provide suggestive evidence that individual candidates, particularly those with prior experience, may have greatly helped facilitate the parties' mobilization efforts. Regardless of whether this was a result of a party being able to utilize a candidate's personal political networks or candidates increasing the overall appeal of a party's ballot, it is clear that there was a strong link between candidates and voter turnout in congressional elections during that era. Moreover, our findings suggest that turnout should not vary by the presence of a quality challenger if there is little evidence of an electoral connection. We see these results as providing an important aspect of the foundation in the broader context of demonstrating that an electoral connection existed throughout the nineteenth century.

Discussion

Our analysis here seeks to address a number of relevant questions about specific factors that influenced the electoral arena throughout the nineteenth century. Understanding which candidates emerge to contest an election is important for evaluating important facets of democracy, such as political competition and electoral accountability. Based on our empirical analy-

ses of candidate emergence, we find that entry decisions for congressional elections during the middle to late nineteenth century are remarkably
similar to behavior observed in the modern era. Experienced candidates
and the political parties that recruited them to run for office appear to have
been sensitive to many of the same strategic factors as their modern-day
counterparts. Although there are important differences between elections
from that era and those held today, our findings offer suggestive evidence
about the relevance of strategic politicians theory (Jacobson and Kernell
1983; Jacobson 1989) across earlier political eras.

Additionally, our analyses of candidate competition find clear and convincing evidence that candidate-specific attributes played a sizable role in
congressional elections throughout the middle to late nineteenth century.
Given the party ballot that was in use throughout most of that century,
previous accounts of congressional elections during the era suggest that
the quality of individual candidates should be less relevant in affecting election outcomes. Although we are not challenging the specifics of the party
ballot that was in use throughout much of the nineteenth century, we find
that candidate effects appear to have been quite influential in affecting the
outcomes of US House elections. Since that era represents a particularly
difficult test case for our hypotheses regarding candidate competition, we
feel quite confident in concluding that experienced candidates during the
nineteenth century were hardly irrelevant in the larger electoral system.
Indeed, our results suggest that candidate experience was a very important
factor in shaping electoral outcomes in that era.

Furthermore, our findings on voter turnout and mobilization help us
better understand the possible mechanism that yielded candidate-specific
effects during the nineteenth century. Much of the previous work on
party organizations in that era discusses the consequential role that party
machines played in mobilizing voters and getting them out to the polls
on Election Day (Bensel 2004). In addition to parties influencing turnout,
our results suggest that individual candidates, especially those with prior
elective experience, may have facilitated the party's mobilization efforts in
light of their appearance on the ballot—especially in an era where candidates running for president did not actively campaign for office. In short,
it appears that voters responded to the quality of individual candidates on
the ballot, given the greater levels of turnout in that period.

What are the broader implications of our findings for understanding
whether an electoral connection might have been present throughout the
nineteenth century? We have found clear examples of both ambition and
responsiveness in that era, despite the use of the party ballot, which previous

studies contend should temper the influence of these qualities during the nineteenth century. Additionally, patterns of candidate emergence, electoral competition, and voter turnout all appear to be influenced by candidate-specific attributes throughout the nineteenth century. Some might argue that increased levels of competitiveness in congressional elections during that period would undercut our broader argument about the electoral connection, but such an argument is somewhat misdirected. An electoral connection implies not that the majority of incumbents will necessarily win but that they can actually be held accountable for their actions and can be replaced if they fail to be responsive to their constituents. In light of the greater levels of competitiveness and turnover in the nineteenth century, it would seem as though a robust electoral connection was in place between the voters and their elected representatives. In the next chapter, we focus more specifically on the components of ambition and autonomy with respect to renomination and turnover patterns during that era.

Appendix for Chapter 4

TABLE 4.A1. Turnout in congressional districts, 1840–88

	Incumbent			Open seat		
	All (SE)	Pres. (SE)	Midterm (SE)	All (SE)	Pres. (SE)	Midterm (SE)
Recruitment adv.	−2.88*	−1.63*	−3.87*	−1.03	−0.98	−0.57
	(0.49)	(0.62)	(0.78)	(0.61)	(0.87)	(0.85)
Margin_{t-1}	−0.09*	−0.12*	−0.07*	−0.07*	−0.05	−0.09*
	(0.02)	(0.02)	(0.03)	(0.02)	(0.03)	(0.04)
Pres. margin	−0.40*	−0.38*	−0.41*	−0.39*	−0.44*	−0.34*
	(0.05)	(0.06)	(0.07)	(0.06)	(0.07)	(0.09)
Gov. elec.	5.57*	5.56*	5.58*	4.73*	4.76*	5.34*
	(0.65)	(0.85)	(1.28)	(0.79)	(1.17)	(1.28)
Pres. elec.	9.61*			8.07*		
	(0.49)			(0.60)		
Pre-Nov.	−2.61*	−3.51*	0.03	−0.61	−2.84*	2.51
	(1.25)	(1.37)	(1.73)	(1.46)	(1.71)	(2.11)
Post-Nov.	−1.80	−7.27*	3.02	0.15	−3.78*	3.40
	(1.41)	(1.57)	(1.92)	(1.76)	(2.26)	(2.34)
Eligible voters (1000s)	−0.11*	−0.02	−0.23*	−0.02	0.09*	−0.12
	(0.04)	(0.03)	(0.06)	(0.06)	(0.05)	(0.09)
Constant	68.46*	75.93*	72.85*	64.04*	65.30*	68.99*
	(3.15)	(2.93)	(4.73)	(3.51)	(3.82)	(5.10)
N	2779	1512	1267	1794	857	937
R^2	0.41	0.41	0.36	0.30	0.26	0.28

Note: Cell entries are regression coefficients from an OLS regression model, with standard errors clustered by congressional district in parentheses. Year-specific fixed effects were estimated but are not reported here. ·

*$p < .05$

TABLE 4.A2. Incumbent margin of victory, 1840–88

	All (SE)	Pres. (SE)	Midterm (SE)
Incumbent Vote$_{t-1}$	0.14*	0.15*	0.15*
	(0.03)	(0.03)	(0.05)
Incumbent Presidential Vote	0.49*	0.62*	0.33*
	(0.04)	(0.05)	(0.06)
Quality Challenger	−3.44*	−1.73*	−4.86*
	(0.35)	(0.40)	(0.56)
Turnout	−0.15*	−0.13*	−0.16*
	(0.02)	(0.02)	(0.02)
Democrat	1.25*	1.27*	1.15
	(0.33)	(0.34)	(0.60)
Constant	33.20*	24.13*	37.59*
	(2.80)	(3.62)	(3.80)
N	2518	1384	1134
R^2	0.47	0.61	0.35

Note: Cell entries are regression coefficients from an OLS regression model, with robust standard errors in parentheses. Year-specific fixed effects were estimated but are not reported here.

*p < .05

FIVE

Nomination and Turnover Patterns in the US House

By most accounts of nineteenth-century congressional politics, the outcome of the 1821 congressional elections in Connecticut would not appear to be particularly notable.[1] After the final votes were tallied, three members of Connecticut's congressional delegation from the 16th Congress—Henry Edwards, John Russ, and Gideon Tomlinson (all Democratic Republicans)—were able to win another term, while two sitting members—Samuel Foot (a Democratic Republican) and Elisha Phelps—lost. As a result, four of the seven members of the Connecticut congressional delegation in the 17th Congress were serving their first term in Congress. Overall, that outcome fits with a general pattern noted in previous accounts of the US House in the nineteenth century, of both frequent member turnover (Kernell 1977; Fiorina, Rohde, and Wissel 1975) and a high proportion of first-term legislators (Polsby 1968). In looking a bit deeper into the historical record, however, a slightly different and arguably more interesting story begins to emerge.

In addition to the five sitting members of Congress previously mentioned, three former congressmen—Lyman Law, Timothy Pitkin, and Thomas S. Williams (all Federalists)—vied to represent Connecticut in the House. Given that the Federalists were on their way out as a national party, it is not surprising that these former representatives were not successful or even electorally competitive. It is important to note, however, that these three cases are hardly unique for Connecticut's congressional elections in the 1820s. Indeed, after losing his seat during the 1821 election, Elisha Phelps made a successful comeback attempt in the 1825 election and served for an additional four years before he once again failed to win reelection. Similarly, Samuel Foot went on to reclaim his seat in the House and served in the 18th Congress. Foot did not run for reelection to the 19th Congress but went on to be elected to the Senate to serve a term from the 20th through the 22nd Congresses. Foot made one final return to the House but only served a partial term in the 23rd Congress before resigning to become the governor of Connecticut.

While Edwards, Russ, and Tomlinson were reelected in 1821, all three would eventually be defeated in a subsequent election. Both Edwards and Russ were defeated in the next election but went on to have very different careers after their respective defeats. After losing his House seat, Edwards was elected to fill a vacancy in the Senate and served out the last four years of the term. Upon completion of his term in the Senate, he went on to spend the next decade in various positions in state government, which included a term as the Speaker of the Connecticut House and multiple terms as governor.[2] In contrast, Russ spent a term in the Connecticut House before leaving legislative and state politics for a county judgeship. Tomlinson, meanwhile, served for another two terms before failing to win his seat back for the 20th Congress. Upon leaving the House, Tomlinson was elected governor of Connecticut, where he served until his election to the Senate for the 22nd through 24th Congresses.

The political careers of the four legislators who first represented Connecticut in the 17th Congress—Noyes Barber, Daniel Burrows, Ansel Sterling, and Ebenezer Stoddard (all Democratic Republicans)—followed some of the same patterns noted above. Barber, who served for 12 years, went on to have the longest career in the House of the four, only leaving when he failed to win reelection to the 24th Congress. Sterling served two terms in Congress before returning to the Connecticut House, but after two years in the state legislature, Sterling made an unsuccessful attempt to return to Congress in Connecticut's 1827 congressional election. Burrows lost his seat in the next election, but his quest for a return to Washington, DC, was far from over, as he ran unsuccessfully for a seat in both the 19th and 21st Congresses. Stoddard served two terms in Congress before leaving to take a seat in the Connecticut Senate. After leaving political life for nearly a decade, Stoddard went on to serve as Connecticut's lieutenant governor for a total of four years.

These cases reveal interesting patterns about the nature of congressional careers and political ambition during the early nineteenth century. First, the fate of Connecticut's incumbent members of Congress highlights the importance of differentiating between the different sources of legislative turnover. Although half of Connecticut's congressional delegation changed between the 16th and 17th Congresses, a majority of the delegation *wanted* to return to Congress. It is therefore important to ensure that our understanding of turnover accounts for members who leave voluntarily versus those who exit the chamber as a result of electoral defeat (Brady, Buckley, and Rivers 1999).

Second, whether a representative left Congress by choice or through electoral defeat, his departure did not mean that he was no longer interested in continuing to serve. In certain cases, the former representative failed to win a second stint in the House, but some former members of Congress were able to win a second, noncontiguous term. For others, the ambition to return to Washington, DC, was channeled into service in the upper chamber of Congress. Lastly, although long terms were not as prevalent as today, some members of Congress did serve relatively long ones during this political era, a reality far different from the conventional view of nineteenth-century legislators.

In this chapter, we provide a more detailed look at the ambition and autonomy of nineteenth-century legislators, in our attempt to identify evidence of an electoral connection across earlier political eras. Most congressional scholars argue that nineteenth-century legislators were not interested in careers in Congress (i.e., they either lacked political ambition or were not autonomous in their decisions to seek reelection). Indeed, previous research points to greater turnover among legislators during the nineteenth century in contrast to the modern Congress, as evidence to support this claim. As we discuss in more detail, we think it is both important and necessary to differentiate between careerism in Congress and careers within the parties. Many legislators were unable to pursue careers in Congress like we regularly observe today, but that does not mean they were less interested in pursuing careers at other levels within the party organizations. We contend that this was a viable alternative for many ambitious politicians during that period in history.

Additionally, much of the prior work on nineteenth-century careers does not account for the different sources of turnover in Congress. We define turnover as consisting of two unique components: voluntary turnover (an incumbent declining to seek another term in office) and involuntary departure. Most prior studies treat these components as roughly analogous quantities. We challenge this perspective and argue that a complete understanding of both turnover and legislators' incentive structure during that era requires an examination of involuntary departure—that is, whether an incumbent unsuccessfully sought another term in office. Our analysis reveals two important and related findings. First, an incumbent was one of the candidates in a majority of the elections held during the period we analyze, which suggests that many incumbents valued continued service in Congress as far back as the early nineteenth century. Second, a sizable portion of legislative turnover during that period was due to greater electoral competition, which means that involuntary departure was an important driving force behind the high turnover rates during that era.

We begin this chapter by reviewing the theoretical motivation for our argument concerning the electoral connection's applicability to congressional developments during the nineteenth century. In particular, we outline the importance of two concepts discussed in Chapter 3—ambition and autonomy—for understanding the importance of legislative turnover in the context of discussions about the electoral connection. From there, we briefly summarize the literature on legislative turnover and identify a variety of factors that are hypothesized to influence membership stability. We then provide the results of an analysis of the importance of autonomy and ambition for member turnover, before discussing the broader implications of our findings for understanding how an electoral connection operated throughout much of the nineteenth century.

Turnover and the Electoral Connection

Understanding legislative turnover and renomination is important if we wish to evaluate the assumption that reelection is the proximate goal for members of Congress. If legislators are unconcerned with renomination, it would be difficult to argue that an impending election would inform or constrain their behavior. Indeed, the conventional wisdom about the nineteenth-century Congress points to higher rates of legislative turnover as evidence that members were not motivated by reelection (Polsby 1968; Swift 1987). We contend, however, that the conventional view of incumbent behavior throughout the nineteenth century is not sufficiently nuanced. In particular, turnover and renomination must be understood in terms of two components of the electoral connection—ambition and autonomy.

Ambition

Ambition is a central theoretical component in the electoral connection (Carson and Jenkins 2011; Mayhew 1974). If legislators view reelection as their proximate goal, it follows that they value a career in Congress as a means to pursue other goals that may be of interest at some future time. Indeed, Mayhew (1974), who begins his foundational work on the electoral connection by examining this point, concludes that "in the modern Congress the 'congressional career' is unmistakably upon us" (14). Under this conceptualization of the electoral connection, ambition is defined strictly in terms of congressional careerism.

Mayhew is hardly alone in equating ambition with a desire for a career in Congress. Kernell (1977) was arguably the most explicit in linking ambition and congressional careerism. In his analysis, he compares the impact of electoral competition, ambition, and the practice of rotation in the nineteenth century and identifies ambition as the primary force behind decreased turnover. The result of this analysis led him to conclude that the "primary source of growing membership stability can be found in the men who ran for office" (690). While electoral competition and rotation were constraints on lengthier congressional careers, the more important missing piece was ambitious legislators who attempted to stay in Congress.

In his study of institutionalization in Congress, Polsby (1968) argues that institutionalized political organizations establish boundaries in order to channel career opportunities. With the development of institutional boundaries, turnover decreases, and a career in the organization becomes more desirable. Brady, Buckley, and Rivers (1999) build on these observations and posit that careerism consists of two components: first, the desire among incumbents to continue to serve; second, the ability of incumbents to choose to pursue reelection. In short, ambition, when framed in terms of congressional careerism, requires legislators both to want to continue serving in the institution and to be able to independently pursue continued service.

When did congressional careerism emerge? To date, most studies examine this question in the context of the US House, and the general agreement is that careerism took hold in the late nineteenth and early twentieth centuries (Brady, Buckley, and Rivers 1999; Carson and Jenkins 2011; Kernell 1977; Polsby 1968). These conclusions are generally based on measures that have a narrow definition of careerists and ambition. For example, some studies omit those incumbents who sought reelection but failed to secure renomination by their party (see, e.g., Brady, Buckley, and Rivers 1999). We argue that the omission of these legislators is problematic for understanding how careerism developed, since these individuals clearly wanted to serve another term in Congress but were denied the opportunity.

A more fundamental concern in this context, however, is the decision to tie ambition solely to congressional careerism. By limiting the focus to only a career in Congress, scholars arguably understate the extent of ambition among nineteenth-century politicians (Carson and Jenkins 2011). Stewart (1989) argues that the portrayal of the nineteenth-century Congress as a revolving door overlooks the fact that members of Congress during that period were not "professional politicians but politicians with a higher priority on local careers than on national ones" (9). During the nineteenth century, it was not uncommon for legislators to view Congress as one stop on their political career, rather than the final destination (MacKenzie 2015). It is thus advisable to conceive of nineteenth-century members of Congress as valuing political careerism over congressional careerism.

Connecticut's congressional delegation from the 16th and 17th Congresses are illustrative of this point. A number of the representatives discussed earlier continued to pursue some type of political career once they left the House. For some legislators, this meant moving to the Senate, but for several others, it meant a return to state or local politics. Carson and Jenkins (2011) provide compelling evidence suggesting that this general pattern was common throughout the early history of the House. Approximately half of the freshmen members of the House in the first 24 Congresses went on to hold another political position after leaving the House, but this number drops to roughly 40 percent for the remainder of the nineteenth century (Carson and Jenkins 2011: 30). Based on these calculations, Carson and Jenkins offer the following observation about the political ambitions of nineteenth-century legislators:

> Overall, these results indicate that a clear "political class" existed in the nineteenth century; although ambitious politicians may not have been congressional careerists in the modern sense, they did establish political life as a vocation. The notion that nineteenth-century politics was populated by "Mr. Smiths," who did their brief tour of duty in Washington amid an otherwise ordinary career wholly outside of politics, is simply incorrect. (31)

In short, ambition was present during the nineteenth century but took a different form than the type of career pattern we associate with ambitious politicians today (see, e.g., Schlesinger 1966).

Autonomy

Although ambition is clearly one of the most important components of the electoral connection, it is not enough that legislators want to maintain a career in Congress. A legislator should be in a position to control his own destiny, which requires that access to renomination must be open and exercised at the incumbent's discretion. The electoral rules in place throughout the nineteenth century represent considerable hurdles, since parties were responsible for slating candidates (Reynolds 2006; Ware 2002). There is no doubt that the party ballot and nomination conventions placed considerable constraints on legislative autonomy.

Even if nineteenth-century incumbents had less control over the decision to run for reelection, a number of factors conditioned the level of discretion. First, parties were not as central to the electoral process through the *entire* nineteenth century. Aldrich (2011) contends that it was "not until 1840 that both parties had come close to being fully organized national, mass-based parties" (109). It was therefore not until the mid-nineteenth century that party organizations arguably became gatekeepers to political careers in the way historians writing about that era often portray them. The cases from Connecticut discussed earlier are illustrative of this point. Before the emergence of mass electoral parties in the mid-nineteenth century, current and former members of Congress were actively pursuing reelection in ways that do not fit with common accounts of nineteenth-century congressional politics but are more reflective of the behavior of legislators in the modern era.

Second, both the party ballot and the party nomination convention could actually work against the parties. Incumbent legislators who were denied a spot on the party ballot were not completely without recourse. Indeed, the lack of state-regulated ballots meant that incumbents or any other candidates could "bolt" the party and create an alternative party ticket (Bensel 2004; Reynolds 2006). Parties would go to great lengths to prevent rogue candidates from stealing votes from the party-backed nominee (Bensel 2004; Rusk 1970); at times, a popular incumbent could pose a threat or at least an annoyance for parties. Although we lack systematic evidence on the extent to which such threats kept a party from jettisoning an incumbent for a different candidate, it is not hard to imagine that such a situation did occur. Similarly, Reynolds (2006) documents the rise of "hustling candidates," who would mount insurgent campaigns during a party's nomination conventions.

Third, higher rates of member turnover do not mean that incumbents were largely absent on Election Day. While incumbents' ability to pursue reelection on their own accord is a relatively recent phenomenon contingent on the development of direct primaries during the early part of the twentieth century, incumbents have always played an important role in

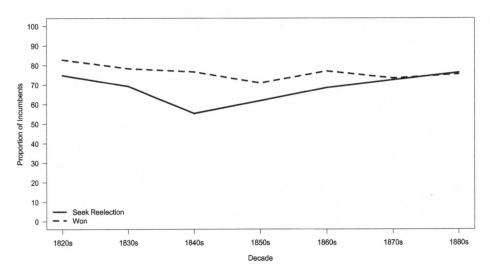

Figure 5.1. Proportion of incumbents seeking reelection, by decade. (Calculated by the authors.)

congressional elections. Figure 5.1 reports the proportion of incumbents who sought reelection (solid black line) and the proportion of incumbents who won reelection (dashed line). Even at its lowest point—the 1840s—the proportion of incumbents who sought reelection always averaged above 50 percent.[3] Thus, the modal election pitted an incumbent against a challenger. Furthermore, approximately three-quarters of incumbents in the 1820s sought reelection, which is comparable to the behavior of incumbents in the 1870s and 1880s. Perhaps incumbent members did not suddenly become more ambitious in the late nineteenth century but, rather, began to exhibit behavior that was comparable to their predecessors from the early part of the century.

The rate at which incumbents sought reelection is particularly important because it highlights a limitation of previous studies of member turnover (Fiorina, Rohde, Wissel 1975; Polsby 1968): namely, focusing exclusively on turnover fails to account for the number of incumbents that desired another term in office but were denied the opportunity (Brady, Buckley, and Rivers 1999). As figure 5.1 demonstrates, most incumbents who sought reelection won another term in office. It is important to note, however, that incumbent reelection rates of between 70 to 80 percent are markedly lower than those observed today (Jacobson and Carson 2016). While it is true that general election defeats were not the main source of membership turnover, it is clear that it was a more important source of membership turnover in that era than in the modern Congress. Indeed, it is difficult to imagine 20 to 25 percent of incumbents losing on Election Day today, and if such an event were to occur, it would probably not be viewed as trivial.

Turnover in the Nineteenth-Century House

Polsby (1968) was among the first to examine the tremendous amount of legislative turnover throughout the nineteenth century. Based on his calculations, the move toward a more stable House membership did not occur until around 1890. Prior to that point, the average representative served just under two terms, and 40 percent or more of the House membership were first-term legislators (Polsby 1968: 146–47). Polsby contends that both a high proportion of first-term members and lower length of service are evidence that the House had failed to establish boundaries, which he viewed as a trademark of institutionalized organizations. After the 1890s, there is a near monotonic increase in the average years served, and the proportion of first-term members fell in each subsequent decade.[4]

Congressional scholars have raised a number of challenges to Polsby's initial findings regarding careerism in Congress. Bogue, Clubb, McKibbin, and Traugott (1976) argue that the median length of service in the early nineteenth century was much more comparable to the late nineteenth and early twentieth centuries. Based on their calculations, the view that the 1890s served as a pivotal turning point is arguably less tenable. Rather, it appears that the 1890s marked a return to legislative career patterns observed in the early nineteenth century. For example, Bogue and his colleagues report that the median length of service was two terms for three of the first four decades of the 1800s and that around 8 to 9 percent of members served four or more terms (291). Those researchers do not find comparable levels of congressional service again until the 1880s, and not until the 1920s had the median service increased by a full term.

Fiorina, Rohde, and Wissel (1975) propose an alternative measure of legislative turnover. Specifically, they note that Polsby's analysis does not control for the addition of new House seats, which is particularly important in the nineteenth century, given the number of new states that joined the union. After adjusting for the creation of new seats, Fiorina and his colleagues find that although turnover was still quite high, it is not the case that turnover decreased monotonically since the start of the nineteenth century. Their adjusted calculations suggest that turnover spiked in the mid-nineteenth century, before starting to trend downward around the 1870s (Fiorina, Rohde, and Wissel 1975: 31–32). These findings fit with subsequent research that identifies the 1870s, rather than the 1890s or early twentieth century, as the starting point for growing congressional careerism (Kernell 1977).

Although Fiorina, Rohde, and Wissel (1975) noted the importance of distinguishing between different types of turnover, Swain, Borrelli, Reed, and Evans (2000) provide one of the most detailed accounts of the different sources of member turnover. Rather than focusing on just overall turnover, they calculate the proportion of turnover from multiple sources, including retirement, death, not getting renominated, and general election defeat.[5] They find that retirement was the main form of congressional turnover for each decade from the 1790s to the 1990s. According to their analysis, turnover as a result of general election defeats, was highest in the period from the 1830s to the 1890s. Indeed, from the 1850s to the 1890s, between one-quarter and almost one-third of legislative turnover was due to general election defeats.

Several studies also find that legislative turnover is higher under different partisan alignments (Fiorina et al. 1975; Swain et al. 2000). In general, these studies are in agreement that overall turnover was highest during the second party system (1824–54), while the third party system (1856–96) featured the second highest level of turnover (Fiorina et al. 1975: 55; Swain et al. 2000: 443). Swain, Borrelli, Reed, and Evans (2000) find that the difference between partisan periods is not uniform across the different types of turnover. There is only one partisan era, the third party period, for which there is a statistically significant difference in the rate of turnover due to retirements. In contrast, turnover from general election defeats spiked under the second and third party systems, before gradually decreasing over time. These differences are notable because even if electoral defeats have never been the primary cause of legislative turnover, their contribution to the overall rate of membership change was highest precisely when previous studies suggest that careerism was nascent at best.

While the aggregate trends in legislative turnover are informative, examining how individual-level factors influence turnover is necessary to a better understanding of the impact of ambition and autonomy on career decisions. There is growing evidence that electoral factors, such as electoral security and redistricting, play an important role in the career decisions of nineteenth-century incumbents (Brady, Buckley, and Rivers 1999; Engstrom 2013; Kernell 1977). Below, we review the findings of these previous studies and provide some preliminary evidence about the impact of redistricting and electoral competition on both voluntary and involuntary turnover.

Redistricting

Research on modern congressional elections identifies redistricting as an important factor for both voluntary and involuntary turnover (Cox and Katz 2002), and it appears to have played a similarly important role in historical congressional elections (Carson, Engstrom and Roberts 2006; Engstrom 2013). Even if incumbent legislators in the nineteenth century were not in complete control over the decision to run for reelection, there is growing evidence that career decisions were influenced by strategic calculations similar to those made by contemporary legislators. Engstrom finds that incumbent legislators in the nineteenth century were less likely to seek another term in office after their districts were redrawn.[6] Since states in that era were less likely to confine redistricting to the election immediately after reapportionment, its impact on legislative turnover could be and often was felt throughout the entire decade (Engstrom 2013: 142–43). Engstrom finds that redistricting also decreased the likelihood of incum-

TABLE 5.1. Effect of redistricting on seeking and winning reelection, by decade

Reapp. cycle	Ran for reelection			Incumbent won		
	Redrawn (N)	Not redrawn (N)	Diff.	Redrawn (N)	Not redrawn (N)	Diff.
1820s	62.62 (110)	74.87 (1000)	12.26*	86.57 (67)	82.47 (736)	4.09
1830s	71.94 (147)	67.96 (1108)	3.98	73.00 (100)	78.47 (734)	5.47
1840s	41.79 (278)	58.32 (940)	16.52*	65.18 (112)	78.99 (533)	13.81*
1850s	49.73 (190)	62.50 (1021)	12.77*	71.74 (92)	71.45 (620)	0.29
1860s	58.55 (156)	69.15 (935)	10.60*	73.03 (89)	77.46 (630)	4.43
1870s	62.07 (291)	74.55 (1183)	12.48*	65.56 (180)	74.91 (861)	9.36*
1880s	72.99 (316)	76.49 (1360)	3.50	71.37 (227)	76.26 (1015)	4.89
Total	59.71 (1488)	69.67 (7457)	9.96*	70.93 (867)	77.08 (5129)	6.15*

Note: Cell entries list the proportion of legislators in each category by whether or not their district was redrawn between elections. The number of legislators in each category is listed in parentheses.
*$p < .05$

bent victory, which suggests that redistricting can influence both voluntary and involuntary exits from Congress.

In table 5.1, we report the proportion of incumbents who ran for reelection and the proportion of reelection-seeking incumbents who won, by whether the incumbent's district was redrawn.[7] Since we are interested in changes in turnover and renomination over time, we report these calculations for each decade as well as for the entire time period we examine. The results reported in table 5.1 comport with Engstrom's overall conclusion about the impact of redistricting on voluntary turnover. There is, however, notable variation across time. For example, the 1840s redistricting cycle, which is the only time the House actually decreased in size following a reapportionment, led to the most pronounced effect, just over 16 percentage points. In contrast, reapportionments in the 1830s and 1880s did not lead to substantive or statistically significant effects for redistricting. When all seven decades are pooled together, the likelihood that an incumbent ran for reelection after his district was redrawn decreases by approximately 10 percentage points.

Although our findings about the impact of redistricting on the decision to run for reelection are similar to Engstrom's (2013) analysis, we reach a slightly different conclusion about the impact of redistricting on involuntary turnover. Based on a pooled analysis of the entire seven-decade period, the proportion of incumbents who won reelection decreases by 6 percentage points between redrawn and unchanged districts. When the results are broken down by decade, however, it becomes clear that the finding for the pooled analysis is heavily influenced by two decades, the 1840s and 1870s. For these two reapportionments, the likelihood that an incumbent won decreases by 13.8 and roughly 9.4 percentage points. In contrast, in districts that were not redrawn, incumbents were actually slightly more likely to win reelection in the 1820s and 1850s and only marginally less likely to do so in the 1830s, 1860s, and 1880s. In short, redistricting was, on occasion, an important source of involuntary turnover, but in most decades, its effect was felt at the margins and was not always in the anticipated direction.

Electoral Competition

In addition to redistricting, the relative level of electoral competition also influences legislative turnover. Kernell (1977) reports a monotonic decrease in turnover from the 1870s to the 1900s due to electoral competition. Indeed, Kernell maintains that decreased electoral competition is the second most important factor, after ambition, for the growth of careerism. More recent studies that focus on the decisions of individual members of Congress find a similarly important role for electoral competition. Whether measured as a general partisan advantage (Brady, Buckley, and Rivers 1999) or a margin of victory (Engstrom 2013), increased electoral security increases the likelihood both that an incumbent seeks another term in office and that he wins reelection.

In the top panel of figure 5.2, we report the average margin of victory for incumbent legislators who won reelection, left the House voluntarily, and exited the House involuntarily. Not surprisingly, incumbents who went on to win reelection had, on average, won by larger margins in the last election. Members of the House who left voluntarily were, on average, less electorally secure than reelected incumbents but more electorally secure than incumbents who ran and lost. There is considerable variation across decades in the magnitude of the difference between these different groups. For the first four decades in the series, there is a difference of approximately 5 percentage points in the average margin of victory between incumbents who won and incumbents who left voluntarily. During this same period, the average difference between those who left voluntarily and involuntarily is nearly 8 percentage points in two of the four decades and just over 10 percentage points in the 1820s. By the 1870s, the average margin of victory for incumbents who left voluntarily is about 3 percentage points higher than incumbents who lost and is around 5 percentage points lower than incumbents who went on to win.

The second panel of figure 5.2 examines the same set of incumbents but reports the proportion in each group who were from marginal districts (where the margin of victory was less than 5 points), by their status at the end of a given Congress. Incumbents who left the House involuntarily were more likely to be from marginal districts, while those who won were consistently less likely to be. The difference between these two groups ranges from a low of 11 points in the 1860s to a high of 20 points in the 1870s. As with margin of victory, incumbents who left voluntarily look most similar to those who won reelection, but by the 1870s, they come to more closely mirror those who left involuntarily.

One potential explanation for the patterns observed in figure 5.2 is that incumbents who left voluntarily in the early nineteenth century likely had a high probability of being reelected. Given that this was a period of comparatively lower legislative turnover, it is possible that these individuals could have returned for another term if they so desired. Once party organizations began to exert greater control over the electoral process, however,

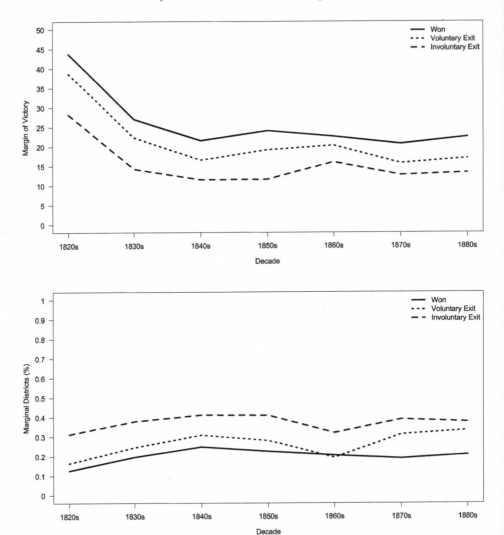

Figure 5.2. Electoral competition and type of departure. (Calculated by the authors.)

the difference between involuntary and voluntary turnover with respect to the average margin of victory began to decrease. Thus, it appears that previous electoral competition has always been an important factor in predicting which incumbents would exit the House involuntarily. Not until the parties emerged as gatekeepers did electoral competition become a more powerful predictor of voluntary turnover.

Involuntary Turnover and Legislative Ambition Revisited

The foregoing review of previous studies and preliminary analyses suggests a number of important implications for our understanding of legislative turnover in the nineteenth century. First, nineteenth-century incumbents exhibit behavior that is more comparable to modern legislators than previous scholarly accounts acknowledge. Based on the individual-level response of incumbents to electoral conditions, Engstrom (2013) concluded, "[I]ncumbents of the nineteenth century, or the parties nominating them, were keenly strategic in deciding when to run for reelection. Indeed, these incumbents appear to be much more like their modern counterparts than is often assumed" (138). The rational response of legislators to the political environment is important to keep in mind, as it relates to understanding legislative turnover throughout the nineteenth century. Indeed, we believe that this response can help to explain why the electoral connection, even if in a more limited form, can coexist with high levels of legislative turnover. If there is a strategic component to nineteenth-century legislative turnover, it suggests candidate and party behavior that is more similar to modern behavior than has previously been recognized.

Second, although previous scholarly accounts acknowledge the importance of parties for low turnover in the nineteenth century, the role of parties has not been fully fleshed out. In some cases, the impact of party has been assessed merely in terms of differences across party systems. While these differences are informative, the studies do not examine how variation in the strength of party organization influences legislative turnover. Furthermore, since several studies focus on the period from the 1870s onward, they have provided, at best, an incomplete picture of legislative turnover. That membership stability in Congress was comparable in the 1820s and 1830s to the 1870s and 1880s suggests a far different story than the one implied by early studies of legislative turnover.[8]

Lastly, ambition has been defined in terms of either the proportion of incumbents running for reelection or the average length of a congressional career. While both these measures have their merits, we believe that it is also important to account for the extent to which former members of the House tried to return to Congress. For example, several former members of Connecticut's congressional delegation attempted to win another term in the House after leaving the chamber. While some members were successful, others were not able to win another term in the House. To our knowledge, prior studies do not examine either of these sets of members of Congress when discussing the ambition of nineteenth-century legislators. We contend that examining both sets is important for understanding the career goals of individual legislators and the role of political parties in limiting career opportunities.

Below, we provide preliminary analyses of the relationship between party organization and legislative turnover and legislative ambition. We believe that the former analysis can provide insights about the extent to which incumbents were able to exercise greater levels of autonomy than researchers have previously recognized. The latter analysis meanwhile offers potentially new insights about the role of ambition among nineteenth-century legislators.

Autonomy and Party Organization

It is clear that nineteenth-century legislators lacked the same type of discretion over their careers that modern members of Congress enjoy. The diminished autonomy is usually attributed to the greater influence and role of political parties. While the logic of that attribution is quite clear, it is important to remember that political parties did not play this role throughout the entire nineteenth century. Indeed, mass electoral parties did not emerge all at once but, rather, grew over time, with the Democrats organizing in some states before others (Chambers and Davis 1978). Prior to the creation of party electoral organizations, incumbents should have been able to exercise greater autonomy over their career decisions. We expect that the baseline probability of an incumbent seeking another term in office should decrease once parties began to act as gatekeepers. We can leverage this variability to better understand how the creation of party organizations influenced the likelihood that incumbents sought another term in office.[9]

As a preliminary test of this expectation, we examine the impact of Democratic party organization in a state on the probability that an incumbent sought another term in office. Our outcome variable for this analysis is coded 1 if the incumbent sought another term in office and 0 otherwise. The main predictor is a variable that indicates whether the Democratic Party organized in the state. We use the classification of party organization by Chambers and Davis (1978) to determine the election in which the Democrats were first organized in a given state. After identifying the relevant election year for each state, we created the variable "Democrats organized," coded 1 in election years where the Democratic Party created electoral organizations and 0 otherwise.

In addition to our main predictor of interest, we include measures to account for electoral competition and redistricting. We measure electoral competition as the incumbent's margin of victory in his last election, which we expect to be positively related to the probability that the incumbent runs for reelection. To account for redistricting, we created the variable "district redrawn," coded 1 when an incumbent's district was altered since he last stood for election and 0 otherwise. As Engstrom (2013) suggests, instances of redistricting should negatively decrease the likelihood that an incumbent runs for reelection. In addition to these covariates, we also control for the number of consecutive terms an incumbent has served and for his age. For our analysis, we focus on four states—New York, Ohio, Pennsylvania, and Virginia—that vary with respect to the election by which the Democratic Party organized.[10] Our analysis includes all elections from 1820 to 1854, which is the last election year in which the Whigs were politically active. We focus on that period to ensure that there is an adequate number of observations in each state for both before and after party organization.

In table 5.2, we report the estimates of a logistic regression model for each state. The coefficient estimate for the variable "Democrats organized" is statistically significant across all four models. More important, the estimated effect of the creation of party electoral organizations is substantively meaningful. In Ohio, for example, the creation of a Democratic organization is predicted to decrease the probability of an incumbent running for

TABLE 5.2. Probability that incumbent seeks reelection, 1820–54

	N.Y. (*SE*)	Penn. (*SE*)	Virginia (*SE*)	Ohio (*SE*)
Democrats organized	−0.503*	−0.711*	−0.523*	−0.963*
	(0.185)	(0.218)	(0.304)	(0.442)
Margin of victory	0.004	0.004	0.002	0.014*
	(0.005)	(0.004)	(0.004)	(0.007)
District redrawn	−0.685*	−0.609*	−0.697*	−0.533*
	(0.251)	(0.259)	(0.304)	(0.309)
Tenure	0.166*	−0.750*	−0.059	−0.085
	(0.087)	(0.129)	(0.058)	(0.094)
Age (logged)	−1.499*	−1.283*	−0.681	−0.403
	(0.469)	(0.550)	(0.648)	(0.734)
Constant	5.553*	7.034*	4.296*	3.150
	(1.760)	(2.102)	(2.469)	(2.745)
N	614	456	332	306
AIC	821.676	559.840	368.232	379.571

Note: Cell entries are coefficients from a logistic regression model, with standard errors reported in parentheses.

*$p < .05$, one-tailed test

reelection, by approximately 18 percentage points. By comparison, redistricting is estimated to lead to a decrease of nearly 9 percentage points in that probability. Our estimates for Pennsylvania also indicate that the creation of party organizations had a larger impact than redistricting. The creation of a Democratic organization in Pennsylvania is estimated to lead to a decrease of just over 17 percentage points in the likelihood that an incumbent seeks reelection, while redistricting is predicted to lead to a decline of approximately 14.5 percentage points in that likelihood. We find a slightly different pattern in New York and Virginia. In New York, party organization and redistricting are estimated to lower the probability of an incumbent running for reelection by 12.5 and 16.9 points respectively. The substantive effects are the smallest in Virginia, where party organization is predicted to lower the probability of an incumbent seeking reelection by 9 points and where redistricting decreases the probability by 12 points.

In short, these findings suggest that the creation of mass parties lowered legislators' autonomy to seek a career in Congress. While the magnitude of the effect is comparable to redistricting, the overall substantive impact may be higher, since parties, once formed, impacted all subsequent elections, while redistricting occurred in a more limited set of elections. When considered in conjunction with the findings reported in figure 5.1, these results suggest that scholars should be mindful not to overgeneralize about the politics of the nineteenth-century House. While parties could limit autonomy, legislators who served in the three to four decades before the creation of mass political parties were not nearly as constrained in their behavior.

Ambition and a Return to the House

Although ambition is a central component to both careerism and the electoral connection, it can be difficult to directly measure. To get around these measurement problems, some scholars employ interviews of potential or actual congressional candidates (Fox and Lawless 2005; Maestas et al. 2006). These interviews can reveal a number of valuable insights about both the formation of ambition and how ambition influences candidacy decisions. Elite interviews are, obviously, not possible with nineteenth-century House elections. We must therefore rely on a more indirect measure of ambition in order to understand the behavior of this particular set of legislators. Following another canonical approach, we use the strategic behavior of incumbents to make inferences about ambition (Carson 2005; Carson and Roberts 2005; Jacobson 1989; Jacobson and Kernell 1983).

We are particularly interested in identifying the conditions under which former members of Congress seek to return for another round of service in the House. Previous studies have not fully examined this dynamic, partly because they do not examine candidate-level data but, rather, focus on aggregate patterns of who entered or exited the House. For example, Kernell (1977) chronicles the growth of ambition by measuring the decade-to-decade change in the proportion of incumbents running for reelection. While we do not question the utility of this approach to studying ambition in the nineteenth century, our point is simply that additional data may provide a more complete view. That at least some former members actively sought to return to the House would be strongly indicative of political ambition that would not be captured by previous research. Furthermore, we believe a full account of *career* ambitions among nineteenth-century legislators requires looking at the frequency with which former members sought to return to the House. Given both more competitive elections and the higher rates of *involuntary* turnover during that era, measures like the average numbers of terms served by incumbent members (see Polsby 1968) may not reveal the full extent of career-seeking behavior among nineteenth-century politicians.

To examine the career ambitions of former members of Congress, we used Dubin's (1998) collection of congressional election returns to identify the number of former members of the House who were candidates in a given election year. For the time period we examine, there were, on average, approximately 31 former members of Congress who were candidates in a given election year. There is considerable variability, however, in the propensity for former legislators to seek a return to the House, with the minimum number of such candidates being 9 and the maximum being 47.

In figure 5.3, we examine the emergence of candidates with prior congressional service, by decade. The 1820s is the high point for the time series, with an average of 40.4 candidates with prior congressional service emerging during the elections contested in this decade. There is a notable decline over the next three decades, with the average falling to a low of 21.1 in the 1850s. After this point, the series trends back upward again, and the average rises in the 1880s to 39.2 candidates with prior congressional experience. While this is comparable to the average for the 1820s, the House grew by over 100 seats in the five decades that separate these time points. The proportion of races where at least one of the challengers was a former member of Congress is thus higher in the 1820s than in the 1880s.

To identify the factors that influenced the strategic behavior of for-

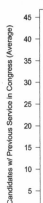

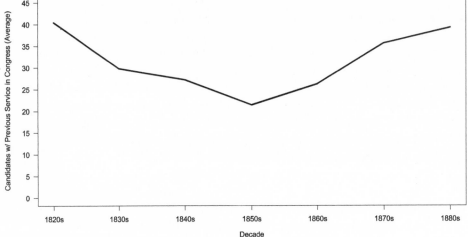

Figure 5.3. Emergence of candidates with prior service in Congress, by decade. (Calculated by the authors.)

mer members, we estimated a series of Poisson regression models where the outcome variable is number of candidates with prior congressional service in a given election year. We expect that an increase in voluntary turnover should result in fewer congressional candidates who are former members of the House. Higher rates of voluntary turnover are evidence that autonomy is either low or being stymied by the parties. We expect former members of Congress to have fewer opportunities to pursue a return to the House. Involuntary turnover is indicative of ambitious legislators, but it is less clear how this would influence candidacy decisions by former representatives. We operationalized turnover as the proportion of incumbents who left Congress, and we created separate measures for both involuntary and voluntary turnover to test our specific expectations.

We also expect that the viability of former members of the US House as congressional candidates should be positively related to their emergence. To account for the viability of candidates with previous congressional experience, we calculated the proportion of legislators who were in their first term of a repeat round of service in the House. This includes any case where a legislator served in a noncontiguous Congress before being elected for a second round of service in Congress (e.g., a legislator who served in the 18th Congress, left the House, and then returned to serve in the House for the 20th Congress). As the proportion of repeat congressmen increases, other former members of the House should be more likely to emerge as candidates.[11]

In table 5.3, we report the results for the regression model previously outlined and an additional model that also controls for the size of the House. The coefficient estimate for voluntary turnover is negative and statistically significant in both models, while the estimate for involuntary turnover is not discernible from zero. An increase in voluntary turnover across the variables' interquartile range leads to a prediction of over 8 fewer candidates with previous congressional experience. As expected, the coefficient estimates for repeat members of Congress are positive and statistically significant in both models. The substantive impact of this factor is somewhat more limited. An increase over the full range of the covariate, from about 3.4 percentage points to 12.3 points, leads to an estimate of 14 more candidates who are former members of the House. The estimate for change from the first quartile (5 percent) to the third quartile (7 percent) is a more modest increase of 3 candidates.

It is important to note that although the covariate for chamber size is statistically significant on a one-tailed test, the substantive impact is still relatively small. Over the full range of the variable "chamber size," which is 178 to 330 seats, the model results predict an increase of approximately

TABLE 5.3. Number of former members of Congress running for the House, 1820–88

	Est. *(SE)*	Est. *(SE)*
Voluntary turnover	–2.622*	–2.347*
	(0.427)	(0.452)
Involuntary turnover	0.053	–0.486
	(0.747)	(0.804)
Repeat MCs (%)	4.694*	5.369*
	(1.774)	(1.816)
Chamber size		0.002*
		(0.001)
Constant	3.958*	3.552*
	(0.212)	(0.305)
N	35	35
AIC	245.123	243.740

Note: Cell entries are regression coefficients from a Poisson regression model, with standard errors in parentheses.

*$p < .05$, one-tailed test

8 candidates. While the estimate is comparable to the other covariates, the magnitude of the change needed to produce a similar effect is arguably greater. Indeed, an increase of 10 percentage points in voluntary turnover seems small in comparison to nearly doubling the size of the House. More important, the relatively small impact of chamber size suggests that factors capturing ambition and autonomy better predict candidate emergence than does the number of elections being contested.

Conclusion

Critics of the contemporary US Congress often decry the rise of career politicians and the supposed entrenchment of power in Washington, DC. For decades, reformers have pushed for ideas such as term limits, in an attempt to limit the ability of representatives or senators to remain in Congress for extended periods of time. Although such reforms would lead to more turnover among elected representatives, there is no guarantee that it would necessarily lead to better representation. What seems to have been overlooked in discussions about reform and the legislative institution is the electoral connection that serves as the primary means by which individuals continue to win reelection to Congress. Regardless of whether members have to run for reelection every two or six years, they must constantly remind voters why they should be allowed to continue to represent them in either the House or the Senate.

In examining legislative turnover across a much wider swatch of history, we have attempted to gain leverage on the importance and role of an electoral connection for the nineteenth-century Congress. As we have shown, legislative turnover was much greater during that era than it is in the modern Congress. Nevertheless, we learned a great deal about two facets of the electoral connection—ambition and autonomy—when we separated out the type of departures that occurred during that period. Members who voluntarily left the House chamber were clearly different, in a number of respects, from those who were forced to depart due to an electoral defeat. The former were often more electorally secure and often pursued other career opportunities in politics after serving one, two, or even three terms in Congress. This finding instructively suggests that members were clearly ambitious during the nineteenth-century and that they operated within the confines of the system of rules then in place.

The findings in this chapter also tell us more about the role and strength of political parties relative to political candidates during the nineteenth century. The strength of party organizations clearly varied by decade during much of that period. Whereas parties were much weaker in the early part of the antebellum era, they witnessed a tremendous growth of influence throughout the middle part of the century, before reforms started to weaken their near monopolistic control near the century's end. Our findings also suggest that party machines cared about winning and recognized that certain types of candidates—those with experience, compared with political amateurs—were substantially more likely to win elections. Regardless of whether candidate ambition was "manufactured" by the party organizations or later motivated by the candidates themselves, we see evidence that candidates were trying to make careers in politics in whatever fashion was encouraged at the time. This is an important finding for our argument about the relevance of an electoral connection during the nineteenth century. In the next chapter, we shift the focus of the discussion to ballot placement and election timing, to better understand how individual candidates could directly influence the outcome of elections in that era.

SIX

Ballots, Election Timing, and the Personal Vote

When the dust settled on the 1844 presidential election, James K. Polk's margin in the popular vote was less than 40,000 votes. Despite the narrow majority, Democrats were able to maintain their outsized majority in the House, largely due to the staggered nature of the congressional election calendar. Unlike contemporary elections, where House and presidential candidates always appear on the same ballot, congressional elections during that period were held before and after the November presidential election. North Carolina, for example, held its congressional elections in August, and Democrats won 6 of that state's 9 seats. Henry Clay, the Whig presidential candidate, carried North Carolina two months later with a little over 52 percent of the vote. Ohio Democrats enjoyed an advantage similar to that of their North Carolina copartisans. Ohio held its congressional election in October, when Democrats won 13 of 21 seats, but Clay won approximately 51 percent of the two-party vote in the next month's presidential election. The Democrats' advantage continued after the November presidential election. In Maryland, which held its congressional elections in October 1845, Democrats picked up 4 seats, even though Clay managed to win the state by over 4.5 points in the presidential election. Indeed, 2 of the 4 seats Democrats won were districts that Clay had carried the previous November. Overall, Democrats' seat losses were concentrated entirely in elections held concurrently with the presidential election, but the party actually gained a seat in the off-November elections.

Differential electoral timing had an even more pronounced impact on the outcome of the 1848 presidential election. Though Zachary Taylor, the Whig presidential candidate, won the popular vote with almost 53 percent of the two-party vote, Democrats managed to gain a small majority in the House. As with the 1844 presidential election, the Democrats' electoral success was achieved by running ahead of their presidential nominee. In Pennsylvania, where Taylor won 51.8 percent of the two-party vote, Democrats managed to gain 2 seats in the October congressional election. Similarly, Lewis Cass, the 1848 Democratic presidential candidate, narrowly won Virginia with 50.8 percent of the vote, but Democrats won 13 of the state's 15 seats in the congressional elections held five months later, in April 1849. As with the 1844 elections, the Democrats secured majority control of the House by dominating the off-November elections. While the Democrats lost 12 seats in congressional races held concurrently with the presidential election, the party won a net of 19 seats in non-November elections from districts that Taylor carried in the November presidential election. If the electoral cycle had been synched, the Whigs may have not only won control of the White House but also retained their House majority.

These cases from the 1844 and 1848 elections highlight how different institutional arrangements could moderate the impact of the party ballot. We believe that examining the variability in the basic structure of elections can be valuable for evaluating the potential for electoral accountability in the nineteenth century. Students of congressional politics generally agree that electoral accountability was significantly enhanced following adoption of the secret ballot in the late nineteenth century. With the elimination of the party ballot that had been in use for several decades, voters could more easily reward or punish elected officials individually, since all candidates for elected offices were listed on the same ballot (see, e.g., Katz and Sala 1996). Nevertheless, recent evidence suggests that a subset of legislators may have been able to develop a "personal" vote with their constituents in the decades prior to adoption of the secret ballot (Carson and Roberts 2013; Finocchiaro and Jenkins 2016). Indeed, some representatives were rewarded or punished selectively based on their level of responsiveness to individual voters. When coupled with emerging evidence of an electoral connection in the nineteenth century (Bianco, Spence, and Wilkerson 1996; Carson and Engstrom 2005; Carson and Jenkins 2011), these phenomena raise a variety of implications for existing accounts of electoral politics during that historical era.

In this chapter, we investigate the preconditions for electoral accountability in the nineteenth century, by examining how candidate-specific factors influence election outcomes. Since electoral accountability requires voters to make decisions based on individual candidates, the extent to which candidate attributes influence election outcomes provides important insights about whether electoral accountability was ever feasible during that era. We do not claim that electoral accountability operated then in the exact same manner as it does today. Indeed, the nature of the electoral institutions during that era can pose considerable barriers to electoral accountability. Our objective here is to document whether the conditions needed for electoral accountability existed, before we conduct a more systematic analysis of accountability itself.

We focus our discussion here on several factors that should influence the level of electoral accountability for individual representatives. First, the collective nature of the party ballot meant that both parties and candidates had an interest in constructing the best party ticket they could (Carson and Roberts 2013). Congressional candidates who could help attract voters or even mobilize supporters had the potential to produce positive electoral returns for the party, even if voters were not voting for them directly. Second, election timing was quite variable prior to 1872, as many House elections were held months before November (or even much later) in a given election year, which raises broad implications for our understanding of congressional election outcomes during that era. Both nonuniform election dates and midterm elections should condition the influence of national politics on congressional elections. The quality of individual congressional candidates should matter significantly more in these cases, since voters in a large subset of races throughout the nineteenth century were not simply making a choice based on which presidential candidate was at the top of the ticket. Finally, the structure of the party ballot varied depending on whether top races (e.g., presidential or gubernatorial) were also being contested at the same time. As with election timing, ballot placement may have important consequences for how individual candidates influence election outcomes.

The Role of Candidates in Nineteenth-Century Elections

Before addressing each of the factors that should influence levels of electoral accountability for the nineteenth century, it is important to emphasize that individual candidates were not expected to structure election outcomes in any way during that period (Formisano 1974, Skeen 1986; Swift 1987).[1] The argument for a more limited role for individual congressional candidates then is buttressed by research suggesting that the party ballot

manufactured greater levels of voter responsiveness to the parties (Engstrom and Kernell 2005, 2014). Since the party ballot made split-ticket
voting difficult, if not impossible, voters were not selecting between different candidates as much as between different political parties (Rusk 1970).
In discussing the importance of this institutional arrangement, Engstrom
and Kernell (2005: 535) conclude that "coattail voting occurred by default"
under the party ballot unless voters went to extraordinary lengths to split
their vote.

As we saw in chapter 4, however, not only were congressional candidates
ambitious, but candidate entry decisions were important determinants of
election outcomes throughout the nineteenth century. Indeed, our earlier
results fit with a growing body of evidence that the attributes of the candidate who was chosen to be a party's nominee for Congress could be quite
consequential in nineteenth-century elections (Carson and Hood 2014;
Carson and Roberts 2013; Carson and Sievert 2017). Similarly, Garand and
Gross (1984; Gross and Garand 1984) find that incumbent candidates consistently outperformed nonincumbent candidates as far back as the 1820s.

How do we reconcile these findings with work by Engstrom and Kernell (2005, 2014) suggesting that the use of the party ticket made the attributes of individual congressional candidates largely irrelevant? We believe
that the answer to this question lies in the unique individual-level variation
in the structure of nineteenth-century elections. Whereas Engstrom and
Kernell (2005, 2014) focus on state-level election returns during presidential election years, we focus on individual congressional elections during
all elections from 1840 to 1888. In doing so, we are able to offer unique
insights on the relationship between candidate-specific attributes and electoral competition during that era.

Our argument does not necessarily conflict with Engstrom and Kernell's (2005, 2014) broader account of electoral politics under the party
ballot. There can be little dispute that the party ballot actively discouraged
individual voters from choosing between individual candidates in *all* races.
Similarly, the party ballot clearly amplified coattail effects for races down
the ticket, since these candidates' fortunes were tied more directly to the
fate of the party's standard-bearer (Engstrom and Kernell 2005). While
these factors might minimize the importance of congressional candidates
relative to modern elections, it does not necessarily follow that these factors were always irrelevant. Our argument can therefore be seen as building
on Engstrom and Kernell's (2005, 2014) analysis, in that we seek to identify
the conditions under which candidate-specific factors were most likely to
influence nineteenth-century congressional election outcomes.[2] In the sec-

tions that follow, we discuss how concern for the overall quality of a party's ballot and variations in election timing and ballot structure could influence the impact of congressional candidates on election outcomes in that era.

The Quality of the Party Ballot

Both congressional candidates and political parties during the nineteenth century were concerned about the overall quality of their party's slate of candidates. According to Kolodny (1998: 17), congressional Republicans first organized a separate congressional campaign organization because of concerns about the deleterious effects of President Andrew Johnson on legislative races. Republicans did not abandon their new organization once a more favorable presidential candidate emerged. They continued to utilize their newly enacted campaign organization rather than entrusting their fate to a presidential campaign.[3] Their fears were well founded, since the party ballot linked the electoral fate of all party members who appeared on the same ballot. For this reason, parties had an incentive to think about the overall "quality" of the ballot they assembled.

Two candidate-specific attributes could enhance the overall quality of a party's ballot. First, incumbent members of Congress who sought another term in office should improve the overall quality of a party's slate. During the period we examine, over three-quarters of the incumbents who ran for reelection were returned to Congress. Although there was some variability in incumbent fortunes, the lowest reelection rate was approximately 59 percent in 1874, and there were 12 elections where at least 80 percent of incumbents were reelected. Furthermore, incumbents routinely outperformed their counterparts in open-seat races. Garand and Gross's (1984) analysis of congressional elections from 1824 to 1980 led them to conclude that "[i]ncumbent winners have always done better than non-incumbent winners" (29), which is consistent with our results. Parties had good reason to believe that including a congressional incumbent on their party ticket could yield real, positive electoral returns for the party's entire slate of candidates. Indeed, we would expect that a party's past electoral performance would be a better predictor of a current election outcome when the party ran an incumbent.

Second, we expect the prior experience of candidates in both open-seat and incumbent-contested races to influence overall ballot quality. In modern elections, both incumbency and candidate quality typically lead to positive electoral returns, partly because the process of winning prior office means that a candidate will know how to run and win a campaign. Experienced candidates also generally have higher levels of name recognition compared with political amateurs seeking elective office. Although both of these explanations are likely to be less relevant in predicting electoral success during an era where party ballots were in use, the party organizations still preferred having a high-quality candidate on the ballot. In a period where voter mobilization was especially crucial for a party's electoral fortunes across all offices (Engstrom 2012), the presence of experienced candidates—and, arguably, their absence—could have important implications for a party's voter mobilization efforts. Although party agents were the central actors in on-the-ground mobilization (Bensel 2004; Ware 2002), the inclusion of candidates with a previous record of service would facilitate this job, as it could give the voters something, beyond simply the party label, to further interest and motivate them in participating in the election. These attributes were no less important in a presidential election year, since presidential candidates traditionally did not campaign themselves and since local party organizations were responsible for managing voter mobilization efforts on behalf of the national campaigns (Aldrich 2011; Kernell 1986).

These expectations are consistent with newspaper accounts of nineteenth-century elections. Indeed, newspaper coverage of congressional nominations and elections during that era frequently offered commentary about how congressional candidates would influence a party's chances in the upcoming election. For example, the *New York Times* (July 7, 1868) described the 1868 congressional nominations in Indiana's Seventh, Eighth, and Eleventh Districts as "foolish nominations" that "will cost the Democracy thousands of votes." Indeed, the "weak" candidates in the Eighth and Eleventh Districts were both amateurs running against candidates with no elective experience. Nineteenth-century congressional party slates were also discussed in terms of overall quality. When discussing the Republican congressional nominees in Michigan, the *Detroit Advertiser* (August 3, 1868) mentioned that the "complete [Republican ticket] is an able and a strong one, and we confidently trust will be elected entire, although not without active work in the First, Fifth, and Sixth Districts." The *Advertiser's* assessment of the elections seems to comport with our own conception of what makes for a higher-quality candidate and a strong party ballot. Each of the candidates on the Republican ticket, which included three incumbents and three candidates in open-seat races, had previously won elected office. Furthermore, the races where the newspaper expected a close contest were all races where a Republican candidate faced off against someone with prior elective experience.

We demonstrated in chapter 4 that attributes of individual candidates shaped electoral competition during the nineteenth century, but we have not directly considered how they contributed to the overall ballot. Carson and Roberts (2013) contend that the collective nature of the party ballot meant that parties who wished to maximize their chance of winning "needed to be concerned about how the candidate for each office on the ballot would affect the collective reputation of the party" (31). Under this arrangement, candidate recruitment efforts could result in spillover effects for down-ballot races and potentially for even higher offices.[4] To examine whether congressional candidates could produce spillover effects for other races, we use Broockman's (2009) approach based on regression discontinuity design (RDD) to test whether congressional candidates had "reverse" coattails in presidential elections.[5] By doing so, we can examine whether sharing a partisan affiliation with the incumbent party boosts a presidential candidate's vote share. The existence of reverse coattails would run counter to the expectations of some prior studies, which contend that presidential candidates, by virtue of being at the top of the ticket, dominated vote choice under the party ballot. While there is no reason to doubt this argument, we also know that local party organizations played a more central role in organizing the presidential campaigns' efforts of voter mobilization (Aldrich 2011; Kernell 1986). It is thus possible that presidential candidates would benefit from having high-quality local candidates who could help turn out loyal partisans and attract other potential supporters.[6]

For our analysis, we take advantage of the variability in election timing during the nineteenth century, which we explore in greater detail below. If congressional candidates did produce spillover effects, we should expect to find these effects *only* for those elections held in November. When the last congressional election was held before or after November, its outcome should not influence presidential vote share, since the congressional candidates in that election were not on the same ballot as their party's presidential candidate. We therefore estimate separate models for elections held before November, in November, and after November in a presidential election year.

In figure 6.1, we report the RDD estimates for our analysis of reverse coattail effects.[7] The results for elections held in November comport with our theoretical expectations, as a presidential candidate's vote share is estimated to increase by 3.4 percentage points when his party won the last

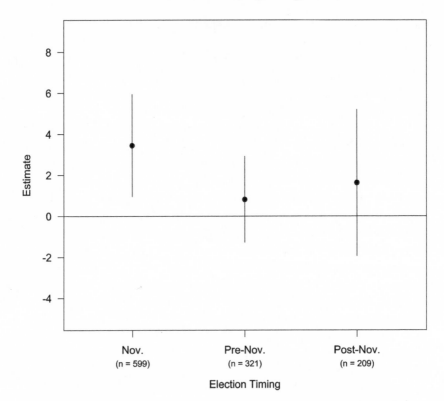

Figure 6.1. Effect of close elections on future presidential vote share. Black dots represent the OLS coefficient estimate for each model. The vertical lines denote the confidence interval of 95 percent for each estimate.

congressional election. It is important to emphasize that this analysis only examines "close" elections, which, in this case, means those won by 5 percentage points or less in the last election. Thus, a boost of roughly 3 percentage points in vote share is substantively quite large and could help tilt such a close race in one party's favor. More important, there is no evidence of reverse coattails in either the pre-November or post-November models, as we expected.

Taken together, the analyses reported in figure 6.1 and chapter 4 show that, contrary to the expectations of previous scholarship, congressional candidates played an important role in structuring election outcomes during the nineteenth century. Indeed, the attributes of individual congressional candidates could produce positive electoral returns for a party, which would have important consequences for a party's entire slate of candidates. Similarly, previous congressional election outcomes, even in potentially competitive districts, could shape a party's fortunes in subsequent elections. We now shift our focus to investigate how election timing and nationalization of elections affected candidate-specific effects in nineteenth-century races.

Election Timing

Today, presidential and House elections are held concurrently, but this was not always the case during the nineteenth century. Throughout much of that period, congressional elections were held outside of November, with some occurring months prior to or even months after the presidential election (Engstrom 2012). In figure 6.2, we report the proportion of congressional elections that were held concurrently with the November presidential election in a given election year. Prior to the 1860 presidential election, less than a third of congressional elections were held at the same time as a presidential election. During presidential election years in the 1840s and 1850s, approximately 40 percent of congressional elections were held in the months after the presidential election, and around 35 percent of races were held before November. By the 1860s, around half of the congressional elections were contested in November. The increase was attributable partly to the secession of the Southern states, many of which held their elections outside of November. In 1872, Congress passed legislation to prohibit the practice of off-November congressional elections, but a few states continued to hold congressional elections at irregular times (Engstrom 2012: 375–76). Both Indiana and Ohio, for example, held their congressional elections in the October before the 1880 presidential election.

In states where congressional elections were held outside of November, voters faced a different decision calculus than suggested by some accounts of nineteenth-century elections. Those voters' choice of ballots in the congressional race did not require them to first choose among the presidential candidates. As a result, the relationship between presidential and congressional vote margins was weaker in those off-November elections despite the use of a party ballot (Engstrom and Kernell 2005, 2014). A diminished correspondence between presidential and congressional vote margins only tells part of the story. In an era where presidential races were often competitive (Burnham 1965), the electoral consequences of holding separate presidential and congressional elections were sometimes considerable. Indeed, the examples from the 1844 and 1848 elections discussed earlier

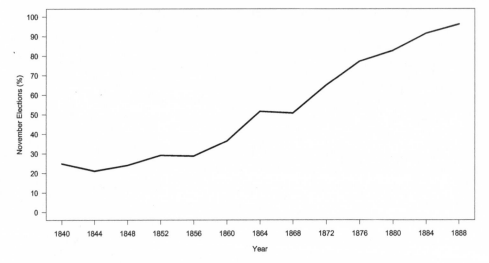

Figure 6.2. Proportion of November elections in presidential years, 1840–88. (Calculated by the authors.)

suggest that differential election timing could influence which party won majority control of the House. Our primary substantive interest here is in differential election timing's potential to condition the relevant factors that shaped election outcomes during that period.

To assess how election timing conditioned the impact of candidate attributes, we estimated separate regression models for elections held before the November election, elections held concurrently with the presidential election, and congressional races contested after the November election. If the presidential election draws voter attention more to the candidates at the top of the ticket, we should see notable differences in the effect of candidate-specific factors across the different time periods. It is important to note, however, that elections held before November could still be nationalized. According to Engstrom and Kernell (2014: 21),

> Where candidates stood for election at the same time, the impact of presidential coattails was direct. But the presidential campaign also intruded into the fall elections prior to November, particularly those held in September and October. . . . A variety of evidence suggests that both voters and the political parties treated voting on these two nearby dates as if they were twin prongs of the same election.

The presidential campaigns and national parties therefore saw at least some of these early races as a proxy or test run for the upcoming presidential election. Indeed, it was not unprecedented for politicians from around the country to descend on these earlier states to boost the party's campaign efforts and secure crucial victories (Engstrom and Kernell 2014: 91). It is not clear, however, that these effects would be felt uniformly across all congressional districts and states. The primary implication, then, is that we should find the largest substantive differences in the post-November period, when the presidential campaign, having already been decided, could not intrude into the congressional campaign.

The results reported in table 6.1 largely comport with our expectation about candidate attributes and their potential effect in off-November elections. Both candidate quality and Democratic incumbency appear to have influenced elections held before November. While the effects are somewhat small in magnitude, the finding of a Democratic advantage is consistent with the anecdotal evidence about election timing and the Democrats' success in Pennsylvania during the 1844 and 1848 election. We do, however, find a more substantial impact of individual candidates in the post-November elections. In these races, a candidate recruitment advantage could net a party an advantage of nearly three percentage points in the election returns. The effect is substantively significant as well when we

TABLE 6.1. Democratic vote share in presidential election years, 1840–68

	Pre-November		November		Post-November	
	Est. (SE)	Est. (SE)	Est. (SE)	Est. (SE)	Est. (SE)	Est. (SE)
Dem. vote$_{t-1}$	0.14*	0.15*	0.18*	0.17*	0.17*	0.20*
	(0.03)	(0.03)	(0.06)	(0.06)	(0.07)	(0.06)
Dem. pres.	0.69*	0.68*	0.72*	0.71*	0.57*	0.56*
	(0.03)	(0.03)	(0.08)	(0.08)	(0.07)	(0.07)
DQA	1.21*	1.44*	0.65	0.82	2.81*	3.48*
	(0.36)	(0.30)	(0.44)	(0.45)	(0.80)	(0.69)
Dem. inc.	1.18*		−1.07		0.56	
	(0.56)		(0.75)		(1.14)	
Non-Dem. inc.	0.38		−1.16*		−1.80	
	(0.47)		(0.53)		(1.24)	
Constant	9.17*	9.62*	6.52*	6.26*	13.47*	12.25*
	(1.54)	(1.47)	(2.81)	(2.83)	(3.30)	(3.22)
N	424	424	366	366	299	299
R^2	0.82	0.82	0.78	0.78	0.57	0.57

Note: Cell entries are regression coefficients from an OLS regression model, with standard errors in parentheses. Year-specific fixed effects were estimated but are not reported here.

*$p < .05$, one-tailed test

consider that approximately 52 percent of the elections held after November were won by three percentage points or less.[8]

We do find weak evidence that candidate-specific factors shaped election outcomes when congressional and presidential elections were held concurrently. Whig/Republican incumbents received a bump of approximately one percentage point in these races, which is arguably consistent with our findings of potential spillover effects reported in figure 6.1. There does not, however, appear to be an independent effect for candidate quality. It is worth noting, lastly, that the coefficient estimate for the presidential vote is slightly larger in the November elections than in the post-November contests. While there was clearly a relationship between the outcome of the November presidential election and the subsequent congressional election in these districts, it was less determinative of the congressional vote in these cases than when the elections were held concurrently.

Nationalization

A key theoretical argument for why electoral accountability should be more limited during the nineteenth century is that the party ballot tied congressional candidates inexorably to their party's presidential candidate. As a result, the attributes of individual candidates are assumed to be inconsequential, because national forces should dominate vote choice. Studies of contemporary congressional elections have also noted the potential connection between nationalization and candidate-specific effects. Jacobson (2015) argues that the rise of candidate-centered elections in the mid-twentieth century was a consequence of the "denationalization" of congressional elections. He contends that "diminishing levels of party loyalty in the electorate" and the "decoupling of congressional and presidential elections" are the driving forces of these developments (861). Over the last several decades, however, House elections have shifted back to being nationalized affairs where congressional candidates are largely subject to national partisan tides (Jacobson 2015: 863–65). While Jacobson's argument is convincing, the era of the party ballot is a particularly fertile period in which to test this proposition, because split-ticket voting, which Jacobson identifies as a key theoretical mechanism that led to denationalized elections in the mid-twentieth century, rarely occurred when presidential and House candidates appeared on the same party ballot (Rusk 1970).

We believe that an examination of two factors—midterm elections and election timing—can be particularly fruitful for understanding the effect of nationalized elections. An interest in the effect of ballot design on split-ticket voting led many previous studies to focus their analysis on presidential elections (Engstrom and Kernell 2005; Rusk 1970). During midterm elections, however, presidential coattails were absent, which should result in less-nationalized congressional elections.[9] Our primary expectation about midterm elections is that the attributes of individual congressional candidates should have a larger effect in midterm elections than in presidential election years.

For an initial test of the effect of nationalization, we begin by comparing the effect of candidate-specific qualities in midterm elections and in presidential election years.[10] To conduct this analysis, we estimated a series of regression models for both presidential and midterm elections, which we report in table 6.2. While the effect of candidate quality is smaller across our different specifications in presidential years, we do find evidence of an effect for quality candidates even in those years, when most of the prior literature suggests such effects should not exist. It is not surprising, though, that the effect is almost two times larger in midterm election years than in presidential election years in both the full-series, incumbent-contested races and open-seat races. One other notable difference is the effect of presidential vote, which is nearly 1.4 times larger in presidential years than in midterm years.

While the results reported in table 6.2 are suggestive of the effects of

TABLE 6.2. Democratic congressional vote by election type, 1840–88

			Incumbents		Open	
	Pres. (SE)	Midterm (SE)	Pres. (SE)	Midterm (SE)	Pres. (SE)	Midterm (SE)
Dem. vote$_{t-1}$	0.16*	0.15*	0.21*	0.19*	0.06*	0.07
	(0.02)	(0.04)	(0.03)	(0.05)	(0.03)	(0.06)
DQA	2.26*	4.02*	2.43*	4.26*	1.68*	3.58*
	(0.25)	(0.30)	(0.34)	(0.45)	(0.36)	(0.41)
Dem. pres.	0.64*	0.47*	0.60*	0.43*	0.72*	0.53*
	(0.04)	(0.04)	(0.05)	(0.05)	(0.04)	(0.07)
South	2.14*	4.78*	2.13*	5.08*	1.76*	4.35*
	(0.49)	(0.62)	(0.64)	(0.78)	(0.69)	(1.08)
Constant	9.94*	21.44*	9.49*	20.26*	11.18*	24.79*
	(1.30)	(1.64)	(1.80)	(2.07)	(1.75)	(3.61)
N	2351	2058	1539	1225	812	833
R^2	0.71	0.53	0.72	.57	0.70	0.47

Note: Cell entries are regression coefficients from an OLS regression model, with robust standard errors in parentheses. Election-year fixed effects are included but are not reported here.
*$p < .05$, one-tailed test

nationalization, the staggered nature of elections during the nineteenth century provide additional leverage on this question. Differential election timing provides a particularly ideal test for examining the effects of congressional elections that are more nationalized. Analyses that focus on modern elections are limited to making comparisons over time, because there is no cross-sectional variation. By turning to historical elections where election timing was not uniform, our analysis can exploit the variation in nationalization *within* the same election year. Congressional elections held in November should be highly nationalized during a presidential election year, which should undermine the impact of candidate attributes. In contrast, nationalization should be lower for congressional elections held after November, once the national contest has been settled. We would thus expect that candidate-specific factors should have a more significant impact on the outcome of congressional contests held after the presidential election. We expect to find greater differences between the effect of candidate quality and district partisanship across midterm and presidential years in November elections than in off-cycle elections. Indeed, by virtue of being synched with presidential contests, elections held in November should be the most nationalized, which means that the removal of presidential coattails should have their greatest effect in these contests.

To conduct this analysis, we estimated a series of regression models where each predictor is interacted with a dummy variable for whether the election took place in a presidential election year.[11] Since the results in tables 6.1 and 6.2 both found a more sizable and consistent impact for candidate quality than incumbency, we only include the former in this analysis, in order to have a more parsimonious model; our findings are substantively the same if we include these additional predictors. We then calculated the marginal effects for candidate quality, which are the first set of marginal effects reported in figure 6.3, to ascertain the effect of each variable in midterm and presidential years. As expected, the differences between election years are far more pronounced for elections held in November. During midterm election years, the marginal effect for a one-unit change in Democratic quality advantage (DQA) is estimated to produce a change of 4.4 percentage points, but the effect drops to 0.77 percentage points in presidential years. Furthermore, the estimate is not statistically significant. The differences between midterm and presidential election years are far more modest, at around 1.3 percentage points for both pre- and post-November elections.

In sum, these findings clearly suggest that candidate-specific effects were larger in congressional races where elections were less nationalized.

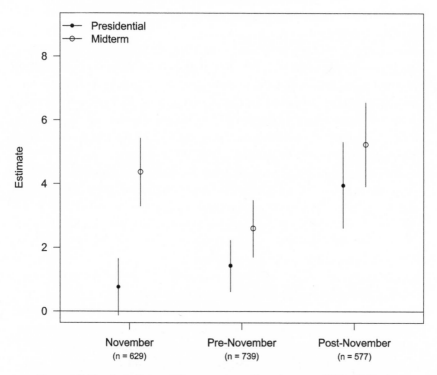

Figure 6.3. Marginal effects of Democratic quality advantage, 1840–68. Black dots represent the OLS coefficient estimate for presidential years, while open circles represent OLS coefficient estimates for midterm years. The vertical lines denote the confidence interval of 95 percent for each estimate.

Our results therefore not only offer support for Jacobson's (2015) argument but also suggest that his theoretical explanation is applicable to congressional elections across a large swath of American history. There is an important difference, however, between the time period we examine and modern elections. During the nineteenth century, nationalized elections were the result of the institutions that governed elections (e.g., the party ballot) rather than of voters *choosing* to cast a vote for presidential and congressional candidates of the same party. The structure of the ballot itself makes that time period a particularly difficult test case in which to find evidence of candidate-specific effects. That we still find evidence of candidate attributes influencing electoral outcomes during that period suggests that the preconditions for electoral accountability were present, even if in a limited form, during the nineteenth century.

Ballot Structure

The electoral connection presumes that voters are able to make choices about whether to support individual members of Congress. It is often assumed that party ballots made such choices difficult, if not impossible, since voters were, in general, forced to choose between parties rather than individual candidates (Rusk 1970). In presidential years, this meant that House members' electoral fortunes were often tied directly to the top of the ticket (Engstrom and Kernell 2014). We might even expect a similar coattail effect in midterm years when congressional and gubernatorial elections coincided, given the obvious partisan connection. Indeed, Engstrom and Kernell (2014) report compelling evidence of gubernatorial coattails throughout the nineteenth century. Despite the clear hurdles to vote choice being influenced by individual legislators, it should not be inferred that it was impossible under the party ballot. There were instances, even in presidential years, where House candidates would not be tied to the coattails of either presidential or gubernatorial candidates.

As noted previously, congressional elections were not always held at the same time as presidential elections. Even when an election was held outside of November, however, the party ballot may have included a gubernatorial race. In presidential elections held between 1840 and 1868, the last presidential election before Congress mandated a uniform election date, there was no presidential or gubernatorial candidate on the ballot in just over 37 percent of off-November elections. In these cases, it is possible that the House race would be a marquee contest on the ballot. Indeed, Engstrom and Kernell (2014: 2) suggest that it was common for House candidates to appear before nongubernatorial statewide candidates and state legislative candidates on the party ballot.

To examine how the ballot structure influenced election outcomes, we first determined which races appeared on the ballot at the same time as the House election. There were four possible race combinations: both the president and gubernatorial elections were on the ballot, only the presidential election was on the ballot, only the gubernatorial election was on the ballot, neither of the top races was on the ballot. We also limited our analysis to only the marginal districts, which we define as those in which the winning candidate received less than 55 percent of the two-party vote. Although our findings are similar if we examine the full set of elections, we chose to examine this subset of races because, by virtue of the higher level of electoral competition, these districts are the ones that may be most susceptible to coattails and, as such, represent a more difficult test case.

Since the results reported in this chapter and in chapter 4 show a consistent effect for candidate experience, our analysis explores whether ballot structure conditioned the effect of candidate quality. We therefore calculated the proportion of House races won by the incumbent party when the party held a quality advantage and when it did not. Such a quality advantage occurs when the candidate for the incumbent party, who may or may not be an incumbent, is the only one to have previously held elected office. There are a number of scenarios under which the incumbent party would not have a quality advantage: if an incumbent faced a quality challenger, if both candidates for an open-seat race have prior electoral experience, or if the candidate for the challenging party has electoral experience but the candidate for the incumbent party does not.

In table 6.3, we report the proportion of races that the incumbent party won when it did and did not have a candidate recruitment advantage. The second and third columns report these figures for both incumbent-contested and open-seat races, while the fourth and fifth columns contain the results for incumbents only. Overall, we find relatively little differences based on ballot structure, regardless of whether we look at all races or only at elections with a congressional incumbent on the ballot. When a party enjoyed a recruitment advantage, it won well over 85 percent of the close elections, irrespective of whether a prominent office was also on the ballot. When a party did not have a recruitment advantage, it still won a majority of races, but the party's win rate dropped to between 50 and 60 percent. In short, candidate-specific attributes had a comparable impact on structuring election outcomes even when coattail effects should be most prominent.

During midterm election years, House candidates' prominence on the

TABLE 6.3. Ballot structure and incumbent party wins in presidential election years

Ballot structure	All races		Incumbents	
	Qual. adv.	No adv.	Qual. adv.	No adv.
Both	88.57	57.14	88.03	54.78
	(175)	(224)	(117)	(115)
Pres. only	88.78	55.97	86.58	53.33
	(107)	(159)	(82)	(90)
Gov. only	88.41	59.00	87.50	54.38
	(95)	(110)	(56)	(34)
Neither	88.48	51.27	87.20	56.33
	(165)	(236)	(125)	(142)

Note: Cell entries list the proportion of legislators in each category by whether or not the incumbent party had a candidate quality advantage. The number of legislators in each category is listed in parentheses.

*$p < .05$

ballot was impacted by the presence of a gubernatorial election rather than by election timing. Since senators were not popularly elected during the nineteenth century, the House race would be the highest office on the ballot unless there was a concurrent gubernatorial election. In the midterm elections from 1842 to 1866, approximately 55 percent of congressional elections were held separately from a gubernatorial contest. The elections of 1850, 1854, and 1866 were the only midterm elections during that period in which a majority of congressional and gubernatorial elections were held concurrently. Even in those years, over 40 percent of the congressional elections were held separately from a gubernatorial contest.

In table 6.4, we again report estimates of the incumbent party's electoral success that are based on ballot structure and candidate quality. Overall, the pattern of results is largely the same as that observed in presidential election years. The incumbent party was nearly always successful when it managed to outdo the opposition party in terms of recruitment. In cases where the other party found an experienced candidate, the incumbent party was considerably less successful. Indeed, we find a slight effect for ballot structure in cases where the candidate from the incumbent party faced an equally experienced candidate. When there was no gubernatorial candidate on the ballot, the incumbent party still won a narrow majority of these races. The incumbent party did not win a majority of the races when they shared the ballot with a gubernatorial candidate. Since the differences between these two categories are small in magnitude, we should not make too much of them, but we still believe that they are worth noting.

Although there is little reason to doubt that the structure of the party ballot could enhance the impact of presidential and gubernatorial coattails, our findings suggest that characteristics of individual congressional candidates mattered. More important, candidate-specific attributes structure

TABLE 6.4. Gubernatorial coattails and incumbent party wins in midterm election years

	All races		Incumbents	
	Qual. adv.	No adv.	Qual. adv.	No adv.
Gov. elec.	88.89	45.42	92.02	47.92
	(216)	(246)	(138)	(96)
No. gov. elec.	84.19	50.12	85.57	53.39
	(107)	(159)	(229)	(206)

Note: Cell entries list the proportion of legislators in each category by whether or not the incumbent party had a candidate quality advantage. The number of legislators in each category is listed in parentheses.

*p < .05

election outcomes in marginal races, which should be the contests that were most likely to be influenced by presidential or gubernatorial coattails. These results are perhaps not surprising when considered in conjunction with our earlier analysis of reverse coattails. While presidential and gubernatorial candidates may have been their party's standard-bearers, the outcome of congressional races still changed, in predictable patterns, based on the candidates who emerged for those races.

Discussion

Electoral accountability requires that voters make choices based on individual candidates. Although this was certainly far more difficult under the party ballot, our findings indicate that the preconditions for accountability via an electoral connection were met even under it. Our findings stand in contrast to prior accounts contending that individual candidates were of little consequence in the era of the party ballot because voters' only option then was to choose between parties at the polls. While there is little reason to doubt what those accounts say about the basic mechanics of the party ballot, we believe that congressional candidates had a far more important role to play than previously acknowledged in the extant literature. Even though voters were generally forced to choose between parties rather than candidates, our findings suggest that candidate-specific attributes influenced election outcomes in nineteenth-century House elections. Indeed, our results provide new evidence to suggest that at least some voters responded to more than just party cues when they decided how to vote on Election Day.

Overall, we find support for our general expectation that both the quality of a party's ballot and variation in the nationalization of elections conditioned the impact of congressional candidates on election outcomes. First, even though voters were not able to directly cast a vote for individual candidates, the party performed significantly better in congressional elections when it recruited experienced candidates to run under the party label. Our findings also raise important questions about the conventional view of the relationship between presidential and congressional elections during the nineteenth century. While winning a close election could benefit a party in subsequent elections, appearing on the same ballot as the party's nominee for Congress could also help the party's presidential candidate. Unlike in the modern era, it appears that presidential candidates in the nineteenth century were sometimes able to benefit from reverse coattails.

Second, our results strongly suggest that midterm elections and non-uniform election timing influenced the extent to which congressional elections were nationalized. The effect of candidate quality was roughly two times larger in midterm elections than in presidential election years. These differences are notable partly because candidates for the House were often included at the very top of the party ballot during midterm elections. Similarly, we found sizable differences between the effects of candidate quality across presidential and midterm elections for congressional elections held in November. That we do not find the same pattern of differences across presidential and midterm years for elections held after November fits with our expectation that nationalization was not only lower for this set of elections but also more constant across time.

The latter set of results is particularly noteworthy since it points to one of the key benefits of studying historical congressional elections. By looking to an era where electoral rules were less uniform, we were able to provide a unique test of Jacobson's (2015) argument about the relationship between the nationalization of congressional elections and candidate-centered politics. Specifically, we were able to leverage the variation in nationalization within the same election year that was a direct result of nonuniform election dates. Although it is not always possible to use historical data for these purposes, we believe that the analysis of historical elections is a particularly promising area.[12] In the future, we hope more scholars of congressional politics will look for historical settings that provide unique variation in the institution or institutional rules they seek to study.

SEVEN

Electoral Accountability
in US House Elections

The 2006 congressional elections were disastrous for the Republican Party. For the first time since 1994, the Democrats managed to win enough seats to gain control of both the House and Senate, as a result of the growing unpopularity of President Bush and the ongoing Iraq War. Several scholars who analyzed the election maintained that public disapproval of the war and the president's falling favorability ratings resulted in significant losses for the Republicans at the polls, demonstrating evidence of electoral accountability. Jacobson (2007) argues that the midterm elections were a referendum on President Bush and that assessments of the war were significant factors to individual voting decisions in congressional races. Grose and Oppenheimer (2007) largely agree with that assessment but add that "voters held individual Republican members of Congress accountable for the local impact of Iraq war deaths in their congressional districts and also held GOP members accountable for their roll-call votes on the Iraq war" (532). Gartner and Segura (2008) support this perspective by demonstrating that local factors such as casualties were crucial to understanding Republican losses in 2006, since that is how voters interpreted national perceptions of the war.

The events of the 2006 election were remarkably similar to another midterm election that was held over 140 years earlier. During the 1862 midterm election, Republican incumbents were punished at the polls throughout the fall, as a result of the growing unpopularity of the Civil War and the increasing number of casualties on the Union side of the conflict. As the tide of the war began to turn in early 1863, Republican House members began to do better at the polls and were more likely to get reelected (Carson et al. 2001).[1] After the electoral dust settled, Republicans managed to hang onto enough seats following the midterm elections to maintain control of the House and pass a number of important initiatives and policies that President Lincoln strongly favored, including the Thirteenth Amendment (outlawing slavery in the United States) and the establishment of the US national banking system.

The remarkable similarity in outcomes between what has historically been viewed as two very different electoral contexts leads us to ask an important question pertaining to democratic accountability and representation: To what extent was it possible to hold members of Congress electorally accountable during the nineteenth century? To be fair, finding evidence of electoral accountability in the modern era can be difficult, since incumbents often use whatever means are available to them to mitigate potential costly actions or missteps (Arnold 1990; Fiorina 1974). The very notion of identifying evidence of electoral accountability during the nineteenth century well before the adoption of the secret ballot and the demise of the party machines poses a formidable challenge in light of these circumstances. Nevertheless, in our efforts to evaluate whether an electoral connection was in place during the nineteenth century, we believe that such an investigation is worthwhile, given the potential to better understand how legislative behavior in conjunction with congressional elections has evolved over time.

In the first section of this chapter, we discuss the importance of electoral accountability in conjunction with the electoral connection and review the challenges of finding evidence of accountability in any era. From there, we expand on our theoretical motivation for how incumbent legislators could be held accountable in an era when party ballots were created and distributed by the political parties. Next, we present three case studies that offer insights about electoral accountability in the nineteenth century. Our first analysis examines tariff politics in the 1870s, while our second case study looks at the politics of slavery in the 1850s. Both slavery and the tariff were major political issues that defined the scope of political conflict throughout large swaths of the nineteenth century. As we will discuss in greater detail below, the saliency of these issues satisfies a key condition for finding evidence of electoral accountability. Our final case study considers the politics of lame-duck sessions with respect to securing peace with Mexico and the eventual repeal of the House gag order related to slavery. While other scholars have already noted the electoral implications of lame-duck sessions (Jenkins and Nokken 2008a, 2008b), the variability in election timing during the early and middle parts of the nineteenth century has important implications for the politics of lame-duck sessions. We conclude this chapter by discussing the broader implications of our findings for democratic accountability and representation in the early American nation.

Electoral Accountability in Congressional Elections

Citizen's ability to ensure the faithfulness of their elected representatives is one of the fundamental challenges of a democratic system of government. Although elections are not the only mechanism through which citizens can influence their representatives, they are one of the main points of contact between the public and the government. The principal-agent problem that results from the use of elections is well known, and it is generally understood that the vote can be a fairly blunt instrument of control. Despite the challenges inherent in relying on elections, there is considerable evidence of electoral accountability—that is, the use of elections to sanction or reward elected representatives for their performance in government.

While our scholarly focus is frequently on whether elected officials are punished at the ballot box for their behavior, it is important to remember that there are two components of electoral accountability. First, accountability requires governmental representatives to act in accordance with the interests of the group that initially elected them (Fearon 1999). Carson and Jenkins (2011) argue that this condition is met when legislators "possess the ability to be responsive; that is, they must be able to provide their constituents with various benefits" (28). Over time, members of Congress created a set of institutions that are particularly well suited for this task (Mayhew 1974).[2] Constituents' benefits can take many forms, including legislation (Schiller 1995), committee assignments (Deering and Smith 1997; Jenkins 1998), and pork-barrel projects (Bickers and Stein 1996; Finocchiaro and Jenkins 2016). Members of Congress can also signal their responsiveness to constituent preferences through their voting record (see, e.g., Bovitz and Carson 2006; Mayhew 1974) or other public statements (Grimmer, Messing, and Westwood 2012). Indeed, several canonical models of roll-call voting argue that constituent interests are one of the key considerations legislators weigh when deciding how to vote (Arnold 1990; Fiorina 1974; Kingdon 1989).

Second, electoral accountability requires that voters be able to reward or punish their elected representatives for their performance in office (Carson and Jenkins 2011; Fearon 1999). While responsiveness imposes certain behavior requirements on elected officials, accountability cannot be realized unless voters meet certain criteria. Voters must be aware of legislators' behavior and then use this knowledge to inform their vote choice (Arnold 1990). While there are a number of challenges to uncovering evidence of the electoral consequences of legislative behavior, Arnold notes that legislative responsiveness can, ironically, be one of the key culprits that makes this task especially difficult.

> The problem is that legislators as a group have not offered congressional scholars much variance to analyze. No legislators have offered to take positions directly opposite their electoral interests so that we may measure the full impact of positions on electoral margins. None have acknowledged selecting their positions by flipping a coin. (Arnold 1990: 37)

One explanation for the relative fidelity of representatives is that the threat of future electoral sanctions can be enough not only to ensure that legislators remain faithful agents but also to afford voters some level of control over their elected officials. Indeed, Mayhew's (1974) seminal argument about legislators behaving as "single-minded seekers of reelection" is premised on precisely this type of anticipatory behavior.

It would be inaccurate, however, to infer that legislators are always able to identify the "correct" position. On some issues, legislators will simply have imperfect information about the position they are expected to adopt (Bianco, Spence, and Wilkerson 1996). In other cases, a series of seemingly unrelated or innocuous votes may end up having electoral consequences when viewed in their totality (Bovitz and Carson 2006). Legislators must therefore "watch the general patterns they create as well as the individual positions they take" (Arnold 1990: 80). Indeed, a legislative voting record that is too ideological or partisan can end up costing an incumbent on Election Day (Canes-Wrone, Brady, and Cogan 2002; Carson, Koger, et al. 2010). Even in these cases, though, it may be difficult to find evidence of accountability in electoral returns, because members of Congress may opt to voluntarily retire rather than face potential voter retribution (Bianco, Spence, and Wilkerson 1996; Carson 2005).

With these challenges and considerations in mind, we want to briefly outline the primary conditions under which electoral accountability is most likely. It is important to begin by noting that most roll-call votes and other congressional actions will remain outside the electoral arena. The first condition, then, is that an issue must reach a certain level of saliency or controversy before it will arouse enough public awareness to inform voting decisions (Arnold 1990; Bovitz and Carson 2006). Saliency is not a sufficient condition for a roll-call vote to have a significant impact on election outcomes, however. Based on an analysis of three decades of House roll calls, Bovitz and Carson (2006) find that only 20 percent of "key votes" had a significant impact on election returns. Roll calls with higher levels of conflict (i.e., smaller majorities) and intraparty disagreement were more likely to result in incumbents being rewarded or punished for their stated position.

Second, if voters are to have the opportunity to hold elected representatives accountable for their behavior, they must have a viable alternative to vote for in the upcoming congressional election (Hollibaugh, Rothenberg, and Rulison 2013). Every two years, a small number of incumbents do not face an opponent in the primary or general election. In many other cases, incumbents face an inexperienced or weak challenger who has little chance of winning, absent some extenuating circumstances (e.g., a scandal or voluntary retirement from Congress). Only in those cases where an incumbent faces an experienced or high-quality challenger are voters given a reasonable alternative if they expect to continue to have their interests represented. Since experienced challengers are often strategic about when they decide to challenge incumbents (Jacobson 1989), there is always a risk that an alternative to an incumbent will not emerge in a given election. Nevertheless, there is systematic evidence that quality challengers do routinely evaluate the positions taken by legislators and are more likely to run when incumbents appear "out of touch" with the district (Carson 2005; Mann and Wolfinger 1980).

Beyond saliency and strategic challengers, voters must also be in a position to hold their elected representatives accountable. For years, the widespread view in the elections literature was that voters were largely ignorant about legislators' policy views (see, e.g., Miller and Stokes 1963). One implication of this finding was that incumbents would be able to vote on legislative matters with little fear of losing reelection as a result of their positions taken on roll-call votes. More recent evidence has begun to cast doubt on this perspective, however, as congressional scholars have found that being perceived as too ideological or voting with the extreme of one's party can significantly reduce one's likelihood of reelection (Canes-Wrone, Brady, and Cogan 2002; Carson, Koger, et al. 2010). Additionally, Ansolabehere and Jones (2010) found that most constituents are able to discern how their legislators behave in office, especially on roll-call votes, and are able to hold their elected officials accountable as a result.[3]

Electoral Accountability Under the Party Ballot

Unlike their modern counterparts, nineteenth-century legislators did not view service in the US House as a long-term career. Many legislators would serve one or two terms in the House before leaving (Kernell 1977; Struble 1979), which meant that a single election during that era could produce dramatic changes in the membership of Congress. The average length of service in Congress gradually increased in the latter half of the nineteenth century but did not exceed three terms until the beginning of the twentieth century (Polsby 1968).[4] The conventional wisdom among congressional scholars was that the dearth of career-oriented legislators meant that representatives lacked strong incentives to pay much attention to the wishes of their constituents (Polsby 1968). From this perspective, electoral accountability was undermined because legislative responsiveness, the first component of electoral accountability, was in short supply.

Over the last two decades, however, a growing body of research has raised important questions about the relationship between constituent interests and legislative behavior (see, e.g., Bianco, Spence, and Wilkerson 1996; Carson and Engstrom 2005; Carson and Jenkins 2011). In discussing the electoral consequences of the Compensation Act of 1816, Bianco, Spence, and Wilkerson provide an insightful critique of the proposition that careerism was a necessary condition for an electoral connection.

> [O]ur findings suggest a need to reopen the debate over the nature of legislator accountability in the early Congress. The conventional wisdom has it that contemporary notions of the electoral connection cannot be applied to the early Congress. Our analysis, admittedly of only one case, suggests that an electoral connection may have operated in the early Congress as well. (Bianco, Spence, and Wilkerson 1996: 167–68)

If legislators were not concerned about electoral backlash, electoral security should not structure the outcome of any votes. Contrary to these expectations, Bianco, Spence, and Wilkerson found a clear correlation between electoral security and voting behavior on the 1816 Compensation Act. Although they acknowledge that their analysis was limited to a single vote, there are clear similarities between this case and the countless examples of electoral vulnerability informing legislators' decision making in the contemporary Congress. For our purposes, these findings provide an important theoretical foundation and suggest that evidence of a marginality effect can indeed provide evidence of legislative responsiveness.

Congressional careers were not the only factor that was posited to undermine electoral accountability throughout the nineteenth century. Congressional scholars generally agree that legislative electoral accountability was significantly enhanced following adoption of the secret ballot in the late nineteenth century. Prior to the use of the secret ballot, political parties exercised significant control over the electoral process. On Election Day, voters were given "party ballots," distributed by the parties, and the votes cast went to a party's *entire* slate of candidates (Bensel 2004; Ware 2002). Furthermore, a party's ability to select its own slate of candidates meant that incumbents had less control over whether they could contest the seat on Election Day. The bigger obstacle for uncovering evidence of accountability, however, is the fact that voters were required to choose between parties rather than candidates (Engstrom and Kernell 2005, 2014; Rush 1970). The relative inability of voters to cast votes for individual candidates constitutes a formidable hurdle in their ability to hold individual legislators accountable at the polls.

A hurdle is only an impediment and does not mean that accountability was impossible. Even before the adoption of the secret ballot, there is evidence of some representatives being rewarded or punished selectively based on their level of responsiveness to individual voters (Bianco, Spence, and Wilkerson 1996; Carson and Engstrom 2005; Carson et al. 2001). Similarly, at least some subset of legislators may have been able to develop a "personal" vote with their constituents throughout the nineteenth century (Carson and Roberts 2013; Finocchiaro and Jenkins 2016). These findings are all the more telling with the growing evidence that candidate-specific attributes structured congressional election outcomes throughout much of the nineteenth century (Carson and Hood 2014; Carson and Roberts 2013). As we demonstrated in chapter 6, there is also evidence of reverse coattails in nineteenth-century presidential elections (Carson and Sievert 2017).

Taken as a whole, these studies suggest that vote choice in the nineteenth century was influenced by congressional candidates to a potentially greater extent than has previously been acknowledged. While these studies suggest that accountability was possible, it is prudent to outline the conditions under which it was most likely to occur. In doing so, we draw on Bovitz and Carson's (2006) findings about electoral accountability in the context of modern House elections. Where relevant, we also outline the similarities and differences between how each condition might operate in the nineteenth century. The first condition we discuss is saliency, because accountability requires that voters are aware of and take action based on actual legislative behavior. We therefore follow Bovitz and Carson's approach and limit the focus of our empirical analyses to salient issues and votes. Although there are a number of options for identifying salient bills and votes, we confine our analysis to public laws that Stathis (2002) identifies as "landmark" legislation.[5]

A second, related condition is the level of conflict on a particular issue. Although there are a number of ways to define conflict, a smaller majority is arguably a good indication that a particular issue was more contentious. A narrow victory may even make it easier for an incumbent's opponents or voters to assign responsibility to the individual legislator for the policy outcome. When a bill passes or fails by a large majority, it is harder to argue that the incumbent could have taken an action to change the outcome. The same cannot be said when a proposal is more closely contested, which could prove to be particularly important in those cases where legislators with imperfect information inadvertently end up on the wrong side of a vote.

The final condition for accountability is the existence of intraparty disagreement on a given issue or vote. If the main political parties are perfectly divided on an issue, it is difficult to distinguish between individual accountability and a national tide against one party. For example, imagine that a highly salient bill becomes law, with all members of the majority party supporting the bill and with all members of the minority party opposing the bill. Under these circumstances, the roll-call vote will provide limited evidence that the incumbent legislators were rewarded or punished on Election Day independent of partisanship. As an empirical matter, this basic identification problem holds true regardless of whether the party ballot or secret ballot is in use, which is another reminder of why it is important to look for evidence of electoral accountability in terms of legislative responsiveness and strategic retirements and not just with respect to election returns. When a vote divides one or both of the parties, however, the intraparty variance makes it possible to distinguish between partisan and legislator-specific effects.

The conventional view of nineteenth-century elections contends that legislators were not rewarded or punished for breaking ranks with their copartisans, because the party ballot forced vote choice to be structured by party rather than individual candidates. While we do not question that the party ballot made the basic mechanics of elections different, we hope to offer a more systematic test of this proposition about electoral accountability. We therefore present several case studies that explore different aspects of electoral accountability on a series of major legislative proposals. Our first case study explores the politics of the Tariff Act of 1872 and the subsequent repeal of this law in 1875. We then present a case study on slavery that examines the Compromise of 1850 and the Kansas-Nebraska Act. Our final case study examines the politics during lame-duck sessions when legislators were brokering a peace agreement with Mexico and lifting the House gag order on slavery. Our main goal is to provide several pieces of evidence in hopes of better understanding both the potential for and limits to electoral accountability in the nineteenth century.

Tariff Politics

Throughout the nineteenth century, tariff legislation, which levied taxes on imported goods, was the main vehicle through which the federal government was able to raise revenue. According to Hansen (1990), the US Department of the Treasury derived as much as 90 percent of its revenue from customs duties. Given the tariff's centrality to the functioning of the federal government, it is not surprising that tariff legislation could be a highly partisan affair (Epstein and O'Halloran 1996; Hansen 1990; Schickler 2001). Indeed, Schickler (2001: 299) goes so far as to argue that the tariff was "the defining partisan issue of the late nineteenth century." Tariff legislation gave rise to partisan conflict largely because the costs of the tariff were not distributed evenly across all sectors of the economy (Madonna 2011). Individuals in export-dependent sectors, such as farmers and laborers, favored lower tariffs. In the federal government, Democratic presidents and legislators were the primary advocates for these groups. Those sectors of the economy that had to compete with imported goods, such as manufacturers and skilled laborers, supported higher tariffs as a means to protect their economic interests against outside competition. During the antebellum period, these interests were represented largely by the Whigs, but the Republicans would also adopt the high-tariff mantel in the postwar period.[6]

The highly partisan nature of tariff politics makes that policy a particularly difficult test case in which to find any evidence of legislator-specific accountability. As we noted earlier, intraparty disagreement is an important condition for uncovering evidence that an individual (not just a party) is being punished. Despite these challenges, tariff legislation was salient and certainly had the potential to lead to retribution on Election Day. In a recent study of nineteenth-century tariff politics, Clarke, Jenkins, and Lowande (2017) examine Speaker Joe Cannon's (R-IL) "thesis" that the majority party would be punished for passing significant tariff legislation before the November elections. Based on an analysis of over 100 years of elections, Clarke and his colleagues conclude that the majority party was punished for tariff reform during the period from 1877 to 1934. When earlier elections are included, however, they find no electoral effects for the adoption of a major tariff bill. Indeed, they posit that "the accountability mechanism . . . did not operate in the same way" in the "pre-Australian era of electoral politics" and that the difference "likely mutes the effect" of tariff reforms (394).

In the analysis that follows, we seek to build on this observation by examining district-level election returns rather than aggregate-level party vote share. While the latter approach is appropriate for testing Speaker Cannon's conjecture, an analysis that focuses on legislators may offer a better test of accountability. Indeed, most theoretical accounts of electoral accountability (e.g., Fearon 1999; Ashworth 2012) are premised on voters rewarding or punishing an individual representative. We accomplish our goal in two parts. First, we begin by examining the electoral impact of the Tariff Act of 1872. After Congress raised tariff rates to help support the Union war effort, the 1872 tariff bill made the first across-the-board cut to duties since the antebellum era. Second, we explore the politics of the Tariff Act of 1875, which repealed the 1872 law. As we discuss in greater detail below, the 1875 tariff bill provides an important reminder that electoral institutions were not the only factor that could serve to undermine electoral accountability in the nineteenth century.

The Tariff Act of 1872

From the late nineteenth century onward, most tariff bills divided the parties almost perfectly. The high levels of party unity can be explained at least partly by the polarization of each party's constituency along lines directly related to tariff politics (Jenkins, Schickler, and Carson 2004). One of the few notable exceptions is the case of the Tariff Act of 1872, in which a coalition of Republicans and Democrats united to pass the first post–Civil War reduction in tariff rates (Taussig 1914). The bill was widely supported by both parties in the South and in states west of the Mississippi. Even President Grant favored the bill's passage.[7] In the rest of the country, however, the bill divided the Republican Party, which had come to favor the higher tariff rates.

Although the bill satisfies the conditions that we have argued make electoral accountability more likely, it is worth outlining why this is a particularly difficult test case. First, the bill was passed in the run-up to the 1872 presidential election, which President Grant won in an Electoral College landslide. Since the party ballot tied congressional candidates' fortunes more directly to the fate of the party's standard-bearer (Engstrom and Kernell 2005), it should be more difficult to find evidence of any legislator-specific effects. Second, the aggregate-level calculation by Clarke, Jenkins, and Lowande (2017: table 1) indicates that the Republicans' national vote share actually increased between 1870 and 1872. We believe there is little reason to expect a vote in favor of the tariff reform to yield positive election returns. Indeed, the Cannon thesis is premised on the idea that tariff revisions led to electoral punishment because they injected uncertainty into the national economy (Clarke, Jenkins, and Lowande, 2017: 384–386). Furthermore, the Republicans who voted in favor of the 1872 tariff law were voting against a more protectionist status quo that their party should have supported. We thus expect Republican incumbents to be punished for supporting the 1872 tariff bill.

To examine the electoral consequences of supporting the Tariff Act of 1872, we used Dubin's (1998) collection of congressional election returns to identify which incumbents ran for reelection in 1872 and their vote share in the 1872 and 1870 elections. Since 1872 was a presidential election year, we also include a measure of district-level presidential vote, which is coded with reference to the incumbent's political party. For example, depending on whether the incumbent was a Democrat or a Republican, the presidential vote share is coded as the vote share of the Democratic or Republican presidential candidate respectively. After identifying the population of incumbents, we merged in data on their vote on the tariff act, with a yea vote coded as 1 and a nay vote coded as 0. Lastly, we also control for whether the incumbent faced a quality challenger (Carson and Roberts 2013).

In table 7.1, we report the results of a series of regression models that estimate the electoral impact of supporting the Tariff Act of 1872. The first column reports the results from a model that includes both Democrats and Republicans. In the pooled model, a vote in favor of the tariff bill is estimated to reduce an incumbent's vote share by 2.5 points. While the Republican Party improved on its performance in 1870, there was no discernible difference between the performance of Democratic and Republican incumbents in 1872. These initial findings support our contention that individual-level data can reveal patterns that are not fully reflected through aggregation.

We also estimated separate models for Republican and Democratic incumbents, which are reported in the second and third columns of table 7.1. As we discussed earlier, Republican incumbents should be punished for voting to lower the tariff rates, because the status quo would be favored by key elements of the Republican constituency. Democratic incumbents voted for an outcome that moved policy in a direction its constituents favored. It is possible, then, that House Democrats would be rewarded for supporting the tariff reforms. Estimating separate models for each party allows us to account more directly for the influence of the concurrent presidential election. President Grant won by a large margin in 1872, which could attenuate the effect of supporting the tariff if the presidential election led to a strong partisan or national tide. By including presidential vote as a control, we are able to determine whether the vote on the tariff had an effect independent of these national forces.

The estimates for the tariff vote in the model with only Republican incumbents are nearly identical to the coefficients from our pooled model. A Republican incumbent who voted for the tariff bill is predicted to receive a vote share approximately 2.5 points lower than an incumbent who opposed the bill. As expected, we also find strong evidence that President Grant's electoral success influenced the outcome in districts with a Republican incumbent. For a one-point increase in Grant's vote share, a Republican incumbent was predicted to see a 0.6-point increase in his vote share. The importance of the presidential election is also evidenced by the fact that the coefficient is over two times larger than the

TABLE 7.1. Incumbent congressional vote on the Tariff Act of 1872

	All (SE)	Rep. (SE)	Dem. (SE)
Tariff vote (yea)	−2.51*	−2.46*	−1.37
	(1.33)	(1.43)	(2.90)
Democrat	0.70		
	(1.56)		
Vote share$_{t-1}$	0.29*	0.24*	0.32*
	(0.09)	(0.11)	(0.16)
Pres. vote share$_t$	0.46*	0.59*	0.25
	(0.09)	(0.10)	(0.17)
Quality challenger	−4.83*	−3.90*	−6.12*
	(1.22)	(1.39)	(2.27)
Constant	17.50*	11.69*	26.58*
	(5.74)	(6.60)	(9.65)
N	135	82	53
R^2	0.50	0.57	0.32

Note: Cell entries are regression coefficients from an OLS regression model, with standard errors reported in parentheses.

*$p < .05$, one-tailed test

estimated effect for an incumbent's previous vote share. Thus, while it was clear that the presidential election structured congressional election outcomes, there is also an independent effect for legislator-specific traits. One possible conclusion from this evidence, then, is that passing tariff legislation may have prevented President Grant from securing an even greater electoral landslide.[8]

Our model estimates for Democratic incumbents reveal two important points about electoral accountability on this particular tariff bill. First, Democratic incumbents were not rewarded for supporting legislation that lowered the tariff rates. Although the coefficient estimate is negative, the standard error is over two times larger than the coefficient estimate. The imprecise estimate can be explained by the fact that the 1872 tariff bill did not appear to divide the Democrats in the same way that it did the Republicans.[9] Second, the null results suggest that being on the wrong side of the presidential election outcome may have made it difficult for Democrats to translate their legislative victory into positive electoral returns. Indeed, members of the House were concerned about being tied to a weak presidential candidate that would drag down the party's slate of candidates (Kolodny 1998). Our results suggest that incumbents' fears were not unfounded. It also indicates that the design of the party ballot may have meant that electoral accountability was exercised asymmetrically.

The Tariff Act of 1875

Prior to the adoption of the Twentieth Amendment in 1933, a Congress would not convene until March 4 of a new year, but the final session of the previous Congress would convene from December of the previous year through early March of the new year.[10] Following the 1872 Apportionment Act, which mandated that all federal elections be held concurrently on the first Tuesday after the first Monday in November, the late session included both legislators who would be returning for the next Congress and those who would not, because of either retirement or electoral defeat. Jenkins and Nokken (2008b: 452) note that the exiting members "were no longer tied to their constituents or parties; yet, they enjoyed all the powers of returning members, most notably the ability to cast roll-call votes, creating a clear 'agency problem' in representation."

These lame-duck sessions are another facet of nineteenth-century politics—in addition to the eras' unique electoral institutions—that posed problems for electoral accountability. Once electoral pressures are removed, either through retirement or defeat, legislators may have an incentive to shirk or modify their behavior (Herrick, Moore, and Hibbing 1994; Jenkins and Nokken 2008a, 2008b). Indeed, if the threat of electoral retribution compelled legislators to be more faithful agents (i.e., responsive), we should expect to see some changes in behavior once the electoral connection was severed. While many studies examine this question in terms of roll-call voting behavior (Carson et al. 2004; Herrick, Moore, and Hibbing 1994; Jenkins and Nokken 2008a, 2008b; Rothenberg and Sanders 2000), these lame-duck sessions could also result in major policy changes. Jenkins and Nokken (2008b) report that over 25 percent of major legislation that became law during the period from Reconstruction to the adoption of the Twentieth Amendment was passed during a lame-duck session.

The Tariff Act of 1875, which repealed the 1872 tariff law, was one such case of a major policy change passed in this manner. After holding a 111-seat majority in the 42nd Congress, the Republican Party suffered a crushing defeat in the midterm election of 1874, which resulted in the party holding a 79-seat deficit in the 43rd Congress. With a majority in both chambers and a Republican in the White House, the Republicans used their final months of unified government to pass legislation that restored customs duties to the levels of the Civil War era. According to Taussig (1914), the Republicans argued that the repeal was a necessary measure to respond to the Panic of 1873.

While the Republicans couched their advocacy of the bill in terms of responding to the economic crisis, Democratic opponents of the bill countered that the majority party was ignoring the results of the recent election. During floor debate on the bill, William O'Brien (D-MD) offered a forceful articulation of the Democratic Party's argument.

> I will state to gentlemen upon the other side that if the faith and honor of the country are at stake at this time, if the pretend emergency sought to be met by this bill is one which really exists, then it is a peril of their own making and their own choosing. . . . *Every charge that has been made by this side against the republican party, I will remark here, has been signally sustained, every one of them, by the judgment of the people at the late elections.* Therefore it does not come with good grace from the other side of the House to say when we oppose this bill that we are acting in bad faith. (3 Cong. Rec. 1414 (1875); emphasis added).

The Democrats, who would soon gain control of the House, clearly viewed the Republican effort as a being in direct contradiction to the recent election results.

While it is beyond the scope of this project to divine the Republicans' true motives for passing this tariff reform when they did, we believe that the tariff bill constitutes a clear example of legislative shirking during a lame-duck session. The 1872 reductions were the result of a compromise to avoid even larger reductions (Taussig 1914: 158–59), and many members of the Republican caucus likely did favor higher tariff rates. Soon to be the House minority party, the Republicans therefore had a strategic incentive to change the status quo back to their party's preference. If they failed to enact a more protective tariff, the incoming Democratic majority would be able to protect the existing status quo. By repealing the 1872 law, however, House Republicans could ensure that either the Republican majority in the Senate or a presidential veto during the 43rd Congress would protect the new status quo. In doing so, they guaranteed that tariff rates would remain high for at least the next two years.

Based on these specific considerations, we view the 1875 tariff reform as an example of legislators adopting behavior that would be inconsistent if the threat of electoral punishment was a distinct outcome. Indeed, the economic crisis was more than a year old when the Republicans introduced the legislation for tariff reform in February 1875. If increased treasury revenues were needed in the wake of the economic panic, which had led to a decrease in imports (Taussig 1914), why did the Republicans wait until the lame-duck session to even introduce the proposal? One potential explanation is that any legislation would have been politically difficult to pass prior to the elections. Indeed, the conference report on the 1875 tariff bill passed with a slim 9-vote majority, with 123 votes in favor and 114 votes against. The vote largely divided the two parties, as all but two of the votes in favor of the reform were cast by Republicans. More important, almost 60 percent of the Republican votes in favor of the reform were cast by legislators who would not be returning to the next Congress. In sum, the importance of these lame-duck legislators is suggestive of the potential for legislative shirking that lame-duck sessions made possible.

Slavery

Few issues defined nineteenth-century American politics more than slavery. Starting with the passage of the Missouri Compromise, however, slavery was largely kept off the legislative agenda for nearly three decades. From the 24th to the 28th Congress, inaction on slavery was actually mandated by a series of gag rules that barred the chamber from addressing abolition of slavery or the slave trade (Meinke 2007). Congressional silence was also encouraged by the general competitiveness of the Second Party System. Unlike the party systems that would follow, both of the major political parties—in this case, the Democrats and Whigs—were largely competitive in all regions of the country (Brady 1988; Ladd 1970). One consequence of the widespread party competition is that neither party could adopt a slavery position, either for or against, without alienating some of its existing members. As a result, both parties had an electoral incentive to focus on other issues and keep the question of slavery off the agenda.

By the 1850s, Congress was no longer able to remain passive on the issue of slavery. Starting with the Compromise of 1850, the sectional hostilities that had been constrained by a competitive party system suddenly began to boil over. The ensuing political crisis produced a "fundamental reshaping of the nature of party competition," which would now be defined on a sectional basis (Holt 1978: 3). Before this new party system emerged, however, Congress dealt with several legislative proposals that led to internal divisions within both parties. As we discussed earlier, intraparty disagreement on an issue increases the likelihood of finding evidence of electoral accountability. Below, we explore the Compromise of 1850 and the Kansas-Nebraska Act with a particular focus on how constituency interests informed legislators' vote choices. In doing so, we build on Meinke's (2007) earlier analysis of how the presence of an abolition constituency informed Northern legislators' vote choice on the gag rule. We are thus particularly interested in examining legislative responsiveness to constituent interests, but we also consider how electoral pressures more broadly informed legislative behavior.

Before turning to our analysis, we first need to outline how we define constituent interests. In his study of the gag rule, Meinke (2007) posits that the presence of an abolitionist organization in a Northern representative's district should lead to a more consistent antislavery voting record. Unfortunately, there is not a direct, district-level measure of abolitionist activity, but Meinke proposes that the presence of an antislavery third-party candidate can serve as a reasonable proxy measure. We utilized Dubin's (1998) detailed compendium of congressional election returns to identify all districts with an antislavery third-party candidate in the relevant election year. We then classified all Northern legislators by whether there was an active abolitionist organization in their district.

The Compromise of 1850

The Compromise of 1850 was not a single piece of legislation but, rather, a package of five bills. In table 7.2, we report the proportions of Northern Whigs and Democrats, by constituency type, who voted in favor of or against each bill. Three of the five proposals—the Texas and New Mexico Act, the Utah Act, and the Fugitive Slave Act—generated some level of intraparty disagreement. In contrast, the admission of California as a free state and the abolition of the slave trade in Washington, DC, were widely supported by all Northern legislators. Since our primary interest is legislative responsiveness, we here focus our preliminary discussion and all subsequent analysis of the Compromise of 1850 on the first set of bills.

The Texas and New Mexico Act settled issues related to the Texas border and established the territorial government of New Mexico. Slavery factored into the politics of this proposal because the bill allowed for "popular sovereignty" on the question of slavery. When New Mexico was admitted to statehood, the question of whether it would allow slaves would depend entirely on the constitution the state chose to adopt. The Utah Act established the territorial government for Utah and included the same popular sovereignty provisions. These bills left open the potential for slavery to expand further west. As expected, both Whigs and Democrats from districts with abolitionist activity were less likely to support either bill than were their copartisans from districts without an abolitionist organization. Although Whigs were generally less supportive of both bills than were Democrats, the change in support between each type of district is of comparable magnitude for both parties. In the case of the Texas and New Mexico Act, the change in support was just over 25 points for Democrats and just under 20 points for Whigs. On the Utah bill, however, the change in support among Whigs (around 35 points) was slightly larger than the change among Democrats (approximately 27 points).

TABLE 7.2. Northern legislators' vote proportions on the bills comprising the Compromise of 1850, by constituency type

Legislation	Abolitionist org., Whigs		Abolitionist org., Dem.	
	Yes (N)	No (N)	Yes (N)	No (N)
TX and NM Act	33.96	53.57	57.14	82.86
	(53)	(45)	(21)	(80)
CA statehood	100.00	100.00	100.00	89.12
	(50)	(47)	(21)	(82)
UT Act	13.63	48.14	57.14	84.84
	(44)	(42)	(21)	(72)
Fugitive Slave Act	2.38	43.48	52.63	80.00
	(42)	(39)	(19)	(79)
DC Slave Trade Act	100.00	82.61	100.00	82.86
	(50)	(36)	(20)	(76)

Note: Cell entries list the proportion of Northern legislators who voted, by constituency type. The number of legislators in each constituency-party combination is listed in parentheses.

The Fugitive Slave Act provided for more stringent enforcement of fugitive slave laws and levied financial penalties on officials who did not enforce the law. Northern Whigs were particularly opposed to the bill, but there were still notable intraparty differences based on constituent preferences. Although a majority of Whigs from districts without an abolitionist organization opposed the bill, only one Whig from a district with an abolition constituency supported the bill. Meanwhile, Northern Democrats largely supported the new fugitive slave law, but nine legislators broke ranks with their party, in favor of their constituency.

While the calculations reported in table 7.2 provide some initial evidence of legislative responsiveness, we also wanted to test for the marginality effect discussed by Bianco, Spence, and Wilkerson (1996). We estimated a series of logistic regression models where the outcome variable was coded 1 if a legislator voted for a bill and 0 if he voted against the bill. As before, our measure of constituent preferences is the presence of an abolitionist organization, which is coded 1 in districts where an antislavery third-party candidate ran in the 1848 election and 0 otherwise. To test for a marginality effect, we include the legislator's margin of victory. A positive coefficient estimate would be consistent with the expectations of a marginality effect. We also control for whether a legislator was a Democrat, since Democratic legislators were, on average, more supportive of all three proposals.

In table 7.3, we report the coefficient estimates for all three models. As expected, the presence of an abolitionist constituency decreased the probability of supporting all three bills, even after controlling for a legislator's partisan affiliation. For the variable of abolitionist organization, the marginal effect ranges from a predicted decrease of 21 points on the Fugitive Slave Act to an estimated decrease of 30 points on the Utah Act. There is also evidence of a marginality effect for all three votes. The marginal effect for the Texas and New Mexico Act, an increase of 19 points, is of comparable magnitude to the effect for the constituency variable.[11] For the other two bills, the marginal effect is about half the size of the estimated effect for constituent preferences. Finally, a legislator's party affiliation appears to be the main determinant of vote choice on two of the three bills. Indeed, the estimated marginal effects for both the Utah Act and the Fugitive Slave Act are consistent with the aggregate patterns evident in table 7.2. For the Texas and New Mexico Act, however, partisanship has an estimated effect that is comparable to our constituency variable. In short, both constituency and electoral considerations demonstrate significant effects that are independent of partisanship and consistent with the behavior of legislators who are responsive to their electoral principals.

The Kansas-Nebraska Act

While the Compromise of 1850 moved the American political system one step closer to party competition defined along regional lines, the Kansas-Nebraska Act was the proverbial nail in the coffin of the Second Party System. While the new territories of New Mexico and Utah were the first to be granted the right of popular sovereignty on the question of slavery, the decision to extend this right to the Kansas and Nebraska territories was more consequential. The Kansas-Nebraska Act repealed the Missouri Compromise, which had banned slavery in the former Louisiana Territory north of the 36°30' parallel. While it was still possible that both territories would decide to ban slavery, the bill created a clear opportunity to reignite sectional hostilities.

Holt argues that Northern opposition to the bill was much more intense because it represented a much more direct threat to Northern legislators and voters.

> But Northern animosities were much more intense in 1854 because the areas involved were not distant like New Mexico but contiguous to populate states. Many Northerners, especially Midwestern farmers, had a real interest in moving to Kansas and Nebraska, and the territorial issue thus had more immediacy than in the 1840s. (Holt 1978: 149)

The proposal's divisiveness in the North was quite evident in the roll-call vote on final passage (see fig. 7.1). While Democrats provided the bulk of

TABLE 7.3. Votes on the Compromise of 1850, 31st Congress

	TX and NM Act		UT Act		Fugitive Slave Act	
	Est. (*SE*)	Marg. eff.	Est. (*SE*)	Marg. eff.	Est. (*SE*)	Marg. eff.
Abolitionist org.	−1.03*	−0.24	−1.68*	−0.30	−1.97*	−0.21
	(0.41)		(0.46)		(0.52)	
Margin$_{t-1}$	0.04*	0.19	0.03*	0.15	0.03*	0.11
	(0.02)		(0.01)		(0.01)	
Democrat	1.28*	0.28	2.06*	0.43	2.56*	0.56
	(0.4*)		(0.46)		(0.53)	
Constant	−0.39		−0.66		−1.33*	
	(0.40)		(0.41)		(0.51)	
N	137		125		119	
PRE	0.29		0.44		0.55	

Note: Cell entries are coefficient estimates from a logistic regression model, with standard errors reported in parentheses.

*$p < .05$, one-tailed test

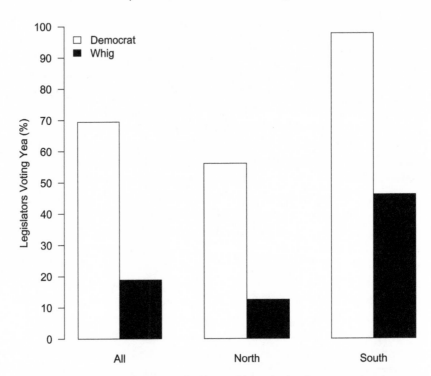

Figure 7.1. Legislators' votes on the Kansas-Nebraska Act, by party and region. (Calculated by the authors, based on roll-call vote 309 in the 33rd Congress.)

votes in favor of passage, the Northern Democrats were internally divided, with 55 voting in favor of the bill and 43 voting against passage. In contrast, only one Southern Democrat voted against the bill. The Whigs were largely unified in their opposition of the bill, and even a slim majority of Southern Whigs opposed it.

While the long-term consequences of the Kansas-Nebraska Act are well known (see, e.g., Holt 1978; Sundquist 1983), our interest here is in exploring the role that constituency and electoral considerations had in shaping both legislators' vote choice and their subsequent career decisions. We begin by examining Northern legislators' vote choice on the Kansas-Nebraska Act. The outcome variable is coded 1 if the legislator voted for passage of the Kansas-Nebraska Act and 0 otherwise. As with our analysis of the Compromise of 1850, we measure constituent preferences by the presence of an abolitionist organization, which is coded 1 in districts where an antislavery third-party candidate ran in the 1852 election and 0 otherwise. We also control for a legislator's previous margin of victory and partisan affiliation.

In table 7.4, we report the coefficient estimates for two logistic regression models. The first model examines all Northern legislators, while the second model includes only Northern Democrats. Just as we saw with roll-call voting on the Compromise of 1850, the existence of an abolitionist constituency decreases a legislator's likelihood of voting for passage of the Kansas-Nebraska Act. The magnitude of the effect is considerably larger on this vote, which suggests that constituency was a more important determinant of vote choice by 1854. Neither model provides any support for a marginality effect, however. The coefficient estimates for marginality are small in magnitude and imprecisely estimated. In the first model, we see strong evidence for the importance of partisanship, with Northern Democrats being more likely to support passage. The second model shows that those Democrats who broke ranks with their copartisans were compelled to do so because of constituent preferences.

As we noted earlier, one of the key challenges to finding evidence of accountability on Election Day is that legislators may opt to choose retirement rather than face the judgment of their constituents. Bianco, Spence, and Wilkerson (1996) suggest that scholars who are interested in studying accountability and the electoral connection should look for evidence of "surplus retirements." The tide of opposition against the bill that swept across parts of the North suggests that legislators who voted for the Kansas-Nebraska Act should be more likely to refrain from running again. Furthermore, retirements should be particularly more pronounced for legislators who shirked their abolition constituency. In table 7.5, we report the proportion of legislators who ran for reelection after the Kansas-Nebraska Act, by vote choice on that act. The first row reports the totals for all

TABLE 7.4. Northern legislators' vote on the Kansas-Nebraska Act

	All (*SE*)	Marg. eff.	Dem. (*SE*)	Marg. eff.
Abolitionist org.	−2.28*	−0.53	−2.02*	−0.48
	(0.45)		(0.47)	
Margin$_{t-1}$	−0.02		−0.01	
	(0.03)		(0.03)	
Democrat	2.10*	0.51		
	(0.51)			
Constant	−0.80*		1.14*	
	(0.49)		(0.40)	
N	143		94	
PRE	0.46		0.41	

Note: Cell entries are coefficient estimates from a logistic regression model, with standard errors reported in parentheses.

*$p < .05$, one-tailed test

Northern legislators. Incumbents who supported the bill were slightly less likely to seek another term in the House, but this difference is not statistically significant.

Once we account for constituency characteristics, however, there is more evidence of a correlation between vote choice and an incumbent's career decisions. Of the 11 legislators who voted against their constituents' preferences, 7 voluntarily departed. By contrast, over 70 percent of the legislators who were responsive to their constituents ran for reelection. Even with the small number of observations in the yea category for constituencies with abolitionist organizations, these differences are statistically significant. When we examine legislators who did not have an active abolition constituency, the correlation between vote choice and running for reelection reverses direction, but the difference is not statistically significant. In sum, the presence of an abolition constituency appears to have had at least some influence on legislators' willingness to run for another term. The more muted constituency effect may be due partly to the fact that the Kansas-Nebraska Act was not the only electorally volatile issue under consideration at the time. For voters in New England and New York, the issues of temperance and nativism were arguably more salient than the expansion of slavery (Holt 1978; Sundquist 1983).

Lame-Duck Sessions

Before the adoption of the Twentieth Amendment in 1933, both chambers of Congress would return to Washington, DC, in the month after the November elections and hold one final session, which lasted until March 3 of the following year. Legislators who had retired or lost in the most recent election retained their full voting rights and proposal powers, which led these legislative sessions to be called "lame-duck" sessions. Several studies have examined these sessions in an effort to gain new insights about how factors like legislative parties, electoral considerations, and presidential pressure influence legislators' voting behavior (Carson and Engstrom 2005; Goodman and Nokken 2004; Jenkins and Nokken 2008a, 2008b). For example, Jenkins and Nokken provide an insightful articulation of the advantages of referencing lame-duck sessions when studying the trade-off between partisan and electoral considerations.

> The lame duck session thus becomes a useful context to study the conflicting bases of member voting behavior: for existing members, both the electoral and partisan connections were effectively severed,

TABLE 7.5. Proportion of incumbents seeking reelection after the Kansas-Nebraska Act, by vote choice

	Vote on Kansas-Nebraska Act	
	Yea (*N*)	Nay (*N*)
Total	56.45	65.22
	(62)	(92)
Constituency		
Abolitionist org.	36.36	71.88
	(11)	(64)
No abolitionist org.	60.78	50.00
	(51)	(28)

Note: Cell entries list the proportion of Northern legislators who ran for reelection, by their position on the Kansas-Nebraska Act. The number of legislators in each category is listed in parentheses.

while for returning members, the electoral connection was greatly reduced (as the next set of elections were almost two years in the future) but the partisan connection remained strong. (Jenkins and Nokken 2008b: 451)

In short, the presence of legislators with differing incentive structures can help scholars identify how electoral motivations inform legislative behavior throughout the nineteenth century. In particular, lame-duck legislators may be more likely to vote in ways that counter the expressed preferences of their constituency (Carson and Engstrom 2005).

One potential consequence is that lame-duck legislators may be pivotal in shaping major policy decisions. According to Jenkins and Nokken (2008b: 452n7), almost 29 percent of the major legislation enacted by Congress between 1877 and 1933 was passed during lame-duck sessions. Based on Stathis's (2002) list of major legislative enactments, we find a similar pattern throughout the early nineteenth century. From the 17th Congress (1821–23) through the 31st Congress (1849–51), approximately 28 percent of landmark legislation was passed during lame-duck sessions. The laws passed during those sessions covered policy areas from the admission of several states and the establishment or annexation of territory to tariff legislation and the federal government's authority to collect custom duties. Of greater interest for our purposes is that legislators during those Congresses did not fall into a simple dichotomy of lame-duck or returning legislator. As we noted in chapter 6, election timing was highly variable during that period, which means that some congressional elections were not held until *after* the end of the final congressional sessions.[12] As such, we are able to observe the behavior of three different legislator types: lame ducks, returning members, and members whose elections had not been held.[13]

While the exact nature of our theoretical expectations for each legislator type could vary depending on the legislation in question, we generally expect that these "pending" legislators will look more similar to returning members than to lame ducks. Our expectation builds on the logic outlined by Jenkins and Nokken (2008b), which contends that lame ducks are not as constrained by partisan or electoral considerations, while electoral constraints remain in place, at least loosely, for returning members. Therefore, legislators whose career and electoral futures remain uncertain share more in common with returning members than with the legislators who will not be returning for the subsequent Congress. With these considerations in mind, we here first examine a case where lame-duck legislators' votes were crucial for the passage of some of these bills. If, as other scholars suggest, lame ducks are no longer subject to electoral sanctions, their behavior may indicate how the removal of electoral constraints shaped policy making during the early nineteenth century. We then examine a case where the House used a lame-duck session to reverse its position on a controversial policy. In doing so, we are particularly interested in how the differential incentive structures faced by these three legislator types influenced their voting behavior.

Appropriation to Secure Peace with Mexico

On March 3, 1847, the final day of the 29th Congress (1845–47), the House approved legislation that appropriated three million dollars for negotiations of a peace agreement with Mexico. While it would be almost another year before a treaty to end the Mexican-American War was ratified, the legislation passed at the end of the legislative session provided necessary resources. Of interest from our perspective, is the role that lame-duck legislators played in securing these funds. Indeed, although the legislation passed by a relatively comfortable margin of 33 votes—115 yeas to 82 nays—passage was dependent on lame-duck legislators. In figure 7.2, we report the numbers of legislators voting for and against the bill who were lame ducks, returning members, or legislators whose election would not be held until after the 29th Congress. Since there were notable regional differences in support for the bill, the first panel shows the patterns for Northern legislators, while the second panel includes only Southern legislators.

As the first panel of figure 7.2 makes quite clear, lame-duck and returning Northern legislators adopted fundamentally different positions on the bill. These differences were largely driven by partisanship: 34 of the 35 lame-duck Northern legislators who voted yea were Democrats, and 24 of the 29 returning Northern legislators who voted nay were Whigs. These numbers should not be surprising when we consider that the Whigs made sizable gains during the pre-November and November elections and would eventually hold a six-seat majority in the 30th Congress. Indeed, the bill's passage was secured almost exclusively by a coalition of lame-duck Northern legislators and Southern Democrats, which accounts for 86 of the 115 yea votes.

Overall, the coalition that helped to push through this policy is arguably consistent with what we would expect from legislators and a party that wanted to enact its most preferred policy once it was freed from electoral constraints. Although the Democrats would win the majority of the congressional elections contested after the close of the 29th Congress, they were already trailing the Whigs and likely knew that they would face an uphill battle to maintain their majority. Furthermore, 16 of the 36 Southern legislators who were in the pending category and voted for the bill would ultimately decide against another run for Congress. While we cannot definitively know whether these legislators had decided to retire at the time this vote was cast, 75 of the 115 votes in support of the bill were from legislators who would not return to the House for the 30th Congress. In short, Democrats who were departing the House and were thus no longer subject to electoral considerations were central to the passage of this bill.

Repeal of the House Gag Order

During the early days of the final legislative session of the 28th Congress (1843–45), former president turned representative John Quincy Adams was finally able to repeal the House's gag order on petitions and memorial related to slavery. Adams tried to have the gag order rescinded at the start of the 28th Congress, when the House adopted a new set of rules, but the order was upheld by a vote of 95 in favor and 91 opposed. Adams was victorious, however, during the lame-duck session, when the vote on repeal passed 108 to 80. While several other studies offer valuable insights about legislators' behavior on the numerous votes related to the gag order (Jenkins and Stewart 2003; Meinke 2007), we are interested here in the voting behavior of the three legislator types discussed above. The vote to repeal the gag order is a particularly interesting case because we can examine the extent to which legislators' positions changed from the initial repeal vote at

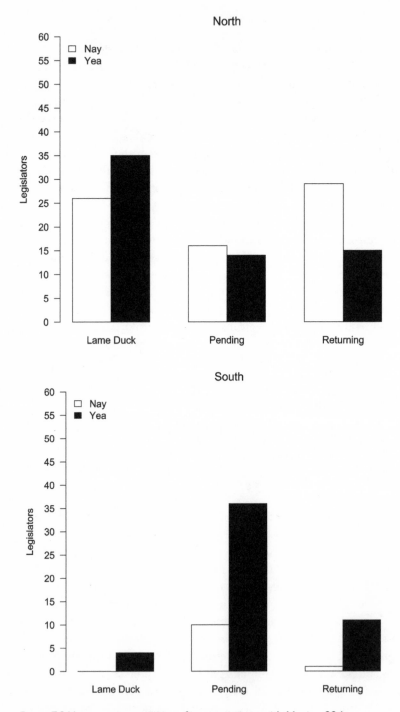

Figure 7.2. Votes on appropriations for negotiations with Mexico, 29th Congress. (Calculated by the authors, based on roll-call vote 637 in the 29th Congress.)

the start of the 28th Congress to the final repeal vote during the lame-duck sessions. Specifically, we are interested in the consistency of legislators' positions on this controversial and contentious House rule.

We began our analysis by identifying the set of legislators who were sitting members of the House for both the initial and the final repeal vote. To examine how electoral considerations might have influenced the repeal of the gag order, we determined whether a legislator was a lame duck, a returning member, or a member whose election had not yet been contested. After classifying each legislator, we examined how his decision on the first repeal vote matched up to his decision during the lame-duck session. Since the vote received effectively no support in the South, we limited our focus to only Northern legislators.[14] The first category reported in table 7.6 includes legislators who adopted a consistent position across the two votes. As expected, lame-duck legislators were the least likely to adopt a consistent position, while legislators whose electoral fate remained unknown were the most likely to do so. These differences, around eight percentage points, are not large in magnitude, which is consistent with other studies finding that legislators had stable positions on the gag order (Jenkins and Stewart 2003).

Arguably more interesting are the observed changes for legislators whose immediate electoral calculations had changed. Indeed, the majority of new

TABLE 7.6. Northern legislators' vote choice on repeal of the House gag order, 28th Congress

Rescind gag order	Legislator type		
Consistent votes	Lame duck	Returning	Pending
Yea-yea	29	33	12
Nay-nay	5	8	14
% of legislator type (N)	64.15	67.21	72.22
	(53)	(61)	(36)
New yea votes			
Nay-yea	3	7	0
Abstain-yea	6	6	4
% of legislator type (N)	16.98	21.31	11.11
	(53)	(61)	(36)
New nay votes			
Yea-nay	1	0	1
Abstain-nay	1	0	1
% of legislator type (N)	3.77	0	5.56
	(53)	(61)	(36)

Note: The cell entries report a comparison of each legislator type's position on the repeal vote at the start of the 28th Congress (roll-call vote 3) and the successful repeal vote (roll-call vote 424) in the final legislative session of the 28th Congress.

yea votes, which includes legislators who either voted against or abstained from voting on the earlier repeal effort, came from either lame ducks or legislators who had already secured another term in the House. Of the 26 new yea votes, 13 were legislators who would be returning to serve in the 29th Congress, 9 were lame ducks, and only 4 were legislators who would be up for reelection after the end of the legislative session. We observe a different pattern when we examine new nay votes, cast by legislators who either voted for or abstained from voting on the earlier repeal effort. Very few legislators switched to a nay vote, which is arguably consistent with the changing political and electoral context surrounding the gag order (Meinke 2007).

In sum, the comparison of legislators' positions on the two repeal votes provides important insights about electoral politics during the lame-duck sessions of the early nineteenth century. First, legislators whose electoral constraints were either weakest or nonexistent were arguably pivotal to the eventual repeal of the gag order. Indeed, the 22 new yea votes from either lame ducks or returning legislators nearly accounts for the entire margin of victory on the last repeal vote. Conversely, legislators who could still be punished electorally provided little in the way of new support and were generally more likely to adopt a consistent position.

Second, votes from lame-duck sessions could have important electoral consequences (albeit smaller in scale) for the composition of the subsequent House. In total, 26 Northern legislators who cast a vote on the lame-duck repeal of the gag order ran for reelection in the months after the end of the 28th Congress. All but one of the 11 legislators who voted against removing the gag order were reelected, but only 7 of the 15 who supported the proposal secured another term in the House. Thus, it appears that changing the status quo may have cost a few legislators their jobs. While we fully recognize that the magnitude of these effects is quite small, it highlights the more complicated politics of lame-duck sessions during the early nineteenth century. While electoral constraints may have been removed for a majority of legislators, the protracted House electoral calendar meant that some of their colleagues would be forced to cast a vote on subjects that could ultimately cost them their House seats.

Discussion

At the heart of debates over representation in Congress is the issue of whether we can effectively hold elected members accountable for their behavior in office. To be fair, this is not a new issue but has existed since the founding of the nation. Legislative scholars suggest that electoral accountability of individual members was significantly enhanced following the adoption of the Australian ballot at the end of the nineteenth century. The argument has a clear intuitive appeal, since these reforms greatly enhanced constituents' ability to vote for or against an individual legislator. Nevertheless, as Arnold (1990) succinctly points out, it can be difficult to find evidence of electoral accountability in the modern era, since legislators are typically quite responsive to the interests of constituents. One important implication of that argument, then, is that the era of party ballots during the nineteenth century should represent the hardest test case for finding evidence of individual legislative accountability.

As demonstrated by the results from the series of case studies analyzed in this chapter, both legislative responsiveness and electoral accountability were possible even when the party ballot was in use throughout the United States. As in contemporary congressional politics, both accountability and responsiveness were more likely on salient issues and in cases where issues split the parties. Indeed, when intraparty divisions emerged on issues like slavery or the tariff, legislators were not afraid to shirk the party line in favor of their constituents. In cases where legislators ignored their constituents, voters appear to have registered their disapproval on Election Day. Building both on our previous work on election timing (Carson and Sievert 2017) and on studies of lame-duck sessions (Jenkins and Nokken 2008a, 2008b), we also found that differences in the electoral rules and the legislative calendar had important implications for how legislators responded to electoral incentives. Like their modern counterparts, nineteenth-century legislators were more likely to vote their preferences (rather than according to their party or constituency) once the electoral bonds were severed.

The evidence for electoral accountability that we report has important implications for the origins and development of the electoral connection in Congress. Prior work has found cases where an electoral connection may have been present during the nineteenth century (see, e.g., Bianco, Spence, and Wilkerson 1996; Carson and Engstrom 2005), although these instances involve hypersalient votes in Congress. The results reported here suggest that an electoral connection may have actually existed on a much larger scale, as reflected by the institutional arrangements in place and the opportunity for voters to reward or punish legislators when they went to the polls. In other words, voters were not always forced to select among candidates indiscriminately during the party ballot era, as was previously believed.

EIGHT

Reevaluating Electoral Incentives in Congress

Since the publication of Mayhew's (1974) classic work on the electoral connection, the conventional wisdom about his argument has viewed it as applying only to modern congressional politics of the post–World War II period. In many respects, this has a certain appeal. This period in history is characterized by powerful committee chairs clearly advantaged by the seniority system in Congress, allowing them to wield tremendous influence in the policy-making process. Political parties have been weaker during much of this era than in the past, leading to greater amounts of independence and self-sufficiency on the part of individual candidates running for office. During the post–World War II era, legislators have regularly utilized the types of activities—advertising, credit claiming, and position taking—that Mayhew outlines in his book. This period has also witnessed a dramatic increase in the number of roll-call votes in Congress, which has forced legislators to go on the record more often and has increased the odds that one or a series of inconsistent roll-call positions could become costly during the next election.

The preceding discussion notwithstanding, there seems to be ample evidence, as presented in this book, that the traditional notion of an electoral connection traces back to earlier political eras. As we discussed at the outset, we believe that the most important first step in analyzing this possibility is to identify what an electoral connection might look like in earlier periods. In specifying the individual, necessary conditions for a Mayhewian electoral connection—ambition, autonomy, responsiveness, and accountability—we find that all were present in a *strict* sense as early as the Gilded Age (1870–1900). In particular, congressional careerism (and strong reelection ambition) emerged around the latter part of the nineteenth century; legislators' autonomy over their own careers solidified with the rise of direct primaries, between 1900 and 1910; and voters' ability to keep individual members accountable was greatly strengthened with the Australian ballot reforms, between 1880 and 1900.[1]

While a formal institutional change did not occur to affect member responsiveness in the same way that changes altered the other three Mayhewian conditions, there is considerable evidence that responsiveness sharpened in the late nineteenth century. As noted, legislative advertising ramped up, and opportunities for members to claim credit via more pork-barrel legislation, as well as more private legislation, increased (see, e.g., Brady, Buckley, and Rivers 1999; Cooper and Young 1989; Finocchiaro 2005; Wilson 1986a, 1986b). In addition, while some argue that responsiveness in the modern era has increased due to the rise of public polling—the claim being that members of Congress better understand constituent demands thanks to poll data—Karol (2007) analyzed Literary Digest interest polls dating back to the 1910s and concluded that the rise of scientific surveys did not lead to an increase in member responsiveness. Thus, it would seem that the electoral connection dates back at least to the latter part of the nineteenth century, rather than being a development of the post–World War II era.

There is evidence to suggest that a weaker or perhaps less formalized version of an electoral connection was present even during the antebellum era. For example, members of Congress appear to have always been politically ambitious; during much of the nineteenth century, they simply pursued political careers (specifically careers within the party) instead of the congressional careers more commonly pursued today. As a result of their general political ambition, evidenced by their voluntary decisions to seek renomination, incumbents actively sought to be responsive to constituents' needs and demands on a regular basis. This was both important and necessary, as members' district constituents might also be state constituents, a strong consideration for members seeking state-level electoral positions (Carson and Roberts 2013; MacKenzie 2015).

Moreover, legislator responsiveness followed from party leaders' political preferences. Party leaders cared about maintaining majority control of Congress (allowing them to pursue their specific policy goals) and wanted to keep districts firmly in the party column, even if the individual placeholder did not desire to make a career out of serving in Congress. Since party leaders could affect legislators' political careers by influencing their ability to earn a place on the party ballot as well as to obtain subsequent state-level positions, legislators had to be cognizant of what party leaders cared about, which was keeping constituents happy and the House seat in the party's hands (Carson and Roberts 2013).[2] Political ambition thus bred significant degrees of responsiveness throughout the nineteenth century and even under certain circumstances in the late eighteenth century.

Severing ties to the party machines, the Australian ballot has been widely viewed as fundamentally altering both the American electoral system and political institutions (see, e.g., Katz and Sala 1996; Rusk 1970; Ware 2002). In the modern era, where all elections are administered by the states, it can be hard to fully appreciate the magnitude of these changes. Indeed, it is important to remember that the Australian ballot was the first in a series of reforms that eventually produced the modern US electoral system. Ballot reforms predate other electoral changes—the direct primary, direct election of US senators, and reporting requirements for federal campaign expenditures—by a decade or more. In this way, ballot reforms were a crucial step in modernizing elections and ultimately facilitated the adoption of subsequent electoral reforms (Ware 2002).

The early nineteenth-century emergence of various institutional structures—party leadership positions, committee and seniority systems, and the property rights norm—suggests that members of Congress valued responsiveness to constituents well before the contemporary era. That incumbents were working to meet the needs of former Revolutionary War veterans as early as the 1810s and 1820s, for example, indicates that legislators recognized the underlying importance of the constituency-representative linkage (see Finocchiaro and Jenkins 2016). The continued emphasis on this type of credit-claiming behavior over the next two centuries further illustrates the importance of an electoral connection across a greater swath of congressional history than previously recognized. Once incentives for legislators to pursue specific goals, such as policy or influence within the chamber, are established, getting reelected becomes very important. Undeniably, the most powerful and influential members of Congress over time tend to be those with the greatest levels of chamber or committee seniority, which has both direct and indirect implications for the emergence and growth of careerism in Congress.

There is also evidence that member autonomy and accountability existed even during the eras of the party convention and party ballot. If incumbents wanted to run for a congressional office, they were not completely constrained by the party-controlled nomination system. Even if they did not receive the party nomination in convention, they could always run an independent (or splinter) campaign by printing and distributing their own ballots, an irregular election route that was always available in the era before the government-regulated ballot. Voters also did not need the Australian ballot to keep members of Congress accountable. Even during the party-ballot era, members could cast a split ticket; such a decision required a more manual effort (e.g., scratching a candidate's name, pasting over a candidate's name, or creating an entire ballot at home), and it ran the risk of upsetting party henchman watching the polls, but the option was always available and occasionally utilized by voters (Reynolds 2006; Ware 2002). Thus, legislators had to be concerned about being voted out of office, should they not be sufficiently responsive to the demands of their constituents. They could not simply rely on the design of the party ballot to insulate them against voter retribution, especially in election years with a strong anti-incumbent sentiment.

The institutional design of the party ballot and the timing of elections during much of the nineteenth century facilitated an electoral connection in ways not previously recognized. As we discuss in chapter 6, congressional elections throughout most of that period were often held months before or months after the presidential election routinely scheduled for early November, which gave voters the chance to vote on the basis of individual candidates at the top of the ticket rather than voting simply for a political party. In the absence of presidential and senatorial candidates on the ballot (the latter of which would not occur until the 1914 election, following passage of the Seventeenth Amendment), representatives for the US House were often the first candidates listed on the ballot, which clearly influenced voters' choices at the polls (Engstrom and Kernell 2014). Individual legislators had to make efforts to be responsive to their constituents throughout the nineteenth century, since voters could, in many cases, hold them individually accountable.

Implications of an Early Electoral Connection

Among the numerous potential implications of the preceding discussion, one stands out in particular—especially as it relates to studies of Congress and American political development more specifically. The identification and uncovering of more systematic evidence suggesting that an electoral connection has been present in Congress across time may lead scholars to revisit our understanding of the institutional development of Congress. The existence of some version of an electoral connection since the nation's constitutional founding, for instance, could help us explain why specific congressional institutions were adopted at certain points in time: they may have been created with the express purpose of enhancing or "firming up" the existing constituency-representative linkage in Congress; that is, some form of an electoral incentive may always have been present in Congress, but the adoption of institutions (or institutional reforms) such as standing committees, the Australian ballot, and the direct primary served to augment the existing linkages already in place.

The takeaway from each of the preceding empirical chapters may also help us address a long-standing puzzle in the context of congressional politics—namely, that property rights may have been around for much longer than has previously been recognized by scholars of legislative politics. Katz and Sala (1996) argue that property rights in Congress really took hold after the adoption of the Australian ballot, near the end of the nineteenth century. Yet Jenkins (1998) found evidence of property rights by the early part of the nineteenth century, when a standing committee system was first being created (Gamm and Shepsle 1989). Based on the evidence in the earlier chapters, it appears that one of the major consequences of creating a standing committee system in the early part of the nineteenth century was that it could have facilitated members' electoral interests to a much larger extent than has previously been recognized. We reinforce this point in an earlier discussion of electoral reform and changes in legislative behavior.

> Lastly, we find no evidence to support the prior claim that changes in the ballot laws should influence committee assignment politics. Contrary to earlier studies, our results provide no evidence that the ballot reforms influenced legislators' interest in, or demand for, committee property rights. This, of course, does not preclude the possibility that these electoral reforms helped to usher in a long-term change in committee assignment politics. Alternatively, our null findings might serve to corroborate studies suggesting that committee property rights were securely in place decades before the ballot reforms were adopted. (Carson and Sievert 2015: 104–5)

Reevaluating Mayhew's Argument

In a short retrospective written 25 years after his seminal book on Congress was published, Mayhew (2001: 251) offered the following assessment of his theoretical argument:

First, the book is a theoretical work that obviously "goes too far." It is a caricature. I knew that at the time, and I planned the book that way on the assumption that pushing a simple argument to its limits can have explanatory utility. I realized in 1974, as I do now, that political reality is very complicated, that no one kind of move can explain everything, and that moves other than this one pointing to an electoral incentive can also have considerable utility.

Despite this broad criticism of his perspective, Mayhew also mentioned that he never would have come to this conclusion about individual legislators had he not served as an APSA Congressional Fellow in 1967–68 and had the chance to observe members of Congress in action. Based on this experience, he believed that his account accurately summarized what he viewed while working on Capitol Hill.

Like Mayhew, we do not believe, nor are we arguing here, that an electoral incentive is the only factor that motivated legislative behavior during earlier political eras. Indeed, as Schickler (2001) maintains in his comprehensive discussion of the "disjointed" nature of congressional development over time, there is rarely a single explanation for institutional change in Congress. Rather, our goal in this book is to demonstrate that there is room for an electoral connection during the nineteenth century and that it actually helps us better understand electoral and institutional development throughout that historical period. In this vein, we think it is worth repeating an earlier quotation from Bianco, Spence, and Wilkerson (1996: 147), who offered the following observation regarding the electoral connection in the context of the nineteenth-century Congress:

> Our premise is simple. It is one thing to argue that a congressional career was less attractive or less feasible in an earlier time than it is today, but another to conclude that members of the early Congress were unconcerned about the electoral consequences of their behavior. We do not believe that the politics of the modern and early Congresses are as different as the conventional wisdom suggests.

The American political system underwent a remarkable array of changes throughout the nineteenth century. The 1828 presidential election ushered in a new two-party system that led to increased participation among those eligible to vote. Over the ensuing decades, large segments of the eligible voting population turned out to vote and regularly participate in elections (Bensel 2004). With each passing election, party organizations grew more influential and, by the 1850s, began to exert considerable influence over candidates and electoral machinery. Following the Civil War, party machines reached a level of influence and control that was unprecedented in American political history. Party bosses controlled access to the party ballot and attempted to recruit the strongest potential candidates to run for office, resulting in high levels of electoral competition for several decades (Carson and Roberts 2013). Nevertheless, their sheer exercise of control led to severe political abuses that would ultimately lead to the demise of the party machines (Ware 2002).

In response to the numerous excesses associated with the party machines in the Gilded Age, progressives pushed for both electoral and institutional reforms, in an attempt to weaken the party bosses' control over the electorate. Adoption of the Australian (or secret) ballot and the later creation of primary elections were two such reforms, which had an immediate and lasting impact on the US electoral landscape. When viewed through the lens of shoring up an *existing* electoral connection in Congress, reform efforts take on new meaning and have important implications for our understanding of electoral accountability and representation in earlier political eras. Such reforms also help us better understand why legislators, who often cared about reelection, would now seek to be even more responsive to constituents during that political era, through the use of increased military pensions, post offices, and public buildings (Finocchiaro 2015, n.d.; Rogowski and Gibson 2015).[3]

To this point, we have sought to better understand how an electoral incentive might have manifested itself in Congress well before the mid-twentieth century. By focusing on the four theoretical components discussed in chapter 3—ambition, autonomy, responsiveness, and accountability—we have provided a foundation for evaluating the individual mechanisms by which an electoral connection could have operated in earlier political eras (see table 8.1). As we showed in the preceding chapters, legislators were clearly ambitious throughout the nineteenth century and were not nearly as constrained in their ability to run for office as scholars

TABLE 8.1. Institutional features that illustrate the electoral connection

Institutional features	Components of the electoral connection
Competitive elections	Ambition, responsiveness
Strategic politicians	Ambition
Voluntary vs. involuntary departures	Ambition, autonomy
Ballot placement	Accountability, responsiveness
Differential election timing	Accountability, responsiveness
Lame-duck sessions	Responsiveness

have previously believed. In their efforts to get reelected, the legislators of that era sought to be responsive to their constituents and could be held accountable, even prior to the adoption of the secret ballot during the late nineteenth century. Such findings are instructive and help us better understand why members pursued a variety of electoral and institutional changes in the nineteenth century and into the twentieth.

While we have here marshaled evidence to suggest an inherent temporal "fluidity" in the electoral linkage, there is still much work to be done to evaluate specifically how (and how much) the electoral connection may have changed over time. Indeed, several questions still need to be addressed more systematically before we have a more complete picture of how electoral politics in Congress have evolved during the past 200 plus years. For instance, why was careerism more political than congressional during much of the nineteenth century? To what extent was the emerging careerism at the end of the nineteenth century tied to issues like congressional compensation? When and under what conditions did legislators begin utilizing their committee assignments to engage in credit-claiming activities, and how did such activities change after the progressive reforms were adopted? When did the candidate-centered electoral system first emerge in Congress? How frequently were members of Congress punished for their expressed positions on roll calls in Congress? Future work providing answers to these important questions can offer valuable, new insights into how the institution of Congress has responded to internal and external changes since the founding of the American political system.

Notes

1. The number of works referencing Mayhew's original argument is too voluminous to include here. See Jacobson 2017 for a recent discussion of Mayhew's contribution to electoral politics and the study of the US Congress.

2. In conversations with Professor Mayhew, he has made it clear that he thinks there is room for an electoral connection outside of the post–World War II era, especially in light of the growing evidence that is emerging in support of such a perspective.

3. In his 1978 review of *The Electoral Connection*, Larry Dodd echoed this sentiment when commenting on Mayhew's book: "The second major problem with Mayhew's argument is its implicit static image of Congress. . . . This picture does mesh well with congressional reality during the 1960s, the period on which Mayhew relies for empirical support. But this view of Congress is an inaccurate characterization if applied to the late nineteenth or early twentieth century; it is also inaccurate today."

4. However, Rudder (1990: 166) argues, "The motive force of [rational actor] theory is, of course, the reelection imperative, an assumption much less applicable in the last century than in this one."

CHAPTER 2

1. As Mann and Wolfinger (1980) note, incumbents typically have an advantage at the polls, since they are often more easily recognized by voters than are challengers.

2. In his 25-year retrospective discussing the significance of *the electoral con-nection*, Mayhew (2001) expressed disappointment that position taking had not received as much attention in the literature as had his ideas about credit claiming.

3. While Mayhew (1974) describes other activities beyond roll-call voting in his discussion of position taking (e.g., floor addresses, speeches, television appearances, press releases), nearly all of the analyses that explore this activity focus exclusively on roll calls.

4. One recent study suggests that being out of step is not a sufficient condition for legislators to be punished on election day. Hollibaugh, Rothenberg, and Rulison (2013) contend that incumbent punishment is conditional on there being a more "in-step" challenger as well.

5. See Carson and Sievert 2015 for a more explicit critique of Katz and Sala's 1996 argument.

6. See Theriault 2003 for a critique of this argument. In short, Theriault argues that representatives opted to reform the civil service system in response to public pressure.

CHAPTER 3

1. In discussing the influence of the political party, Mayhew (1974: 99) offers an important and related observation: "What is important to each congressman, and vitally so, is that he be free to take positions that serve his advantage. There is no member of either house who would not be politically injured—or at least who would not think he would be injured—by being made to toe a party line on all poli-cies (unless of course he could determine the party line). There is no congressional bloc whose members have identical position needs across all issues."

2. Our argument here is not unlike the argument in the literature examining the specific conditions for institutionalization for either the US Congress or the presidency (see, e.g., Polsby 1968; Ragsdale and Theis 1998). Having three of the four conditions explicitly met during a historical era, for instance, would provide evidence for arguing that an electoral connection could be relevant outside of the modern era.

3. This idea is consistent with Madison's famous argument, from *Federalist No. 51*, that "ambition must be made to counteract ambition."

4. Kernell (1977: 676) posits that congressional careerism may extend back even earlier, as antebellum Southern politicians likely saw the benefit of "extended polit-ical service in protecting [their] 'peculiar institution.'"

5. Kernell (1977: 691) discusses this nineteenth-century career pattern: "A typ-ical career sequence early in the nineteenth century would be local office, state house, U.S. House, and back to the state house. If the individual were lucky, some-

where along the line a government sinecure, or a judgeship, would be available. Or if he climbed the career ladder—and the top rungs appear to have formed early—he would manage to win a gubernatorial or senatorial seat."

6. Even during the period of strong party bosses and machine-era politics in the nineteenth century, there is almost no systematic evidence suggesting that individual ambition was tempered by the party-centered nature of the electoral process. Just because individual candidates had to seek out the approval of the party organization to earn a position in Congress did not mean that they failed to value that position once elected. There is strong evidence that nineteenth-century party bosses desired strong candidates on the ticket as much as the candidates needed the parties to facilitate their careers in Congress (Carson and Roberts 2013).

7. One limitation of the data reported in figure 3.1 is that it only denotes whether members of Congress won election to another office after leaving Congress. It does not tell us how many of these legislators ran for but did not win election to another office. The results reported in figure 3.1 may thus underestimate the extent to which members of Congress desired a continued career in politics even after leaving Congress.

8. In addition to the increased desire for a career in Congress, MacKenzie (2015) finds that late nineteenth-century and early twentieth-century members of the House had long precongressional careers in politics.

9. Politicians of this earlier era recognized immediately the effects of direct primary elections on House membership. As House Speaker Champ Clark (1920: 220) stated, "The primary election method . . . helps the sitting member retain his seat if he is at all worthy of it." Clark's extended quote is cited in Kernell 1977 and 2003.

10. There are exceptions, of course. Independents may skirt the renomination process or lose renomination and still win reelection. Joseph Lieberman's 2006 reelection to the Senate after he lost the Democratic nomination in Connecticut is one such example. But such cases are exceedingly rare.

11. Kernell (1977) estimates that only 4 percent of all congressional careers during the 1850s were ended due to rotation, only 3 percent in the 1870s and 1880s, and just 1 percent in the 1890s. For a critique of Kernell's methodology, see Price 1998.

12. Kolodny (1998) argues that congressional campaign committees were formed immediately following the Civil War in an attempt to prevent congressional candidates from being subsumed by weak presidential candidates at the top of the party ticket. She notes that congressional candidates were also instrumental in stumping on behalf of the party and energizing voters, especially since presidential candidates of this era did not actively campaign for office.

13. In response to the increased levels of money being spent on elections in the direct-primary era, some states passed laws to restrict various forms of political

advertising. Other laws (so-called corrupt practices acts) attempted to place dollar limits on campaign expenditures and to force disclosure of how funds were being spent. The escalating costs of campaigns even led some states to reemploy a form of the convention system (for a short time).

14. Pre–Seventeenth Amendment US Senate elections provide additional evidence that direct nominations and elections were by no means necessary conditions for high levels of campaign spending. According to Schiller, Stewart, and Xiong (2013), campaign spending in these races, usually in the form of payments to state legislatures, could outpace spending in modern US Senate elections.

15. In discussing policy responsiveness generally in Congress during the 1870s, Thompson (1985: 123, 125) states, "Most legislators tried earnestly to hold up their end of the representational relationship by pledging to work explicitly in behalf of what they perceived to be their constituencies' policy interests. Speeches, eulogies, memoirs journalistic accounts, and, for those who kept them, diaries and correspondences all attest to the pervasiveness of such behavior. . . . There is a clear consensus that House members demonstrated awareness of and concern for their constituencies' needs and tried, whenever possible, to act responsively."

16. Wilson (1986a) notes that members in this era also sought committee assignments that would allow them to craft legislation on rivers and harbors in such a way to ensure that elements would be beneficial to their districts; being on the "right" committee would thus provide them with a more credible mechanism to claim credit with their constituents.

17. Civil War pensions were funded mainly by the revenue surpluses generated by postbellum protective tariffs.

18. Cooper and Young (1989: 99) make a similar point in explaining why nineteenth-century members of Congress worked to please their constituents, though they did not often pursue congressional careers: "It is arguable that before 1880 the political careers of members were focused broadly on state politics rather than narrowly confined to their House constituencies. Hence, members could well be interested in service to their states and localities, even if they were not as concerned about reelection to the House as they became in the twentieth century."

19. Keyssar (2000: 28) notes that most states had adopted a written-ballot requirement for voting by the mid-nineteenth century. Before then, many parts of the country allowed for oral voting: "[M]en assembled before election judges, waited for their names to be called, and then announced which candidates they supported."

20. For lists of states and their adoption dates (as well as the variant of the Australian ballot that was adopted), see Evans 1917; Albright 1942; Engstrom and Kernell 2005.

21. Katz and Sala (1996), for example, find that House members were more likely

to invest in specific policy expertise (and to seek to hold on to the *same* committee assignments) after the advent of the Australian ballot, as a way to enhance their credit-claiming opportunities with constituents.

22. Bensel 2004 details the types of activities in which party henchmen engaged during the nineteenth-century heyday of machine-era politics.

23. See Reynolds and McCormick 1986 for perhaps the most thorough analysis of ticket splitting in the era of party ballots. They examine ten counties in New York and New Jersey every two years from 1880 through 1910 and find that the incidence of split-ticket voting occurred as much as 25 percent of the time in certain parts of the states.

24. National political coverage in newspapers was also extensive in the eighteenth century, as rival partisan presses emerged throughout the country. Moreover, eighteenth-century newspaper politics often had a bare-knuckle, lurid quality— similar to tabloid journalism today—which often piqued public interest (see Pasley 2001).

25. Mann and Wolfinger (1980: 629) summarize this argument best: "It would be a mistake, however, to conclude that issues and roll-call voting have no importance for congressional elections. The low salience of issues may reflect in part the efforts of the incumbent to avoid being dramatically out of step with district sentiment. In order to preserve a favorable public image, incumbents may act to forestall vociferous criticism on policy grounds. Incumbents must state positions on issues to satisfy local groups that are important for endorsements, campaign contributions, and volunteers. House members realize that the best way of ensuring their continued reelection is to discourage serious opposition. This requires making peace with those in the district who might otherwise underwrite a vigorous challenge. Finally, most politicians operate at the margin, not at the base. A loss of two or three percent of the vote as a result of a vote or a position taken on an issue will give them pause."

CHAPTER 4

1. While the anti-Nebraska opposition was represented by different parties in different states—the Republican Party in Wisconsin and Michigan, the Anti-Nebraska Party in Ohio, the People's Party in Indiana, the American Party or Know-Nothing Party throughout the East Coast, or some form of fusion ticket— the result was largely the same. Across the North, Democrats were swept out of office.

2. According to Sundquist (1983: 44), the Democratic caucus was even weaker than its seat share would indicate, as their candidate for Speaker received a mere 17 votes.

3. Both the American Party and the Free-Soil Party had previously won seats in the House, and the latter nominated Martin Van Buren as its presidential candidate in 1848.

4. Cohen, Karol, Noel, and Zaller (2008) examine the prior political experience of the 21 anti-Nebraska candidates in Ohio who won in the 1854 election. While that analysis was motivated by different considerations, those scholars' findings suggest that a majority of the candidates had some type of prior elective experience.

5. We focus on Illinois, Michigan, and Wisconsin in our analysis, because candidates ran as Republicans, rather than as part of a general anti-Nebraska coalition, in each of these states.

6. While five of the Republican candidates were incumbents who switched parties, seven of the remaining nine experienced candidates served at least one term in the state legislature, while the other two candidates served in other lower-level offices. There is some anecdotal evidence that prior legislative experience was viewed as more valuable than other forms of prior electoral experience. James H. Woodworth's (R-IL) most recent electoral experience prior to being elected to the 34th Congress (1855–57) was as mayor of Chicago, a position he held from 1848 to 1850. Before serving as mayor, however, Woodworth spent a total of eight years in the state legislature, with five years of service in the Illinois House of Representatives and three years in the state senate. The *Chicago Tribune* (September 22, 1854) only noted Woodworth's legislative experience in its coverage of his nomination: "He is not without legislative experience, either, having served a term in the Senate of this State, where he was noted for his practical business talent."

7. See Jacobson and Carson (2016) for more recent evidence of strategic candidate behavior in the contemporary era.

8. A number of different scenarios presented challenges for election-to-election comparisons. In some states, either the local parties simply did not adopt the national party labels, or the main scope of conflict was defined by factional competition within the same party. It was also not uncommon for only one party, typically the Jacksonians, to be formally organized. When this occurred, typically only one candidate ran under a party label, while any other challengers ran without a party label.

9. Our coding rules regarding party affiliation for the construct of this variable are the same as those used for the two-party vote.

10. In 1832, Henry Clay appeared on the ballot in Ohio but not in Pennsylvania, where the non-Democratic candidate was the Anti-Masonic candidate William Wirt.

11. Our substantive interpretations remain the same if we estimate an ordered logistic regression model instead of using a linear model.

12. The emergence of third parties is a common issue when studying congres-

sional elections in this era. Overall, only 3.9 percent of elections held during this period featured a third-party candidate who won or was the opposition candidate. In these cases, we attempted to determine whether the third-party candidate either caucused with one of the major parties or later affiliated with a major party in a later Congress or election. Our results are not contingent on including these cases.

13. One exception is elections in the Southern states during the 1850s, which typically featured a Democrat and an American Party candidate. Although the American Party is usually treated as a third party, it is effectively one of the two major parties in congressional elections in the South. We therefore treat the American Party as a major party in these races.

14. We were not able to collect this measure in cases where district lines cross county borders or where there are multiple districts within a county. The first case is quite rare in this period, and the latter typically occurs in urban areas.

15. Furthermore, the inclusion of the turnout covariate increases the overall fit of all three models.

CHAPTER 5

1. Prior to 1872, congressional elections were held not on the same day in November but at various points before and after that month (see Engstrom 2012). Connecticut was one of several states that held their elections in the post-November period. We examine the consequences of differential election timing in greater detail in chapter 6.

2. At the time of Edwards's election, Connecticut governors only served one-year terms. He won his first gubernatorial election in 1833, lost his reelection bid in 1834, and went on to win three more terms before retiring from politics.

3. The election of 1842–43, which was the first election after the 1840s reapportionment in which the House actually decreased in size, was the only election where less than 50 percent of incumbents ran for reelection.

4. MacKenzie (2015) finds a similar increase in the number of years members of the House spent in politics during their pre-congressional careers.

5. Swain et al. (2000) include a fifth category of turnover: unknown cases. They describe the unknown category as "those cases of turnover for which the exact cause could not be determined. Most unknown cases involved situations where members either failed to gain nomination or retired" (437). For our empirical analyses, we have tried our best to identify the fate of the incumbent legislators who fall into the unknown category. Over the time period we examine, 1820 to 1888, there were 1,084 cases in the unknown category. We used Dubin's (1998) collection of congressional election returns to identify whether the incumbent was a candidate for reelection. Overall, we found 145 cases where the incumbent ran unsuccessfully

for reelection, 2 cases where the incumbent was reelected, 1 case of resignation, and 1 instance of the incumbent going to the Senate. The most common outcome, comprising 922 cases in total, was the incumbent not running for reelection. We were not able to identify the fate of the incumbent in the remaining 13 cases.

6. Fiorina, Rohde, and Wissel (1975) had previously noted the impact of redistricting on overall legislative turnover. However, Engstrom's 2013 analysis focuses on the decision of individual legislators and examines all instances of redistricting, rather than only reapportionment.

7. Following Engstrom's coding rule (2013: 68), we do not code the former Confederate states as having drawn new districts when they rejoined the Union.

8. We are not the first to observe that legislative turnover has not followed a single downward trend since the early Congresses. Indeed, the response to Polsby 1968 by Fiorina, Rohde, and Wissel (1975: 31) was notable partly because it demonstrated that congressional scholars "should not assume that turnover . . . has been declining monotonically since 1800."

9. Aldrich (2011) adopts the same approach to examine how the creation of party electoral organizations influences voter turnout.

10. The Democratic Party was first organized in Ohio by 1828, in New York and Virginia by 1832, and in Pennsylvania by 1836 (Chambers and Davis 1978).

11. These analyses utilize data from Inter-university Consortium for Political and Social Research and McKibbin 1997.

CHAPTER 6

1. See Rogowski and Gibson 2015 for evidence of electoral accountability prior to the adoption of the secret ballot.

2. Furthermore, the structure of the party ballot itself should make it difficult to find *any* evidence of candidate-specific effects, which implies that the nineteenth century represents a particularly difficult test case.

3. Democrats started a congressional campaign committee not long after the Republicans. Kolodny (1998) argues that the Democrats' decision was motivated not by countering a presidential candidate but by wanting to limit a Republican resource advantage.

4. See Carson and Roberts 2013: 30–35 for a more detailed discussion of this point.

5. RDD exploits the "as-if" random assignment of winners and losers in close elections to obtain an estimate of the consequences of winning an election at time $t-1$ on outcomes at time t (Eggerset al. 2015; Lee 2008). The key theoretical and empirical assumption is that candidates on either side of the electoral threshold

(i.e., 50 percent) will not be systematically different, save for their treatment status (Caughey and Sekhon 2011; Lee 2008). We follow the standard convention for RDD analyses and only include those races in which the previous margin of victory was less than five points. See Carson and Sievert 2017 for a more detailed discussion about this analysis and for tests of whether the empirical assumptions of RDD models are met for these data.

6. After the 1860 presidential election, a *New York Times* correspondent reported that local Democratic Party officials in California pointed to candidate recruitment as a key factor in Abraham Lincoln's narrow victory over Stephen Douglas in that state. The California Democrats contended that if they had "placed in nomination for municipal and legislative offices, as good, as trusty citizens as the Republicans chose, they would have carried the State" for Douglas (*New York Times*, December 26, 1860).

7. The reported estimates are from a quadratic specification where the cutoff is a margin of victory of less than five percentage points. Our substantive interpretation remains the same if we use a local linear or higher order polynomial specification. Similarly, the results are the same when we employ bandwidths of 1 and 2.5 instead of a bandwidth of 5.

8. We calculated this figure by identifying the number of races where the Democratic vote share was between 47 and 53 percent, which was 291 elections, and dividing this by the total number of races, which was 560.

9. While a type of coattail effect might occur in midterm years when congressional and gubernatorial elections coincided, these cases should not result in a nationalizing effect.

10. Given that presidential candidates were at the top of the party ballot and that voter turnout in this era was higher in presidential years (Engstrom 2012), the assumption that nationalization was, on average, greater during presidential election years is theoretically justified. This is not to say that some midterm elections, such as that in 1862, were not also nationalized.

11. In an effort to facilitate the interpretation of the resulting interactions, we centered our measure of lagged congressional vote and presidential vote at 50.

12. For other examples of using historical data to test theories about modern politics, see Engstrom 2012; Finocchiaro and Jenkins 2016; MacKenzie 2015.

CHAPTER 7

1. As we discussed in chapter 6, congressional elections prior to the 1870s were held on different dates and sometimes even months apart, based on the preferences of the states that were responsible for scheduling them.

2. Mayhew (1974: 81–82) emphasizes, "[I]f a group of planners sat down and tried to design a pair of American national assemblies with the goal of serving members' electoral needs year in and year out, they would be hard pressed to improve on what exists."

3. Speculating on why their findings differ from those of Miller and Stokes (1963), Ansolabehere and Jones (2010) explain that they have a more representative sample of constituents across districts and that the issues they focused on in their survey-based design were more likely to be familiar to voters.

4. In contrast to Polsby (1968), Bogue et al. (1976) found that the median length of service in the early nineteenth century was more comparable to the late nineteenth and early twentieth centuries.

5. While there are alternative measures of "major" or "landmark" legislation in Congress (e.g., Clinton and Lapinski 2006), Stathis (2002) covers more of the time period we examine than do other available options. Furthermore, other studies of historical elections and congressional development rely on the Stathis list for similar reasons (Clarke, Jenkins, and Lowande, 2017; Lynch and Madonna 2013).

6. Ladd (1970: 151) argues that the Republican Party became the "party of business" due to "war-created ties" and its majority status throughout much of the late nineteenth century.

7. See the House roll-call file for the 42nd Congress, http://voteview.com (accessed August 28, 2017).

8. See Carson and Sievert 2017 for an analysis of reverse coattails under the party ballot.

9. Almost half of the votes in favor of the tariff reform came from Democrats, but less than a third of the votes against the bill were cast by Democratic legislators.

10. For example, the final session of the 43rd Congress met December 7, 1874, through March 3, 1875. The first session of the 44th Congress started on March 5, 1875, only two days after the close of the 43rd Congress.

11. Since margin is not a discrete variable, we calculated the marginal effect as the difference in the predicted probability between the covariate's first and third quartiles.

12. During the 1840s and 1850s, around one-third of congressional elections were held after March 3, which was the final day of the legislative session.

13. While the last category includes both legislators who ran for reelection and legislators who retired, we included them in a single, "pending" category for two reasons. First, the number of legislators in this category is often quite small, and further stratification would reduce the number of observations even more. Second, our argument is that, on average, these legislators will look more like returning members than lame-duck legislators, and this coding decision actually works against finding evidence in support of our theoretical expectations.

14. Thomas Clingman (Whig-NC) was the lone Southern representative to vote in favor of repealing the gag order. Clingman did run for reelection but was defeated, despite having won by almost 14 percentage points in the previous election.

CHAPTER 8

1. As we discuss in the preceding chapters, various institutional features (e.g., ballot placement, differential election timing, and lame-duck sessions) made it possible to hold individual legislators accountable prior to the adoption of the Australian ballot. Nevertheless, the passage of the secret ballot made it easier for constituents to reward or punish legislators at the polls.

2. Prior to the adoption of the Australian ballot in the late nineteenth century, political parties, rather than individual states, printed and distributed ballots for voters to use when they went to the polls. These party-controlled ballots provided the parties with considerable influence over access to the ballot (Carson and Roberts 2013). For instance, parties could regulate who participated in the elections as well as monitor who individual citizens were voting for when they showed up at the polls on Election Day. This arrangement made voters, candidates, and elected officials more dependent on the parties in a way not found in the contemporary electoral system.

3. Such arguments also support the claim that legislative self-interest and the accompanying policy consequences are not confined to the modern era. This is consistent with Aldrich's (2001: 255) own impressions of Mayhew's work 25 years after it was published: "The lesson was simple: The electoral imperative had shaped the design of the institution, because it is the Members themselves who get to shape the inner workings of their institution. Whenever opportunity arises to modify that design, Members would, naturally, choose from the set of possible changes those that are more likely to make the electoral connection tighter."

References

Abramowitz, Alan. 1975. "Name Familiarity, Reputation, and the Incumbency Effect in a Congressional Election." *Western Political Quarterly* 28 (4): 668–84.

Albright, Spencer D. 1942. *The American Ballot.* Washington, DC: American Council on Public Affairs.

Aldrich, John H. 2001. "Congress: The Electoral Connection: Reflections on Its First Quarter-Century." *PS: Political Science and Politics* 34 (2): 255–56.

Aldrich, John H. 2011. *Why Parties: A Second Look.* Chicago: University of Chicago Press.

Alexander, De Alva Stanwood. 1916. *History and Procedure of the House of Representatives.* Boston: Houghton Mifflin.

Alford, John R. and John R. Hibbing. 1981. "Increased Incumbency Advantage in the House." *The Journal of Politics* 43 (4): 1042–61.

Alston, Lee J., Jeffery A. Jenkins, and Tomas Nonnenmacher. 2006. "Who Should Govern Congress? Access to Power and the Salary Grab of 1873." *Journal of Economic History* 66 (3): 674–706.

Alvarez, R. Michael, and Jason L. Saving. 1997. "Deficits, Democrats, and Distributive Benefits: Congressional Elections and the Pork Barrel in the 1980s." *Political Research Quarterly* 50 (4): 809–31.

Ansolabehere, Stephen, John Mark Hansen, Shigeo Hirano, and James M. Snyder Jr. 2010. "More Democracy: The Direct Primary and Competition in U.S. Elections." *Studies in American Political Development* 24 (2): 190–205.

Ansolabehere, Stephen, and Philip E. Jones. 2010. "Constituents' Responses to Congressional Roll-Call Voting." *American Journal of Political Science* 54 (3): 583–97.

Ansolabehere, Stephen, James M. Snyder Jr., and Charles Stewart III. 2000. "Old Voters, New Voters, and the Personal Vote: Using Redistricting to Measure the Incumbency Advantage." *American Journal of Political Science* 44 (1): 17–34.

Ansolabehere, Stephen, James M. Snyder Jr., and Charles Stewart III. 2001. "Candidate Positioning in U.S. House Elections." *American Journal of Political Science* 45 (1): 136–159.

Anzia, Sarah F. 2012. "Partisan Power Play: The Origins of Local Election Timing as an American Political Institution." *Studies in American Political Development* 26 (1): 24–49.

Arnold, R. Douglas. 1990. *The Logic of Congressional Action*. New Haven, CT: Yale University Press.

Ashworth, Scott. 2012. "Electoral Accountability: Recent Theoretical and Empirical Work." *Annual Review of Political Science* 15: 183–201.

Balinski, Michel L., and H. Peyton Young. 2001. *Fair Representation: Meeting the Ideal of One Man, One Vote*. 2nd ed. Washington, DC: Brookings Institution.

Banks, Jeffrey S., and D. Roderick Kiewiet. 1989. "Explaining Patterns of Candidate Competition in Congressional Elections." *American Journal of Political Science* 33 (4): 997–1015.

Baughman, John, and Timothy Nokken. 2011. "The Electoral Connection and Participation on House Roll Call Votes, 1819–1921." Paper presented at the Annual Meeting of the American Political Science Association.

Benedict, Michael Les. 1985. "Factionalism and Representation: Some Insight from the Nineteenth-Century United States." *Social Science History* 9 (4): 361–98.

Bensel, Richard F. 2003. "The American Ballot Box: Law, Identity, and the Polling Place in the Mid-Nineteenth Century." *Studies in American Political Development* 17 (1): 1–27.

Bensel, Richard F. 2004. *The American Ballot Box in the Mid-Nineteenth Century*. New York: Cambridge University Press.

Berglof, Eric, and Howard Rosenthal. 2005. "The Political Origin of Finance: The Case of U.S Bankruptcy Law." Unpublished manuscript, Princeton University.

Berglof, Erik, and Howard Rosenthal. 2007. "Power Rejected: Congress and Bankruptcy in the Early Republic." In *Process, Party, and Policy Making: New Advances in the Study of the History of Congress*, eds. David W. Brady and Mathew D. McCubbins. Stanford: Stanford University Press.

Bianco, William, David Spence, and John Wilkerson. 1996. "The Electoral Connection in the Early Congress: The Case of the Compensation Act of 1816." *American Journal of Political Science* 40 (1): 145–71.

Bickers, Kenneth N., and Robert M. Stein. 1994. "Congressional Elections and the Pork Barrel." *Journal of Politics* 56 (2): 377–99.

Bickers, Kenneth N., and Robert M. Stein. 1996. "The Electoral Dynamics of the Federal Pork Barrel." *American Journal of Political Science* 40 (4): 1300–1326.

Bogue, Allan G., Jerome M. Clubb, Carroll R. McKibbin, and Santa A. Traugott. 1976. "Members of the House of Representatives and the Process of Modernization, 1789–1960." *Journal of American History* 63 (2): 275–302.

Bovitz, Gregory L., and Jamie L. Carson. 2006. "Position-Taking and Electoral Accountability in the U.S. House of Representatives." *Political Research Quarterly* 59 (2): 297–312.

Box-Steffensmeier, Janet, Laura Arnold, and Christopher Zorn. 1997. "The Strategic Timing of Position Taking in Congress: A Study of the North American Free Trade Agreement." *American Political Science Review* 91 (2): 324–38.

Brady, David. 1973. *Congressional Voting in a Partisan Era*. Lawrence: University Press of Kansas.

Brady, David. 1988. *Critical Elections and Congressional Policy Making*. Stanford: Stanford University Press.

Brady, David, Kara Buckley, and Douglas Rivers. 1999. "The Roots of Careerism in the U.S. House of Representatives." *Legislative Studies Quarterly* 24 (4): 489–510.

Brady, David, Judith Goldstein, and Daniel Kessler. 2002. "Does Party Matter? An Historical Test Using Senate Tariff Votes in Three Institutional Settings." *Journal of Law, Economics, and Organization* 18 (1): 140–53.

Broockman, David E. 2009. "Do Congressional Candidates have Reverse Coattails? Evidence from a Regression Discontinuity Design." *Political Analysis* 17 (4): 418–34.

Burnham, Walter Dean. 1965. "The Changing Shape of the American Political Universe." *American Political Science Review* 59 (1): 7–28.

Cain, Bruce, John Ferejohn, and Morris Fiorina. 1987. *The Personal Vote: Constituency Service and Electoral Independence*. Cambridge, MA: Harvard University Press.

Canes-Wrone, Brandice, David Brady, and John Cogan. 2002. "Out of Step, Out of Office: Electoral Accountability and House Members' Voting." *American Political Science Review* 96 (1): 127–40.

Canon, David T., and Charles H. Stewart, III. 2001. "The Evolution of the Committee System in Congress." In *Congress Reconsidered*, ed. Lawrence C. Dodd and Bruce I. Oppenheimer, 163–89. 7th ed. Washington, DC: CQ Press.

Carpenter, Daniel, and Colin D. Moore. 2014. "When Canvassers Became Activists: Antislavery Petitioning and the Political Mobilization of American Women." *American Political Science Review* 108 (3): 479–98.

Carpenter, Daniel, and Benjamin Schneer. 2015. "Party Formation through Petitions: The Whigs and the Bank War of 1832–1834." *Studies in American Political Development* 29 (2): 213–34.

Carson, Jamie L. 2005. "Strategy, Selection, and Candidate Competition in U.S. House and Senate Elections." *Journal of Politics* 67 (1): 1–28.

Carson, Jamie L., Michael H. Crespin, Jeffery A. Jenkins, and Ryan J. Vander Wielen. 2004. "Shirking in the Contemporary Congress: A Reappraisal." *Political Analysis* 12 (2): 176–79.

Carson, Jamie L., and Erik J. Engstrom. 2005. "Assessing the Electoral Connection: Evidence from the Early United States." *American Journal of Political Science* 49 (4): 746–57.

Carson, Jamie L., Erik J. Engstrom, and Jason M. Roberts. 2006. "Redistricting, Candidate Entry, and the Politics of Nineteenth-Century U.S. House Elections." *American Journal of Political Science* 50 (2): 283–93.

Carson, Jamie L., Erik J. Engstrom, and Jason M. Roberts. 2007. "Candidate Quality, the Personal Vote, and the Incumbency Advantage in Congress." *American Political Science Review* 101 (2): 289–301.

Carson, Jamie L., Charles J. Finocchiaro, and David W. Rohde. 2010. "Consensus, Conflict, and Partisanship in House Decision Making: A Bill-Level Examination of Committee and Floor Behavior." *Congress and the Presidency* 37 (3): 231–53.

Carson, Jamie L., and M. V. Hood III. 2014. "Candidates, Competition, and the Partisan Press: Congressional Elections in the Antebellum Era." *American Politics Research* 42 (5): 760–83.

Carson, Jamie L., and Jeffery Jenkins. 2011. "Examining the Electoral Connection across Time." *Annual Review of Political Science* 14: 25–46.

Carson, Jamie L., Jeffery A. Jenkins, David W. Rohde, and Mark A. Souva. 2001. "The Impact of National Tides and District-Level Effects on Electoral Outcomes: The U.S. Congressional Elections of 1862–63." *American Journal of Political Science* 45 (4): 887–98.

Carson, Jamie L., Gregory Koger, Matthew J. Lebo, and Everett Young. 2010. "The Electoral Costs of Party Loyalty in Congress." *American Journal of Political Science* 54 (3): 598–616.

Carson, Jamie L., and Jason M. Roberts. 2005. "Strategic Politicians and U.S. House Elections, 1874–1914." *The Journal of Politics* 67 (2): 474–96.

Carson, Jamie L., and Jason M. Roberts. 2013. *Ambition, Competition, and Electoral Reform: The Politics of Congressional Elections across Time.* Ann Arbor: University of Michigan Press.

Carson, Jamie L., and Joel Sievert. 2015. "Electoral Reform and Changes in Legislative Behavior: Adoption of the Secret Ballot in Congressional Elections." *Legislative Studies Quarterly* 40 (1): 83–110.

Carson, Jamie L., and Joel Sievert. 2017. "Congressional Candidates in the Era of Party Ballots." *Journal of Politics* 79 (2): 534–45.

Caughey, Devin, and Jasjeet S. Sekhon. 2011. "Elections and the Regression Discontinuity Design: Lessons from Close US House Races, 1942–2008." *Political Analysis* 19 (4): 385–408.

Chambers, William N., and Philip C. Davis. 1978. "Party Competition and Mass Participation: The Case of the Democratizing Party System, 1824–1852." In *The History of American Electoral Behaviour*, 174–97. Princeton: Princeton University Press.

Clark, Champ. 1920. *My Quarter Century of American Politics*. Vol. 1. New York: Harper.

Clarke, Andrew J., Jeffery A. Jenkins, and Kenneth S. Lowande. 2017. "Tariff Politics and Congressional Elections: Exploring the Cannon Thesis." *Journal of Theoretical Politics* 29 (3): 382–414.

Clausen, Aage. 1973. *How Congressmen Decide: A Policy Focus*. New York: St. Martin's.

Clemens, Austin C., Michael H. Crespin, and Charles J. Finocchiaro. 2015. "The Political Geography of Distributive Politics." *Legislative Studies Quarterly* 40 (1): 111–36.

Clinton, Joshua, and John Lapinski. 2006. "Measuring Legislative Accomplishment, 1877–1994." *American Journal of Political Science* 50 (1): 232–49.

Cohen, Marty, David Karol, Hans Noel, and John Zaller. 2008. *The Party Decides: Presidential Nominations before and after Reform*. Chicago: University of Chicago Press.

Conybeare, John A. C. 1991. "Voting for Protection: An Electoral Model of Tariff Policy." *International Organization* 45 (1): 57–81.

Cooper, Joseph, and Cheryl D. Young. 1989. "Bill Introduction in the Nineteenth Century: A Study of Institutional Change." *Legislative Studies Quarterly* 14 (1): 67–105.

Cover, Albert D., and Bruce S. Brumberg. 1982. "Baby Books and Ballots: The Impact of Congressional Mail on Constituency Opinion." *American Political Science Review* 76 (2): 347–59.

Cox, Gary W., and Jonathan N. Katz. 1996. "Why Did the Incumbency Advantage in US House Elections Grow?" *American Journal of Political Science* 40 (2): 478–97.

Cox, Gary W., and Jonathan N. Katz. 2002. *Elbridge Gerry's Salamander: The Electoral Consequences of the Reapportionment Revolution*. New York: Cambridge University Press.

Crook, Sara Brandes, and John R. Hibbing. 1997. "A Not-So-Distant Mirror: the 17th Amendment and Congressional Change." *American Political Science Review* 91 (4): 845–53.

Dallinger, Frederick W. 1897. *Nomination for Elective Office*. Harvard Historical Studies 4. New York: Longmans, Green, and Co.

Deering, Christopher J., and Steven S. Smith. 1997. *Committees in Congress*. 3rd ed. Washington, DC: CQ Press.

Desposato, Scott W., and John R. Petrocik. 2003. "The Variable Incumbency Advantage: New Voters, Redistricting, and the Personal Vote." *American Journal of Political Science* 47 (1): 18–32.

Dodd, Lawrence C. 1978. "Review of *Congress: The Electoral Connection* by David R. Mayhew." *American Political Science Review* 72 (2): 693–95.

Dubin, Michael J. 1998. *United States Congressional Elections, 1788–1997: The Official Results of the Elections of the 1st through 105th Congresses.* Jefferson, NC: McFarland.

Dubin, Michael J. 2003. *United States Gubernatorial Elections, 1776–1860.* Jefferson, NC: McFarland.

Eggers, Andrew C., Anthony Fowler, Jens Hainmueller, Andrew B. Hall, and James M. Snyder. 2015. "On the Validity of the Regression Discontinuity Design for Estimating Electoral Effects: New Evidence from over 40,000 Close Races." *American Journal of Political Science* 59 (1): 259–74.

Engstrom, Erik J. 2006. "Stacking the States, Stacking the House: The Politics of Congressional Redistricting in the Nineteenth Century." *American Political Science Review* 100 (3): 419–28.

Engstrom, Erik J. 2012. "The Rise and Decline of Turnout in Congressional Elections: Electoral Institutions, Competition, and Strategic Mobilization." *American Journal of Political Science* 56 (2): 373–86.

Engstrom, Erik J. 2013. *Partisan Gerrymandering and the Construction of American Democracy.* Ann Arbor: University of Michigan Press.

Engstrom, Erik J., and Samuel Kernell. 2005. "Manufactured Responsiveness: The Impact of State Electoral Laws on Unified Party Control of the Presidency and House of Representatives, 1840–1940." *American Journal of Political Science* 49 (3): 531–49.

Engstrom, Erik J., and Samuel Kernell. 2014. *Party Ballots, Reform, and the Transformation of America's Electoral System.* New York: Cambridge University Press.

Epstein, David, and Sharyn O'Halloran. 1996. "The Partisan Paradox and the U.S. Tariff, 1877–1934." *International Organization* 50 (2): 301–24.

Erikson, Robert S. 1971. "The Electoral Impact of Congressional Roll Call Voting." *American Political Science Review* 65 (4): 1018–32.

Evans, Eldon Cobb. 1917. *A History of the Australian Ballot System in the United States.* Chicago: University of Chicago Press.

Fearon, James D. 1999. "Electoral Accountability and the Control of Politicians: Selecting Good Types versus Sanctioning Poor Performance." In *Democracy, Accountability, and Representation*, ed. Adam Przeworski, Susan Stokes, and Bernard Manian, 55–97. New York: Cambridge University Press.

Feldman, Paul, and James Jondrow. 1984. "Congressional Elections and Local Federal Spending." *American Journal of Political Science* 28 (1): 147–64.

Fenno, Richard F., Jr. 1973. *Congressmen in Committees.* Boston: Little, Brown and Co.

Fenno, Richard F., Jr. 1978. *Home Style: House Members in Their Districts.* Glenview, IL: Scott Foresman.

Finocchiaro, Charles J. 2005. "Credit-Claiming in the Partisan Era: An Exploration of Private Legislation in the U.S. House." Paper presented at the Annual Meeting of the American Political Science Association.

Finocchiaro, Charles J. 2006. "Party Politics, Civil War Pensions, and the Development of the U.S. Congress." Paper presented at the Annual Meeting of the American Political Science Association.

Finocchiaro, Charles J. 2015. "The Public Buildings Boom: Distributive and Partisan Politics in the Modernizing Congress." Paper presented at the Congress and History Conference at Vanderbilt University, Nashville, TN.

Finocchiaro, Charles J. n.d. *Of Pork Barrels and Personalism: The Nineteenth-Century Roots of the Modern American Congress.* Unpublished manuscript.

Finocchiaro, Charles J., and Jeffery A. Jenkins. 2016. "Distributive Politics, the Electoral Connection, and the Antebellum U.S. Congress: The Case of Military Service Pensions." *Journal of Theoretical Politics* 28 (2): 192–224.

Finocchiaro, Charles J., and Scott A. MacKenzie. 2018. "Making Washington Work: Legislative Entrepreneurship and the Personal Vote from the Gilded Age to the Great Depression." *American Journal of Political Science* 62 (1): 113–31.

Fiorina, Morris P. 1974. *Representatives, Roll Calls, and Constituencies.* Boston: D.C. Heath.

Fiorina, Morris P. 1989. *Congress: Keystone of the Washington Establishment.* 2nd ed. New Haven, CT: Yale University Press.

Fiorina, Morris P., David W. Rohde, and Peter Wissel. 1975. "Historical Change in House Turnover." In *Congress in Change,* ed. Norman Ornstein, 24–57. New York: Praeger.

Foner, Eric. 1995. *Free Soil, Free Labor, Free Men: The Ideology of the Republican Party before the Civil War.* New York: Oxford University Press.

Formisano, Ronald P. 1974. "Deferential-Participant Politics: The Early Republic's Political Culture, 1789–1840." *American Political Science Review* 68 (2): 473–87.

Fowler, Anthony. 2015. "A Bayesian Explanation for Incumbency Advantage." Unpublished Manuscript, University of Chicago.

Fox, Richard L., and Jennifer L. Lawless. 2005. "To Run or Not to Run for Office: Explaining Nascent Political Ambition." *American Journal of Political Science* 49 (3): 642–59.

Froman, Lewis A., Jr. 1963. *Congressmen and Their Constituencies.* Chicago: Rand McNally.

Gaddie, Ronald Keith, and Charles S. Bullock III. 2000. *Elections to Open Seats in the U.S. House: Where the Action Is.* Lanham: Rowman and Littlefield.

Gaines, Brian J., and Timothy P. Nokken. 2001. "The Presidential Shadow on Midterm House Elections: Presidential Support, Presidential Agendas, and Seat Loss." Paper presented at the Annual Meeting of the Midwest Political Science Association.

Gamm, Gerald, and Kenneth Shepsle. 1989. "Emergence of Legislative Institutions: Standing Committees in the House and Senate, 1810–1825." *Legislative Studies Quarterly* 14 (1): 39–66.

Garand, James C., and Donald A. Gross. 1984. "Changes in the Vote Margins for Congressional Candidates: A Specification of Historical Trends." *American Political Science Review* 78 (1): 17–30.

Gartner, Scott S., and Gary M. Segura. 2008. "All Politics Are Still Local: The Iraq War and the 2006 Midterm Elections." *PS: Political Science and Politics* 41 (1): 95–100.

Gienapp, William E. 1986. "Who Voted for Lincoln?" In *Abraham Lincoln and the American Political Tradition*, 50–97.

Goodman, Craig, and Timothy P. Nokken. 2004. "Lame-Duck Legislators and Consideration of the Ship Subsidy Bill of 1922." *American Politics Research* 32 (4): 465–89.

Grimmer, Justin, Solomon Messing, and Sean J. Westwood. 2012. "How Words and Money Cultivate a Personal Vote: The Effect of Legislator Credit Claiming on Constituent Credit Allocation." *American Political Science Review* 106 (4): 703–19.

Grose, Christian R., Neil Malhotra, and Robert Parks Van Houweling. 2015. "Explaining Explanations: How Legislators Explain Their Policy Positions and How Citizens React." *American Journal of Political Science* 59 (3): 724–43.

Grose, Christian R., and Bruce I. Oppenheimer. 2007. "The Iraq War, Partisanship, and Candidate Attributes: Variation in Partisan Swing in the 2006 U.S. House Elections." *Legislative Studies Quarterly* 32 (4): 531–57.

Gross, Donald A., and James C. Garand. 1984. "The Vanishing Marginals, 1824–1980." *The Journal of Politics* 46 (1): 224–37.

Hansen, John Mark. 1990. "Taxation and the Political Economy of the Tariff." *International Organization* 44 (4): 527–51.

Herrick, Rebekah, Michael K. Moore, and John R. Hibbing. 1994. "Unfastening the Electoral Connection: the Behavior of US Representatives when Reelection is No Longer a Factor." *The Journal of Politics* 56 (1): 214–27.

Hollibaugh, Gary E., Lawrence S. Rothenberg, and Kristin K. Rulison. 2013. "Does It Really Hurt to Be Out of Step?" *Political Research Quarterly* 66 (4): 856–67.

Holt, Michael F. 1978. *The Political Crisis of the 1850s.* John Wiley & Sons.

Holt, Michael F. 1992. *Political Parties and American Political Development from the Age of Jackson to the Age of Lincoln*. Baton Rouge: Louisiana State University Press.

Huckabee, David C. 1989. "Reelection Rates of House Incumbents: 1790–1988." Washington, DC: Congressional Research Service, Library of Congress.

Inter-university Consortium for Political and Social Research and Carroll McKibbin. 1997. *Roster of United States Congressional Officeholders and Biographical Characteristics of Members of the United States Congress, 1789–1996: Merged Data*. ICPSR 07803-v10. Ann Arbor, MI: Inter-university Consortium for Political and Social Research. https://doi.org/10.3886/ICPSR07803.v10

Irwin, Douglas A. 2006. "Antebellum Tariff Politics: Coalition Formation and Shifting Regional Interests." Unpublished manuscript, Dartmouth College.

Jacobson, Gary C. 1987. "The Marginals Never Vanished: Incumbency and Competition in Elections to the U.S. House of Representatives, 1952–1982. *American Journal of Political Science* 31 (1): 126–41.

Jacobson, Gary C. 1989. "Strategic Politicians and the Dynamics of U.S. House Elections, 1946–86." *American Political Science Review* 83 (3): 773–93.

Jacobson, Gary C. 1993a. "Deficit-Cutting Politics and Congressional Elections." *Political Science Quarterly* 108 (3): 375–402.

Jacobson, Gary C. 1993b. "Getting the Details Right: A Comment on 'Changing Meanings of Electoral Marginality in U.S. House Elections, 1824–1978.'" *Political Research Quarterly* 46 (1): 49–54.

Jacobson, Gary C. 2007. "Referendum: The 2006 Midterm Congressional Elections." *Political Science Quarterly* 122 (1): 1–24.

Jacobson, Gary C. 2015. "It's Nothing Personal: The Decline of the Incumbency Advantage in US House Elections." *The Journal of Politics* 77 (3): 861–73.

Jacobson, Gary C. 2017. "The Electoral Connection, Then and Now." In *Governing in a Polarized Age: Elections, Parties, and Political Representation in America*, ed. Alan Gerber and Eric Schickler, 35–64. New York: Cambridge University Press.

Jacobson, Gary C., and Jamie L. Carson. 2016. *The Politics of Congressional Elections*. 9th ed. Lanham: Rowman and Littlefield.

Jacobson, Gary C., and Samuel Kernell. 1983. *Strategy and Choice in Congressional Elections*. 2nd ed. New Haven, CT: Yale University Press.

Jenkins, Jeffery A. 1998. "Property Rights and the Emergence of Standing Committee Dominance in the Nineteenth-Century House." *Legislative Studies Quarterly* 23 (4): 493–519.

Jenkins, Jeffery A., and Michael C. Munger. 2003. "Investigating the Incidence of Killer Amendments in Congress." *Journal of Politics* 65 (2): 498–517.

Jenkins, Jeffery A., and Timothy P. Nokken. 2008a. "Legislative Shirking in the Pre-Twentieth Amendment Era: Presidential Influence, Party Power, and

Lame-Duck Sessions of Congress, 1877–1933." *Studies in American Political Development* 22 (1): 111–40.

Jenkins, Jeffery A., and Timothy P. Nokken. 2008b. "Partisanship, the Electoral Connection, and Lame-Duck Sessions of Congress, 1877–2006." *Journal of Politics* 70 (2): 450–65.

Jenkins, Jeffery A., and Brian R. Sala. 1998. "The Spatial Theory of Voting and the Presidential Election of 1824." *American Journal of Political Science* 42 (4): 1157–79.

Jenkins, Jeffery A., Eric Schickler, and Jamie L. Carson. 2004. "Constituency Cleavages and Congressional Parties: Measuring Homogeneity and Polarization, 1857–1913." *Social Science History* 28 (4): 537–73.

Jenkins, Jeffery A., and Charles Stewart III. 2001. "Sophisticated Behavior and Speakership Elections: The Elections of 1849 and 1855–56." Paper presented at the Annual Meeting of the Midwest Political Science Association.

Jenkins, Jeffery A., and Charles Stewart III. 2003. "The Gag Rule, Congressional Politics, and the Rise of Anti-Slavery Popular Politics." Paper presented at the Annual Meeting of the Midwest Political Science Association.

Jenkins, Jeffery A., and Charles H. Stewart III. 2012. *Fighting for the Speakership: The House and the Rise of Party Government*. Princeton: Princeton University Press.

Johannes, John R., and John C. McAdams. 1981. "The Congressional Incumbency Effect: Is It Casework, Policy Compatibility, or Something Else? An Examination of the 1978 Election." *American Journal of Political Science* 25 (3): 512–42.

Johnson, Ronald N., and Gary D. Libecap. 1994. *The Federal Civil Service System and the Problem of Bureaucracy: The Economics and Politics of Institutional Change*. Chicago: University of Chicago Press.

Karol, David. 2007. "Has Polling Enhanced Representation? Unearthing Evidence from the Literary Digest Issue Polls." *Studies in American Political Development* 21 (1): 16–29.

Katz, Jonathan N., and Brian R. Sala. 1996. "Careerism, Committee Assignments, and the Electoral Connection." *American Political Science Review* 90 (1): 21–33.

Kernell, Samuel. 1977. "Toward Understanding 19th Century Congressional Careers: Ambition, Competition, and Rotation." *American Journal of Political Science* 21 (4): 669–93.

Kernell, Samuel. 1986. "The Early Nationalization of Political News in America." *Studies in American Political Development* 1 (1): 255–78.

Kernell, Samuel. 2003. "To Stay, to Quit, or to Move Up: Explaining the Growth of Careerism in the House of Representatives, 1878–1940." Paper presented at the Annual Meeting of the American Political Science Association.

Kernell, Samuel, and Gary C. Jacobson. 1987. "Congress and the Presidency as News in the Nineteenth Century." *Journal of Politics* 49 (4): 1016–35.

Kernell, Samuel, and Michael P. McDonald. 1999. "Congress and America's Political Development: The Transformation of the Post Office from Patronage to Service." *American Journal of Political Science* 43 (3): 792–811.

Key, V. O., Jr. 1954. "The Direct Primary and Party Structure: A Study of State Legislative Nominations." *American Political Science Review* 48 (1): 1–26.

Keyssar, Alexander. 2000. *The Right to Vote: The Contested History of Democracy in the United States.* New York: Basic Books.

King, Gary. 1991. "Constituency Service and Incumbency Advantage." *British Journal of Political Science* 21 (1): 119–28.

Kingdon, John W. 1989. *Congressmen's Voting Decisions.* 3rd ed. New York: Harper and Row.

Kolodny, Robin. 1998. *Pursuing Majorities: Congressional Campaign Committees in American Politics.* Norman: University of Oklahoma Press.

Kuklinski, James H. 1977. "District Competitiveness and Legislative Roll-Call Behavior: A Reassessment of the Marginality Hypothesis." *American Journal of Political Science* 21 (3): 627–38.

Ladd, Everett Carll. 1970. *American Political Parties: Social Change and Political Response.* New York: W. W. Norton.

Lee, David S. 2008. "Randomized Experiments from Non-random Selection in US House Elections." *Journal of Econometrics* 142 (2): 675–97.

Lee, Frances. 2016. *Insecure Majorities: Congress and the Perpetual Campaign.* Chicago: University of Chicago Press.

Lynch, Michael S., and Anthony J. Madonna. 2013. "Viva Voce: Implications from the Disappearing Voice Vote, 1865–1996." *Social Science Quarterly* 94 (2): 530–50.

MacKenzie, Scott A. 2014. "From Political Pathways to Legislative Folkways: Electoral Reform, Professionalization, and Representation in the US Senate." *Political Research Quarterly* 67 (4): 743–57.

MacKenzie, Scott A. 2015. "Life before Congress: Using Pre-congressional Experience to Assess Competing Explanations for Political Professionalism." *Journal of Politics* 77 (2): 505–18.

Madonna, Anthony. 2011. "Winning Coalition Formation in the U.S. Senate: The Effects of Legislative Decision Rules and Agenda Change." *American Journal of Political Science* 55 (2): 276–88.

Maestas, Cherie D., Sarah A. Fulton, L. Sandy Maisel, and Walter J. Stone. 2006. "When to Risk It? Institutions, Ambitions, and the Decision to Run for the U.S. House." *American Political Science Review* 100 (2): 195–208.

Mann, Thomas E., and Raymond Wolfinger. 1980. "Candidates and Parties in Congressional Elections." *American Political Science Review* 74 (3): 617–32.

Martis, Kenneth C. 1989. *The Historical Atlas of Political Parties in the United States, 1789–1989.* New York: Macmillan.

Matthews, Donald R., and James A. Stimson. 1975. *Yeas and Nays: Normal Decision-Making in the U.S. House of Representatives.* New York: Wiley.

Mayhew, David R. 1974. *Congress: The Electoral Connection.* New Haven, CT: Yale University Press.

Mayhew, David. 2001. "Observations on *Congress: The Electoral Connection* a Quarter Century after Writing It." *PS: Political Science and Politics* 34 (2): 251–52.

McCormick, Richard P. 1966. *The Second American Party System: Party Formation in the Jacksonian Era.* Chapel Hill: University of North Carolina Press.

McDonald, Michael P., and Samuel Popkin. 2001. "The Myth of the Vanishing Voter." *American Political Science Review* 95 (4): 963–74.

McIver, John P. 2006. "Congressional Bills and Resolutions: 1789–2000." In *Historical Statistics of the United States: Millennial Edition Online*, ed. Susan B. Carter, Scott S. Gartner, Michael R. Haines, Alan L. Olmstead, Richard Sutch, and Gavin Wright. New York: Cambridge University Press.

Meinke, Scott R. 2007. "Slavery, Partisanship, and Procedure in the U.S. House: The Gag Rule, 1836–1845." *Legislative Studies Quarterly* 32 (1): 33–57.

Meinke, Scott R. 2008. "Institutional Change and the Electoral Connection in the Senate: Revisiting the Effects of Direct Election." *Political Research Quarterly* 61 (3): 445–57.

Miller, Warren E., and Donald E. Stokes. 1963. "Constituency Influence in Congress." *American Political Science Review* 57 (1): 45–56.

Miller, William Lee. 1995. *Arguing about Slavery: John Quincy Adams and the Great Battle in the United States Congress.* New York: Vintage.

Niemi, Richard, Simon Jackman, and Laura Winsky. 1991. "Candidacies and Competitiveness in Multimember Districts." *Legislative Studies Quarterly* 16 (1): 91–109.

Nyhan, Brendan, Eric McGhee, John Sides, Seth Masket, and Steven Greene. 2012. "One Vote Out of Step? The Effects of Salient Roll Call Votes in the 2010 Election." *American Politics Research* 40 (5): 844–79.

Ostrogorski, Moisei. 1964. *Democracy and the Organization of Political Parties.* Vol. 2. New Brunswick, NJ: Transaction.

Pasley, Jeffrey L. 2001. *"The Tyranny of the Printers": Newspaper Politics in the Early American Republic.* Charlottesville: University of Virginia Press.

Pincus, Jonathan J. 1975. "Pressure Groups and the Patterns of Tariffs." *Journal of Political Economy* 83 (4): 757–78.

Pincus, Jonathan J. 1977. *Pressure Groups and Politics in Antebellum Tariffs.* New York: Columbia University Press.

Polsby, Nelson W. 1968. "The Institutionalization of the U.S. House of Representatives." *American Political Science Review* 62 (1): 144–68.

Poole, Keith T., and Howard Rosenthal. 2007. *Ideology and Congress*. New Brunswick, NJ: Transaction.

Powell, Lawrence N. 1973. "Rejected Republican Incumbents in the 1866 Congressional Nominating Conventions: A Study in Reconstruction Politics." *Civil War History* 19 (3): 219–37.

Price, H. Douglas. 1971. "The Congressional Career Then and Now." In *Congressional Behavior*, ed. Nelson Polsby, 14–27. New York: Random House.

Price, H. Douglas. 1975. "Congress and the Evolution of Legislative 'Professionalism.'" In *Congress in Change: Evolution and Reform*, ed. Norman J. Ornstein, 2–23. New York: Praeger.

Price, H. Douglas. 1998. "House Turnover and the Counterrevolution to Rotation in Office." In *Explorations in the Evolution of Congress*, by H. Douglas Price, ed. Nelson W. Polsby. Berkeley: Institute of Governmental Studies Press.

Prior, Markus. 2006. "The Incumbent in the Living Room: The Rise of Television and the Incumbency Advantage in U.S. House Elections." *Journal of Politics* 68 (3): 657–73.

Pritchard, Anita. 1986. "An Evaluation of CQ Presidential Support Scores: The Relationship between Election Results and Congressional Voting Decisions." *American Journal of Political Science* 30 (2): 480–95.

Ragsdale, Lyn, and John J. Theis III. 1997. "The Institutionalization of the American Presidency, 1924–92." *American Journal of Political Science* 41 (4): 1280–1318.

Reynolds, Andrew, and Marco Steenbergen. 2006. "How the World Votes: The Political Consequences of Ballot Design, Innovation, and Manipulation." *Electoral Studies* 25 (3): 570–98.

Reynolds, John F. 2006. *The Demise of the American Convention System, 1880—1911*. New York: Cambridge University Press.

Reynolds, John F., and Richard L. McCormick. 1986. "Outlawing 'Treachery': Split Tickets and Ballot Laws in New York and New Jersey, 1880–1910." *Journal of American History* 72 (4): 835–58.

Rogowski, Jon C. 2016. "Presidential Influence in an Era of Congressional Dominance." *American Political Science Review* 110 (2): 325–41.

Rogowski, Jon C., and Chris Gibson. 2015. "Returns to Sender? Legislative Accountability and the Expansion of the U.S. Postal System, 1876–1896." Unpublished Manuscript, Washington University.

Rohde, David W. 1979. "Risk-Bearing and Progressive Ambition: The Case of Members of the United States House of Representatives." *American Journal of Political Science* 23 (1): 1–26.

Rohde, David W. 1991. *Parties and Leaders in the Postreform House*. Chicago: University of Chicago Press.

Rothenberg, Lawrence S., and Mitchell S. Sanders. 2000. "Severing the Electoral

Connection: Shirking in the Contemporary Congress." *American Journal of Political Science* 44 (1): 316–25.

Rudder, Catherine. 1990. Review of *Budget Reform Politics*, by Charles Stewart III. *Congress and the Presidency* 17 (2): 165–67.

Rusk, Jerrold G. 1970. "The Effects of the Australian Ballot Reform on Split Ticket Voting: 1876–1908." *American Political Science Review* 64 (4): 1220–38.

Schaffner, Brian F. 2006. "Local News Coverage and the Incumbency Advantage in the U.S. House." *Legislative Studies Quarterly* 31 (4): 491–511.

Schickler, Eric. 2001. *Disjointed Pluralism: Institutional Innovation and the Development of the U.S. Congress*. Princeton: Princeton University Press.

Schiller, Wendy J. 1995. "Senators as Political Entrepreneurs: Using Bill Sponsorship to Shape Legislative Agendas." *American Journal of Political Science* 39 (1): 186–203.

Schiller, Wendy J. 2006. "Building Careers and Courting Constituents: U.S. Senate Representation, 1889–1924." *Studies in American Political Development* 20 (2): 185–97.

Schiller, Wendy J., and Charles Stewart III. 2014. *Electing the Senate: Indirect Democracy before the Seventeenth Amendment*. Princeton: Princeton University Press.

Schiller, Wendy J., Charles Stewart III, and Benjamin Xiong. 2013. "U.S. Senate Elections before the 17th Amendment: Political Party Cohesion and Conflict, 1871–1913." *Journal of Politics* 75 (3): 835–47.

Schlesinger, Joseph. 1966. *Ambition and Politics: Political Careers in the United States*. Chicago: Rand McNally.

Schmeckebier, Laurence F. 1941. *Congressional Apportionment*. Washington, DC: Brookings Institution.

Sellers, Patrick J. 1997. "Fiscal Consistency and Federal District Spending in Congressional Elections." *American Journal of Political Science* 41 (3): 1024–41.

Serra, George, and David Moon. 1994. "Casework, Issue Positions, and Voting in Congressional Elections: A District Analysis." *Journal of Politics* 56 (1): 200–213.

Silbey, Joel H. 1985. *The Partisan Imperative: The Dynamics of American Politics before the Civil War*. Oxford: Oxford University Press.

Silbey, Joel H. 1991. *The American Political Nation, 1838–1893*. Stanford: Stanford University Press.

Skeen, C. Edward. 1986. "*Vox Populi, Vox Dei*: The Compensation Act of 1816 and the Rise of Popular Politics." *Journal of the Early Republic* 6 (3): 253–74.

Smith, Culver H. 1977. *The Press, Politics, and Patronage: The American Government's Use of Newspapers, 1789–1875*. Athens: University of Georgia Press.

Squire, Peverill, Keith E. Hamm, Ronald D. Hedlund, and Gary F. Moncrief. 2005. "Electoral Reforms, Membership Stability, and the Existence of Committee Property Rights in American State Legislatures." *British Journal of Political Science* 35 (1): 169–81.

Stathis, Stephen W. 2002. *Landmark Legislation, 1774–2002.* Washington, DC: CQ Press.

Stewart, Charles H., III. 1989. *Budget Reform Politics: The Design of the Appropriations Process in the House of Representatives, 1865–1921.* New York: Cambridge University Press.

Stewart, Charles H., III. 2001. *Analyzing Congress.* New York: W. W. Norton.

Stonecash, Jeffrey M. 2013. *Party Pursuits and the Presidential-House Election Connection, 1900–2008.* New York: Cambridge University Press.

Struble, Robert. 1979. "House Turnover and the Principle of Rotation." *Political Science Quarterly* 94 (4): 649–67.

Sullivan, John L., L. Earl Shaw, Gregory E. McAvoy, and David G. Barnum. 1993. "The Dimensions of Cue-Taking in the House of Representatives: Variation by Issue Area." *Journal of Politics* 55 (4): 975–97.

Summers, Mark W. 2004. *Party Games: Getting, Keeping, and Using Power in Gilded Age Politics.* Chapel Hill: University of North Carolina Press.

Sundquist, James L. 1983. *Dynamics of the Party System: Alignment and Realignment of Political Parties in the United States.* Washington, DC: Brookings Institution.

Swain, John W., Stephen A. Borrelli, Brian C. Reed, and Sean F. Evans. 2000. "A New Look at Turnover in the U.S. House of Representatives, 1789–1998." *American Politics Quarterly* 28 (4): 435–57.

Swift, Elaine K. 1987. "The Electoral Connection Meets the Past: Lessons from Congressional History, 1789–1899." *Political Science Quarterly* 102 (4): 625–45.

Taussig, Frank William. 1914. *The Tariff History of the United States.* New York: G. P. Putnam's Sons.

Theriault, Sean M. 2003. "Patronage, the Pendleton Act, and the Power of the People." *Journal of Politics* 65 (1): 50–68.

Thompson, Margaret Susan. 1985. *The "Spider Web": Congress and Lobbying in the Age of Grant.* Ithaca: Cornell University Press.

Valelly, Richard M. 2004. *The Two Reconstructions: The Struggle for Black Enfranchisement.* Chicago: University of Chicago Press.

Wallis, John J. 2004. "American Government and the Promotion of Economic Development in the National Era, 1790 to 1860." Unpublished Manuscript, University of Maryland.

Wallis, John J., and Barry R. Weingast. 2005. "Equilibrium Impotence: Why the States and Not the American National Government Financed Infrastructure Investment in the Antebellum Era." Unpublished Manuscript, University of Maryland.

Ware, Alan. 2002. *The American Direct Primary: Party Institutionalization and Transformation in the North.* New York: Cambridge University Press.

Wilkins, Arjun. 2012. "Electoral Security of Members of the U.S. House, 1900–2006." *Legislative Studies Quarterly* 37 (3): 277–304.

Wilson, Rick K. 1986. "An Empirical Test of Preferences for the Political Pork Barrel: District Level Appropriations for River and Harbor Legislation, 1889–1913." *American Journal of Political Science* 30 (4): 729–54.

Wittrock, Jill N., Stephen C. Nemeth, Howard Sanborn, Brian DiSarro, and Peverill Squire. 2008. "The Impact of the Australian Ballot on Member Behavior in the U.S. House of Representatives." *Political Research Quarterly* 61 (3): 434–44.

Wright, Gerald C., Jr. 1978. "Candidates' Policy Positions and Voting in U.S. Congressional Elections." *Legislative Studies Quarterly* 3 (3): 445–64.

Zagarri, Rosemarie. 1987. *The Politics of Size: Representation in the United States, 1776–1850*. Ithaca: Cornell University Press.

Index